The Work of Inclusion

T&T CLARK STUDIES IN SOCIAL ETHICS, ETHNOGRAPHY, AND THEOLOGY

Over the last half century, there have been numerous calls for Christian theology and ethics to take human experience seriously—to delve into particular economic, socio-political, racial-ethnic, and cultural contexts from which theological and moral imagination arises. Yet actual theologies that draw upon descriptive-rich, qualitative methods—methods that place such particularity at the center of inquiry and performance—are few and scattered. **T&T Clark Studies in Social Ethics, Ethnography, and Theology** is a monograph series that addresses this gap in the literature by providing a publishing home for timely ethnographically-driven theological and ethical investigations of an expansive array of pressing social issues, ranging from armed conflict to racism to healthcare inequities to sexuality/gender and discrimination to the marginalization of persons with disabilities. The scope of the series projects, taken together, is at once global and intensely local, with the central organizing conviction that ethnography provides not only information to plug into a theology, but a valid and vibrant way of *doing* theology.

The Work of Inclusion

An Ethnography of Grace, Sin, and
Intellectual Disabilities

*Lorraine
Cuddeback-Gedeon*

t&tclark

LONDON · NEW YORK · OXFORD · NEW DELHI · SYDNEY

T&T CLARK
Bloomsbury Publishing Plc
50 Bedford Square, London, WC1B 3DP, UK
1385 Broadway, New York, NY 10018, USA
29 Earlsfort Terrace, Dublin 2, Ireland

BLOOMSBURY, T&T CLARK and the T&T Clark logo are trademarks of
Bloomsbury Publishing Plc

First published in Great Britain 2023

Cover design: Terry Woodley
Cover image courtesy Barbara Pickut

A catalogue record for this book is available from the British Library.

A catalog record for this book is available from the Library of Congress.

ISBN: HB: 978-0-5676-9830-8
PB: 978-0-5676-9829-2
ePDF: 978-0-5676-9832-2
ePUB: 978-0-5676-9831-5

Typeset by Deanta Global Publishing Services, Chennai, India

To find out more about our authors and books visit www.bloomsbury.com and
sign up for our newsletters.

For everyone at "Payton," especially K and J—and always, for Will.

CONTENTS

ACKNOWLEDGMENTS

At the completion of a project which repeatedly emphasizes interdependence and support among people and institutions, I cannot offer enough thanks for the many types of care and support I have received while shaping this work. First and foremost, I must thank "Payton," for opening its doors to me and this project. Cheryl Schade, Marilyn Florey, and the Human Rights Commission were instrumental in making this work possible. I want to offer special thanks to Barbara Pickut, who connected me with Emily, the talented artist who made the cover of this book. Of course, I owe my deepest debt to the clients of Payton who befriended me and trusted me with their stories. K, J, K, M, and F—I hope I have done justice to all you have shared with me.

In the process of my research, I have had to be something of a jack of all trades: ethnographer, theologian, social ethicist, and historian. On this last point, I want to thank the Local and Family Histories division of the St. Joseph County Public Library for their archives, through which I was able to triangulate the historical narrative in Chapter 1. I am also grateful to the Burke Library at Union Theological Seminary, which gave me two afternoons working with Ada Maria Isasi-Díaz's archives as I wrestled with the deeper implications of ethnography and solidarity. The entire premise of this book, especially its method, is possible thanks to the wisdom and mentorship of Todd Whitmore, who took me on as an "apprentice" and guided me through everything from IRB approvals to final drafts in the messy, rewarding work of ethnography. The opportunity to publish came largely from Todd's encouragement to submit to this series. The support, advice, and patience he and the other series editors—Aana Vigen and Traci West, AnneMarie Mingo—provided as I navigated the completion of this project through a pandemic and a career change is very, very much appreciated.

Writing is a team sport, and pieces of this manuscript have been workshopped and revised several times over to my relief and their great improvement. Brian Hamilton provided the necessary jumpstart I needed on Chapter 1 when I was just starting the shift from dissertation to book. I am indebted to Emily Reimer-Barry and Simeiqi He for the opportunity to workshop Chapter 3 with CTEWC colleagues. Chapter 4 benefited greatly from the discussants and reviewers within the Society of Christian Ethics. I have many other interlocutors that have shaped ideas, big and small, throughout the initial writing and ongoing revisions of this work—many of whom may not even realize the impact their words and work have had. I am grateful for Elisabeth Kincaid, Layla Karst, Jaisy Joseph, Leo Guardado, Kyle Lambelet, Robby Kiley, Jack Trammell, Sarah Barton, Miguel Romero, Mary Jo Iozzio, Devan Stahl, and especially Tim Snyder, who has read many tangled drafts as this project moved from proposal, to dissertation, to book, all while helping me find the motivation to keep the practice of writing, bit by bit.

When life changes came and I needed advice and discernment, I turned to Becky Czarnecki, Megan Urbaniak, and Jessica Ochoa—thank you for the wisdom and love you still provide, ten years after our M.Div. When I needed humor, hope, and a found family (even at a pandemic-distance), I relied on Sarah Morini, Emily Perez de Alejo, Beth Chen, and Lizzy Leong. Finally, to Chris Gedeon: oftentimes as worried as I was about whether I would finish this book, your gentle encouragement and endless support has made the impossible, possible.

Introduction

The Payton Workshop (all names changed) is a factory, and it is predictably noisy. But in my first days there, I discovered layers of noise: unpredictable, complex, dissonant.[1]

First you hear the expected background noises of the factory. An ongoing humming, like the blowing of air through some massive ductwork up on the ceiling. But there is no air conditioning, although it is June and the hot days of summer are just starting. To cool the space when the temperature rises, a series of large standing fans are placed throughout the workshop, varying from one foot to almost three feet across. They rotate back and forth, their slow nods moving air but not ruffling the workstations. This mostly works, though I've been told there have been times when the workshop had to be closed as the heat was too unbearable. Given the high temperatures around the heavy machines, I find this unsurprising.

Underneath the machinery, music emerges. Many of the sections have radios playing, and the music surfaces intermittently against the general thuds and clanks of work and chatter. The local Top 40 station plays on most radios, but as you move between areas some different songs and sounds play. Hip-hop at one desk fades into a nostalgic 80s hair band ballad at another.

In all this noise, I often have to ask people to repeat themselves—and it makes me feel terrible. The workers at Payton Workshop, "clients" of the larger Payton Center organization, have various kinds of intellectual and developmental disabilities. Some can speak clearly, though maybe at a slow, halting pace as they search for words. Others have significant communicative delays, ranging from stutters to too many vowels and not enough consonants to almost completely nonverbal.

When I don't understand, I apologize that I didn't get it the first time and humbly ask for them to repeat themselves. On some occasions, I have had to ask five times or more before I think—think—I get the main idea. On a few

---

[1]My ethnographic research began in 2014, with part-time observation work (about two to six hours a week) at the Payton Center with their Adult Recreation program, particularly their art class and theater class. Additional observation work took place over approximately six months at Payton Industries, a job placement center and sheltered workshop. In addition to my participant observation, I completed interviews with staff, clients, and family members of Payton, and all research was completed with approval from both the Internal Review Board of the University of Notre Dame and Payton Center's own internal IRB, their Human Rights Commission.

occasions, other clients have stepped in as translators. This prevents tiresome repetition, but certainly holds problems of its own—are these translations accurate? Or are they just trying to interject into the conversation with a stranger on the workshop floor?

Every interaction I have at Payton echoes this struggle, off and on the workshop floor. I have to sift through layers—of noise, of communicative blocks, of intentions explicit, implicit, real, and imagined. Fieldwork is messy, and the just-this-side-of-chaotic environment at Payton Industries brings that to the fore. And still, I chose this site, I chose to include fieldwork as an integral part of my theological project, in a discipline not known for doing so.

Disability holds a tenuous position in theology. Historically, people with disabilities are often viewed as passive recipients of charity, providing opportunities to meet our Christian obligation toward works of mercy and charity. A recent turn in the literature has challenged the presumption of passivity in disabled bodies, largely thanks to the disability rights movement. Disabled theologians have written from their own experiences with disabilities, and call theology to a new accountability that takes seriously their agency. Yet, theological reflections on intellectual and developmental disabilities are commonly written not by self-advocates, but by caregivers, family, or friends. Disabled voices are muted, with their presence only seen through the impact they have on the nondisabled writer. This is the gap I want to start closing with my work.

So I chose this workshop, this place, this community, as a way of overcoming the tendency to write *about* people with IDD (especially as objects of charity), rather than working *with* this community as subjects seeking their own human flourishing. By taking up this posture of listening, my ethnographic work uncovers patterns of grace and sin as seen and experienced by the Payton community on its own terms. This is a necessary task for our churches to become spaces that represent every part of the multifaceted Body of Christ.

Defining Disability

Before outlining the larger sense of my argument, a few preliminary definitions need to be given. "Disability" is a complex word and phenomenon: the early origins of the concept are generally attributed to the nineteenth century which saw the advance of statistics, eugenics, and "normal." Normal begets "abnormal," the term from which Lennard Davis argues there is a clear line to "disability." Prior to normal, one might have spoken of an ideal, but an ideal was, by definition, unreachable. Even if the ideal was in some sense aspirational, it was not prescriptive. Normal, by contrast, was prescriptive, with expectations that bodies and behaviors had to meet. This was seen most clearly in the co-option of normal and abnormal by the eugenics movement of the early twentieth century, a time when rapid changes in the United States threatened the hegemony of the white middle class.[2]

Though scholars like Davis situate disability as a concept defined by social norms, for much of its early history disability was seen as a medical problem. Throughout its development, disability has volleyed between at least two conceptual models, though many more exist in the literature.[3] Until recently, the most commonly accepted model was medical, which sees disability as a physiological problem rooted in an individual's body. If someone loses a limb, he or she is "cured" with a prosthetic; if he or she has an intellectual disability, the "cure" is an education that makes one a productive, contributing citizen, rather than a dependent.

Competing with the medical model is the social model of disability, which argues for a conceptual distinction between an impairment and a disability. Whereas impairments are physiological, disabilities are not. Rather, disability is the result of how society enables or disables people according to their kind(s) of impairment(s). Someone who uses a power chair may have a physical *impairment*, but that person is only *disabled* by a building without a ramp. When there is a ramp, they can come and go as freely as any able-bodied person. In some situations what is regarded as a "disability" may provide advantages: Deaf people signing to one another in a loud venue will communicate more easily than hearing people trying to shout at each other. Since what constitutes disability is socially constructed, it would be remediated not (only) by medical interventions, but by making social spaces more accessible, whether through the removal of architectural barriers or through education that removes stigma and stereotypes.

While I rely on the social model of disability in this work, it must be noted that there is often resistance, even within disability studies itself, to a new hegemony of a social model.[4] There is particular resistance to rendering IDD as "socially constructed," since the impact that profound IDD can have on a person's capacities seems to transcend the kind of help that assistive technology or curb cuts offer someone with a physical disability. I want to acknowledge the reality of these difficulties for intellectually disabled persons. If the presumption of accessibility is to make everyone

---

[2]This concept originated with Davis, but Allison Carey's work addresses the link between eugenics and the desire for a bourgeois cultural hegemony, in much greater detail. See Allison Carey, *On the Margins of Citizenship* (Philadelphia: Temple University Press, 2009), 52–82. See also Lennard Davis, *Enforcing Normalcy: Disability, Deafness, and the Body* (New York: Verso, 1995), 35.

[3]Mary Jo Iozzio and Miguel Romero, "Preface: Engaging Disability," *Journal of Moral Theology* 6, Special Issue 2 (2017): 1–9.

[4]Tom Shakespeare and Nicholas Watson, "The Social Model of Disability: An Outdated Ideology?," in *Exploring Theories and Expanding Methodologies: Where We Are and Where We Need To Go*, ed. Sharon Barnartt and Barbara Altman (Bingley: Emerald Group Publishing Limited, 2002): 9–28.

in the disability community independent and self-sufficient, then there is a significant number of people who may never meet that criterion.

Nonetheless, there are ways in which the social model is still applicable to people with IDD. The social model does not deny the material reality of an impairment, whether to a hand, foot, or brain. Rather, the fundamental argument of the social model is that these impairments are unjustly given a negative social value. This can be seen in how the definition of "intellectual disability" has shifted over time. For example, people born to certain social classes, or women determined to be of "incorrigible" moral character were, at one point in history, understood to be "feebleminded," the diagnostic precursor to IDD.[5] This is obviously not how we would define intellectual disability today. Moral philosopher Licia Carlson addresses this by arguing that IDD is an "interactive kind": that is, a kind that is continuously shaped by social forces, particularly by relationships with others. As an interactive kind, we can maintain a level of material realism to the phenomenon of intellectual disability, but also retain socially constructed elements that shape how people with IDD are valued and integrated into communities.[6]

If we accept that IDD is also subject to social construction, then we can also accept that people with IDD can benefit from the constructive possibilities of the social model and the politics associated with it. With this preliminary conceptual framework in mind, I offer a broad definition for how I am using intellectual and developmental disability: a set of impairments and behaviors that arise from delayed intellectual development, resulting in persons being unable to attend to the everyday tasks of life without a significant level of assistance from caregivers (paid or unpaid). This definition is designed to reflect the heterogeneity of my fieldwork: Payton Center serves a wide array of people—some who have identifiable conditions like Down Syndrome, some on the Autism spectrum,[7] and some with dual diagnoses of intellectual disability and mental illness.[8] Some people at Payton also have physical impairments. This brief, certainly not comprehensive, list should serve to highlight the complexity of IDD, both at my field site and elsewhere.

The limits of my definition also echo my fieldsite, Payton. In the workshop, I was mostly engaging with "high functioning" (in a diagnostic

---

[5]Licia Carlson, *The Faces of Intellectual Disability* (Bloomington: Indiana University Press, 2010), 53–84; Carey, *On the Margins of Citizenship*, 52–82.
[6]Carlson, *The Faces of Intellectual Disability*, 94–5.
[7]It should be noted that the current DSM-V locates Autism as a separate disorder from intellectual and developmental disabilities. While severe cases of Autism can result in a person functionally having an IDD, it is diagnostically considered a behavioral, not cognitive disorder. That being said, Autistic advocates have been at the forefront of the neurodiversity movement, which does aim to include forms of IDD, as well.
[8]Mental illness can be considered a disability under the ADA; however, Payton only takes clients if they have an IDD. Someone with a diagnosis of mental illness but without IDD would not qualify for Payton services.

sense) clients, people who are capable of labor and vocational rehabilitation. This means I am not dealing directly with people considered profoundly intellectually disabled, that is, people who have extremely limited forms of verbal or symbolic communication. My intention is not to exclude such people as insignificant because they are not represented by my fieldsite. On the contrary, I argue that by attending to Payton, we can open a space that takes seriously the agency, limited as it may seem, of people with profound intellectual disabilities, as well—something addressed in more detail in Chapter 3.

The Risk of Taking a Liberationist Approach to IDD

My decision to use ethnographic research as a part of this project comes from my commitment to doing theology that liberates. Like its peers in Black theologies, Latin American liberation theologies, and feminist theologies, disability liberation theology emerged from social movements that resisted oppression. The most influential entry in the genre is Nancy Eiesland's *The Disabled God*.[9] The impact of this text cannot be underestimated: Eiesland's work is cited in almost every other book written on theology and disability, whether in agreement or critical argument with it. Eiesland wrote about disability not just as something that theology needed to respond to, but as something that could teach and correct theology. She set up three key tasks, with the first being the de-ideologization of theology by identifying sites of ableism in theology and Christian practices. Second, she strongly advocates for the importance of narratives about the experience of disability from people who have disabilities—she uses the rhetoric from the disability rights movement, "nothing about us without us" to express this. Finally, the need for these narratives about disability points to an issue beyond orthodoxy and into that essential element of liberation theology: orthopraxis. Liberation theologies posit that theology and praxis need one another; for Eiesland, this means that ableist theologies beget ableist practices. While not all liberation theologies engage politics in an activist sense, Eiesland's engagement with praxis is clearly informed by her activist background, centering on the ways that churches failed to support the Americans with Disabilities Act and how sacramental and liturgical church practices continue to exclude disabled persons.

Following in Eiesland's footsteps, a liberationist approach to intellectual disability must also take up a hermeneutical task, by deconstructing ableism

---

[9]Nancy L. Eiesland, *The Disabled God: Toward a Liberatory Theology of Disability* (Nashville: Abingdon).

in theology and engaging the "sitpoint" of people with disabilities; it is also a political project, aiming to change concrete, exclusionary practices.[10] The deconstructive task for theologies of disability is uncontroversial: there is a long list of bad theologies that have perpetuated exclusion, including (but not limited to) bad Thomisms that exclude people with IDD from the Eucharist, collapsing the *imago dei* into the rational will, associating physical healing with one's strength of faith, and pure ableism preventing disabled people from taking up ministerial roles. However, the second part of the hermeneutic task—including the voices and knowledge of disabled people at the center of theological discourse—is somewhat contested, especially by theologians concerned with IDD.

Alongside and in response to Eiesland, another genre of disability theologies has developed, which questions the role that disabled identity plays in the production of theology: I call these postliberal theologies of disability. Experiences with intellectual disability are found more frequently in this second genre and are strongly influenced by the anti-liberalism of Stanley Hauerwas, whose *Suffering Presence* continues to influence subsequent work.[11] Where liberation theologies take up the abled-disabled distinction to draw forward differences in power, these theologies seek our shared humanity by emphasizing what is universal in human persons. They use the language of the social model of disability (though not always the underlying philosophical presuppositions) to explore how disability highlights a shared human vulnerability and interdependence.

These insights raise important critiques for the politics of a liberal, capitalistic society. Yet, the embedded critiques of the liberationist genre reveal a misunderstanding of the task of liberation theology. First, postliberal theologies express skepticism concerning the political task: more precisely, politics is considered insufficient compared to the real, final end of theology—love of neighbor and communion with God.[12]

---

[10]Rosemarie Garland Thompson proposes the neologism "sitpoint theory," derived from the autobiographical work of Nancy Mairs, who is also central to Eiesland's constructive theology. See: Eiesland, *The Disabled God*, 40–8; Rosemarie Garland Thompson, "Integrating Disability, Transforming Feminist Theory," *NWSA Journal* (now *Feminist Formations*) 14, no. 3 (2002): 1–32; Nancy Mairs, *Waist-High in the World: A Life Among the Nondisabled* (Beacon Press, 1997).

[11]Stanley Hauerwas, *Suffering Presence: Theological Reflections on Medicine, the Mentally Handicapped, and the Church* (Notre Dame: University of Notre Dame Press, 1986). Examples of postliberal work include Brian Brock, *Wondrously Wounded: Theology, Disability, and the Body of Christ* (Waco: Baylor University Press, 2019); Hans S. Reinders, *Receiving the Gift of Friendship: Profound Disability, Theological Anthropology, and Ethics* (Grand Rapids: William B. Eerdmans Publishing Co., 2008); Reinders, *The Future of the Disabled in Liberal Society: An Ethical Analysis* (Notre Dame: University of Notre Dame Press, 2000).

[12]John Swinton, "Who Is the God We Worship? Theologies of Disability: Challenges and New Possibilities," *International Journal of Practical Theology* 14, no. 2 (2011): 273–307; Deborah Beth Creamer, *Disability and Christian Theology: Embodied Limits and Constructive Possibilities* (New York: Oxford University Press, 2009).

Where politics does come forward, as in Jason Reimer Greig's examination of medical ethics and L'Arche, it is identified as the politics of particular faith communities *contra* liberal society.[13] Rights language and macro-level legislative advocacy is deemed too "thin" to respond adequately to the needs of the disabled community.[14] Liberation theologies of disability that draw on the disability rights movement are criticized for focusing on macro-political representation and independence, rather than relationship, to the detriment of the IDD community.

Postliberal and liberationist theologies of disability also sit in tension over the hermeneutic task at hand. Where liberationists draw a mutually critical correlation between theology and the experience of disability, postliberals give theology the primacy of place, even if there are some bad theologies to deconstruct (as, for example, Hans Reinders does with his theological anthropology). This is not about preserving power or truth for theology, but presumptions that postliberal theologies make about the ability of the IDD community to participate in doing theology. Hans Reinders illustrates this with his treatment of Kelly, an encephalitic woman.[15] Since Kelly is missing the part of her brain that accounts for emotions or symbolic thought, Reinders takes it as a given that she cannot take part in doing theology, as liberationists (and arguably postliberals) would understand it. Kelly has no capacity for self-representation (so Reinders argues) and cannot give an account of her experience.

Kelly does present a challenge for liberationists, but one that I argue is not insurmountable.[16] Liberation theologies do privilege the epistemic position of marginalized communities, and most liberationists write from a sense of shared identity with the community from which their liberation theology comes from (e.g., Eiesland, a disabled woman, writes a disability liberation theology). Strictly understood, "nothing about us without us" might exclude the nondisabled from writing disability theologies. Deborah Creamer touches on this debate, nothing that within disability studies there is a strong expectation—even moral sensibility—that one must have a disability to be able to write about it.[17] Clearly, that's a proposition that most theologians writing about intellectual disability reject, because it seems self-evident that the IDD community cannot do theology. So, nondisabled theologians step up to the proverbial plate. However, there are examples of liberationist theologies (meaning, they take up deconstructive, reconstructive, and political tasks through the specific lens of the experience

---

[13]Jason Reimer Greig, *Reconsidering Intellectual Disability: L'Arche, Medical Ethics, and Christian Friendship* (Washington: Georgetown University Press, 2016).

[14]John Swinton, "From Inclusion to Belonging: A Practical Theology of Community, Disability and Humanness," *Journal of Religion, Disability & Health* 16, no. 2 (2012): 172–90.

[15]Reinders, *Receiving the Gift of Friendship*, 19–23.

[16]I discuss this more fully in Chapter 3.

[17]Creamer, *Disability and Christian Theology*, 5–6.

of disability) by nondisabled allies and caretakers. Amos Yong's *Theology and Down Syndrome* is explicitly framed as a "liberative" approach to intellectual disability, though Yong himself is not intellectually disabled.[18] Yong even includes the voices of people with Down Syndrome through the use of social science texts and biographies, in addition to reflections on his own experience with a brother with Down Syndrome. Yet he and others struggle to make the shift from using experiences of disability as supplementary evidence to integrating them into the *process* of theology, which Eiesland and those like her are able to do more easily by virtue of their firsthand experiences.

My strategy for bridging this gap is ethnography: a method developed by cultural anthropologists, where a researcher is embedded in a community for a year or more as a "participant observer." The goal of an ethnography is "thick description"—an immersive description in which the ethnographer attempts to understand the inner logics of a community. I am not intellectually disabled, but I do not take it for granted that the IDD community cannot be a part of doing theology—even academic theology. If the heart of a liberationist method is the epistemic privilege of the poor, then as theologians we owe it to people on the margins to ensure that their standpoints and sitpoints are integrated in our work. We should also contemplate how we might challenge the academic structures that marginalize the IDD community.[19] Now, ethnography is not a morally neutral tool, and cultural anthropologists have long wrestled with the intertwining of their discipline with the legacies of power and oppression.[20] Nonetheless, the rise of theological ethnography within Christian ethics has been consistently employed with the intent of taking seriously the epistemic privilege of the communities in which we do our fieldwork.[21] Ethnographic methods help harness two other invaluable tools offered by liberationists: solidarity and orthopraxis.

---

[18]Amos Yong, *Theology and Down Syndrome: Reimagining Disability in Late Modernity* (Waco: Baylor University Press, 2007), 9–14.
[19]Lorraine Cuddeback-Gedeon, "'Nothing About Us Without Us': Ethnography, Conscientization, and the Epistemic Challenges of Intellectual Disability," *Practical Matters Journal* 11 (2018): 1–18. http://practicalmattersjournal.org/2018/08/03/nothing-about-us-without-us-ethnography-conscientization-and-the-epistemic-challenges-of-intellectual-disability/.
[20]In fact, one method of coping with that legacy has been to adopt neutrality as the discipline's primary moral stance, though there are dissenting viewpoints (such as Nancy Scheper-Hughes) that want to see cultural anthropologists take on more responsibility for the injustices they inevitably encounter. See Todd David Whitmore, "'If They Kill Us at Least the Others Will Have More Time to Get Away': The Ethics of Risk in Ethnographic Practice," *Practical Matters* 3 (2010): 1–28. http://practicalmattersjournal.org/wp-content/uploads/2015/09/Whitmore.If-They-Kill-Us.pdf; Nancy Scheper-Hughes, "The Primacy of the Ethical: Propositions for a Militant Anthropology," *Current Anthropology* 36, no. 3 (1995): 409–40.
[21]Emily Reimer-Barry, "The Listening Church: How Ethnography Can Transform Catholic Ethics," in *Ethnography as Christian Theology and Ethics*, ed. Christian Scharen and Aana Marie Vigen (New York: Continuum, 2011), 97–117.

Solidarity, Reflexivity, and Intellectual Disability

I have said ethnography is an imperfect tool: as the ethnographer I am inevitably mediating the experiences of the people I encounter. I do not propose that ethnography offers a "pure" distillation of experiences of intellectual disability, if such a thing even existed. However, ethnography does help a theologian recognize their social locations and implicit biases (something which is a part of theology even without doing ethnography). An essential component of ethnography is the *reflexivity* of the ethnographer; in a liberationist valence, reflexivity might be compared to the process of *conscientization* that results in solidarity with the poor.

Solidarity can be a frustratingly oblique concept, and social refrains such as "#SolidarityIsForWhiteWomen" remind us that it is not a term to be used lightly.[22] Gustavo Gutierrez defines solidarity as an act of sacrifice, a "specific action, a style of life, a break with one's social class."[23] He understands solidarity as a love of neighbor modeled on the sacrifice of Christ; it is also a part of *conscientization* on the way to making and living the preferential option for the poor.[24] As an action, solidarity does not need to be politically *effective*, but it must be *transformative*. Ada Maria Isasi-Díaz builds on Gutierrez by defining solidarity as mutuality and shared praxis between the privileged and the poor, but she moves away from the sacrificial elements Gutierrez highlighted, like voluntary poverty. Instead, Isasi-Díaz insists on the political effectiveness that Gutierrez does not. She argues that solidarity requires that no oppressed group be left behind when mobilizing for action, which is something she shares in common with the mission of disability advocates.[25] This bears important repercussions for the accusation that liberation theologies of disability ignore the IDD community—if they are true to building solidarity, then no one should fall behind.

The practice of solidarity that Isasi-Díaz describes is a dialog between the oppressed and oppressors, where "the first word in this dialog is uttered by the oppressed."[26] A privileged ally must engage in critical self-examination, and offer a response that "is born of the critical consciousness of those who allowed themselves to be critiqued and who take responsibility for their own consciousness."[27] This description of solidarity resembles an ethnographer's reflexivity: unsurprising given that Isasi-Díaz was a pioneer of "ethnomethodology." And like an ethnographer, Isasi-Díaz reflects on her

---

[22]Ada Maria Isasi-Díaz, "Solidarity: Love of Neighbor in the 1980s," in *Feminist Theological Ethics: A Reader*, ed. Lois K. Daly (Louisville: Westminster John Knox Press, 1994), 78.
[23]Gustavo Gutiérrez, *A Theology of Liberation: History, Politics, and Salvation* (Maryknoll: Orbis Books, 1988), 172.
[24]Gutiérrez, *A Theology of Liberation*, 171–2.
[25]Isasi-Díaz, "Solidarity," 81.
[26]Isasi-Díaz, "Solidarity," 82.
[27]Isasi-Díaz, "Solidarity," 83.

own role and privilege as an academic theologian alongside the *mujeristas* she does theology with:

> But I have had to accept the fact that I am both an insider and an outsider in the community of Hispanic Woman. I have struggled to distinguish what I hold in common with the respondents (because I am a woman and Hispanic) from what is different, that is, class, age, role, degree of formal education, and so forth. It is important to recognize that identities are always complex and multifaceted, and, therefore, no researcher is ever totally an insider.[28]

Isasi-Díaz speaks to the challenges of neither suppressing her own knowledge and training, nor letting that experience become the primary lens through which she encounters the experiences of other *mujeristas*. And what of the researcher who, unlike Isasi-Díaz, is more outsider than insider (like myself)? For them, Isasi-Díaz advises that the "less the professional theologian is an insider, the more she must . . . allow herself to be deeply engaged by the community so that she can, as much as possible, come to understand the community from within."[29] This means that my social location and accompanying biases as a nondisabled theologian must be disrupted, challenged, and questioned. I must embrace epistemic humility, and set aside expectations of what grace, sin, and flourishing look like. Moreover, I have to ask myself in what manner my work *effectively* contributes to that flourishing.

Yet my context within the IDD community raises additional questions for solidarity: it does not seem as if we have properly answered postliberal criticisms of liberationists. If solidarity is a conversation in which the marginalized speak the first word, can this create space for Kelly—who has no language—to participate in theology? If solidarity must result in effective action that contributes to flourishing, can Kelly participate? It might seem,

---

[28]Isasi-Díaz, *En La Lucha = In the Struggle: A Hispanic Women's Liberation Theology* (Minneapolis: Fortress Press, 1993), 88.

[29]Isasi-Díaz, *En La Lucha*, 89. Given that this follows on Isasi-Díaz's discussion of accountability, that is bringing her work back to the community so they can affirm its accuracy, it is likely that she would see accountability as a critical component to avoiding "equivocation," or the instrumentalization of the oppressed by an outsider-professional theologian. Describing the work of a theologian as that of a "theological technician," Isasi-Díaz suggests the following to avoid problems of instrumentalization: "The writer needs to write in a very simple way, using extensive direct quotes from what the community has said. . . . The material needs to be organized rather than systematized according to one preconceived construct. . . . The organization of the material should be around central words/ideas which are repeated often in the conversation and carry emotional weight." "Towards a Hispanic Women's Liberation Theology" address for the Maryknolls in November 1986, pgs 17–20, Series 2, Box 2, Folder 3 Ada María Isasi-Díaz Papers, Archives of Women in Theological Scholarship, The Burke Library (Columbia University Libraries) at Union Theological Seminary, New York, NY.

given what I've laid out thus far, that the answer is no, and liberation theologies fail at their own task of cultivating solidarity by leaving Kelly behind. I would argue, however, that this assumes language is the only way to engage theology—and on this point, recent engagements of Christian ethics with both ethnography and disability have been helpful in understanding the role of embodied experience.

Ethnography and Embodied Revelation

For many Christian theologians using ethnography, the method is a way of exploring the *ongoing* role of revelation and the ways revelation exists in our very bodies. Mary McClintock Fulkerson argues that we only come to know revelation through the body, for "it is the body, with its corporeal bifurcation, that *provides* orientation in the world (left-right, up-down, front-back) . . . [t]he world *takes shape* through our bodies."[30] In *Places of Redemption,* Fulkerson uses "place," defined as a "convergence of practices" shared by embodied persons, to illustrate how redemption is made visible over time.[31] Given the multiplicity of layers to a community's experience of place, this does not create neatly packaged continuity, but reveals redemption amid conflict and contradiction. I take Fulkerson's understanding of place and the messiness of revelation as a central premise of this work: ethnography reveals God's work in this world to be a messy art.

Moreover, Fulkerson uses embodied experience as described by Pierre Bourdieu's *habitus* to challenge the dominance that discursive knowledge holds in theology as a discipline. This is inspired by Fulkerson's own encounters with people with IDD:

> an account of tradition and practices must take seriously the full continuum of human experience, particularly the nondiscursive ordering that constitutes place. . . . Take Daphne and other members of group homes [for people with IDD] at Good Samaritan who do not have language capacities. Daphne cannot tell stories, nor is her behavior likely to qualify for a "coherent and complex form of socially established cooperative human activit[y]," as the definition of practice requires. Indeed, taking Daphne's practices seriously is not itself a long-practiced habit in the US.[32]

---

[30]Mary McClintock Fulkerson, *Places of Redemption: Theology for a Worldly Church* (New York: Oxford University Press, 2007), 25.
[31]Fulkerson, *Places of Redemption*, 21–8.
[32]Fulkerson, *Places of Redemption*, 40.

Fulkerson rightly points out that prioritizing discursive communication over non-discursive communication excludes people with significant IDD not just from academic theology, but recognizing how they, too, engage in practices and traditions of the church. The challenge and opportunity of ethnography is that it allows bodies to become as central as texts:

> even though she cannot talk, Daphne's squeals in the [liturgical] service are messages. She is communicating. To count her as a potential contributor to tradition, however, requires changes in the categories, including what counts as practice. . . . In one sense that means an account of tradition that includes the contributions of bodies. However, written traditions are not only in need of supplementation by interpreting bodily practices. A definition of tradition must itself reflect the wider character of communication.[33]

Coming to recognize Daphne as an active, participatory member of the Good Samaritan community makes adjustments to both the content and transmission of tradition and, therefore, of revelation. Daphne's personhood, subjectivity, and agency challenge centuries of tradition that have not fully recognized people with IDD as rightly belonging in church life. Our bodies—weak and vulnerable though they may be—are holders of revelatory grace and wisdom.

By recognizing embodiment as revelatory, it is possible for Kelly, despite Reinders's assumptions, to take part in doing theology, though she will need both persons and structures willing to do the slow, careful work of recognizing and translating her bodily practices. This means that theologians doing such work must employ not only reflexivity, but careful forms of accountability.

Accountability and Reflexivity

Where Fulkerson engages the revelatory power of the non-discursive, Christian Scharen's "carnal theology" embraces the concrete, gritty details of the theologian's behavior in the field.[34]

Scharen emphasizes the importance of embodiment in perception and the accompanying need for rigorous self-reflection.[35] Scharen explores

---

[33]Fulkerson, *Places of Redemption*, 41–2.
[34]Christian Scharen, "Ecclesiology 'From the Body': Ethnographic Notes toward a Carnal Theology," *Perspectives on Ecclesiology and Ethnography*, ed. Pete Ward (Grand Rapids: William B. Eerdmans Publishing Co., 2012), 50–70.
[35]Christian Scharen, *Fieldwork in Theology: Exploring the Social Context of God's Work in the World* (Grand Rapids: Baker Academic, 2015). See in particular his second chapter on Bachelard and third chapter on Merleau-Ponty.

the reflexivity needed for this work through Loïc Wacquant's "radicalized *habitus*" and "apprenticeship" approach to fieldwork, which "flip[s] the standard position in fieldwork of participant observation so that it becomes observant participation."[36] Wacquant and Scharen both make the body itself a tool of theological work, whether boxing or interviewing informants.[37] The difference between Scharen and Wacquant is in the kind of *habitus* that Christians are asked to take on: Scharen argues that *kenosis*, "dispossession," as the defining attribute of a Christian *habitus*.[38] The act of dispossession allows the critical lens of reflexivity to work.

Accountability, however, is not solely a matter of reflexivity—it involves the communities in which we do fieldwork, too. Aana Vigen defines accountability with four practical elements: (1) a commitment to following-up with informants and avoidance of misappropriation and misinterpretation; (2) the obligation to describe someone or something well, in all its complexity; (3) prioritizing the collaborators; and finally, (4) that the research itself "ought to matter in some way to the positive transformation of society."[39] Taken together, reflexivity and accountability prevent the ethnographic research from becoming symbolically and discursively violent—whether by simply being a "pornographic" account of the struggles and lives of people on the margins, or by becoming a "tautology," that is instrumentalizing the data to prove pre-established ideas.[40] Making a community's feedback integral to the process also preserves the collaborative nature of ethnographic work and theology.

Vigen's specific practices of accountability do have limits and some critics. Fulkerson, for example, admits that she did not bring her writing back to Good Samaritan, a decision born of both time and her knowledge of the racial dynamics at the parish. She asserts that she was using an interpretive framework to describe the dynamics of the church which many of the informants would not have had access to. She questions:

> have I crossed the line of "accountability"? If so, should every interpretation by the ethnographer require assent/collaboration? But

---

[36]Scharen, *Fieldwork in Theology*, 100.

[37]For an outline of a method of qualitative interviewing that Scharen provides as both formative and theological, see: Eileen R. Campbell-Reed and Christian Scharen, "Ethnography on Holy Ground: How Qualitative Interviewing Is Practical Theological Work," *International Journal of Practical Theology* 17, no. 2 (2013): 232–59. Campell-Reed and Scharen both place a high value on establishing trust with their interview subjects, preserving their dignity and agency, and ensuring their stories are genuinely heard. Everything from environment to questions to expectations for the focus group participants is integrated into these concerns.

[38]Scharen, *Fieldwork in Theology*, 106.

[39]Aana Marie Vigen, *Women, Ethics, and Inequality in U.S. Healthcare: "To Count among the Living"* (New York: Palgrave Macmillan, 2006), 95–6.

[40]Christian Scharen and Aana Marie Vigen, *Ethnography as Christian Theology and Ethics* (New York: Continuum, 2011), 20–1.

these questions are connected to the inevitable re-framings that come with theological/ ethical employment of ethnography. Even to "interpret" what folks without language are communicating, if one had the skills of reading nonsymbolic communication, would be a reframing that could not be safely or adequately confirmed.[41]

Fulkerson's questions resonate with my own work. I was a theologian doing fieldwork in a secular nonprofit, and so I had a set of concepts and questions that were unfamiliar to many of the clients, staff, and administrators. I've experienced dynamics of privilege and power in my fieldsite that leave me unsure of how to enact accountability with Payton. These obstacles were both structural, in that Payton as an organization often had different priorities than I did, and interpersonal, in that the clients I worked with at Payton were so eager to be a part of my research that I was often unsure if they would effectively counter or challenge my interpretation of the events that happened. With respect to Vigen's definition of accountability, I feel confident that I have strived to do the work of description well, "in all its complexity"; I also prioritize the stories and perspectives of the clients (insofar as I had access to them). Where I have felt lacking in this work is in the follow-up, and the hoped-for contribution to "a positive transformation for society."

When I first started writing my dissertation, I attended a seminar with anthropologists where the issue of feedback among informants came up over our dinner conversations. There were a lot of different views on the topic—with some embracing the practice and others more hesitant, worried about making their informants responsible for conclusions that it was clear had originated with the researcher. The American Anthropological Association (AAA) takes that position that

Anthropologists should not withhold research results from research participants, especially when those results are shared with others. However, restrictions on disclosure may be appropriate and ethical, such as where study participants have been fully informed and have freely agreed to limited dissemination, or where restrictions have been placed on dissemination to protect the safety, dignity, or privacy of research participants or to minimize risk to researchers.[42]

---

[41]Christian Scharen and Aana Marie Vigen, "Roundtable on Ethnography as Christian Theology and Ethics: Ethnography Audacious Enough to Witness," *Practical Matters Journal* 6 (2013): 5.

[42]American Anthropological Association, "Code of Ethics 2012," *AmericanAnthro.org*, available online: https://www.americananthro.org/LearnAndTeach/Content.aspx?ItemNumber =22869&navItemNumber=652#openandhonest (accessed October 1, 2019).

This does not explicitly address the issue of feedback, per se, but it does suggest that the default position of the ethnographer ought to be one of transparency and openness. AAA frames the question through relationships, with the hope that developing trust between researcher and informant creates opportunities to learn more deeply about their culture, their worldview, and even about places where informants might have misled the researcher. It is not clear, from this statement, how AAA would respond to the questions Fulkerson raises about informants with limited language and symbolic thought. Vigen would likely add that as Christian ethicists, we have a stronger obligation to those we encounter in the field, especially when they come from marginalized communities, to recognize their dignity as collaborators in this project. I suspect she would say that in whatever form I could communicate my findings, I should do so.

This is one element of accountability in which I feel I may have failed. There were structural barriers to contend with: primarily, limitations of access. I had no access to my informants outside of Payton as an institution. In fact, once I began, my access within Payton was limited to clients who were able to give their own informed consent (rather than a guardian), since I encountered concerns about HIPAA privacy that had not been raised when I went through Payton's IRB. While many clients had phones, email, and access to social media, concerns for their privacy prevented me from collecting that information. This meant that when my teaching responsibilities kept me from being on site, I also lost the ability to communicate with clients, or with many staff. I was also sensitive (perhaps overly so) to the fact that I was a guest in Payton's space, so I was personally reluctant to ask more of them: more time with clients, an opportunity to present research, etc. The options I could come up with all seemed to create burdens for Payton, and so they went unpursued. I am not sure this was the right moral judgment, but it is the one I made that I must continue to wrestle with and question. Throughout this text, I am confronted by the question: *have I done enough?*

I did find a partial, limited solution for making concrete contributions to flourishing through my teaching. Following my dissertation defense, I took up a postdoctoral position where I spent the year teaching a community-based learning course for undergraduates. In that course I was able to keep collaborating with Payton, thereby leveraging what social capital I had to meet needs that Payton expressed—in this case, volunteers for their social programs. I also shared the knowledge this work gave me with those who might carry it forward. In the name of transparency, I must admit I am still dissatisfied with this. Useful as it was for Payton, it served the institution rather than the clients themselves.

I have identified here some obvious struggles, both pragmatic and theoretical, to integrating the voices of people with IDD into the doing of theology. Taking up ethnography is a risk: a risk of encounter, a risk in getting it right (or wrong). It has provided the foundation to ask important theological questions about flourishing in the lived—and living—experience of IDD communities. Payton becomes a place where sin, struggle, and grace are visible through the everyday lives of the clients and staff. I ask these questions in the ultimate hope that we can generate practices that make our communities more inclusive, loving places.

Daring to Identify Grace

Given the discussion so far, my attempt in this book to identify grace highlights the risk of ethnography—it is always risky to use etic vocabulary in an ethnography. Nonetheless, I make the case that over time Payton becomes a place where grace is revealed in the very ordinary lives of the clients I worked with. Even as I clarify some of the boundaries and borders of what may be grace, I follow Elizabeth Dreyer by using:

> "description" rather than "definition" because the nature of the task requires a category as open ended as possible. The situation will frustrate those who like things clean, neat, organized, and labelled. It will delight the person who is more comfortable with open boundaries, ragged edges, and endless possibilities.[43]

Dreyer's use of description is not unlike its role in ethnography: it remains ambiguous and riddled with tensions. Such is the nature of fieldwork, and such is the nature of locating grace within limited, fallible, and vulnerable human lives.

Dreyer offers seven broad principles as the foundation of her description of grace: (1) "grace is universal"; (2) "grace is relational"; (3) "grace is corporate"; (4) "God is the source of grace, and humans are recipients"; (5) "God freely initiates grace"; (6) "the presence of sin indicates the need for the presence of grace"; and finally (7) "grace has consequences, has real effects on a person's life."[44] It is this final component that justifies my exploration of grace through the work of ethnography. Dreyer—echoing what we saw from Isasi-Díaz, Fulkerson, Scharen, and Vigen—indicates that grace must have some material, detectable presence in the world. This strengthens the need for a liberation theology of intellectual disability, since liberation is rooted in praxis, in concrete practices that improve human flourishing in both a material and a spiritual sense. Liberation becomes a place where grace is visible in the world.

Now, it must be said that liberation and grace are not co-extensive; nonetheless, liberation certainly depends on God's grace, and where the

---

[43]Elizabeth Dreyer, *Manifestations of Grace* (Wilmington: M. Glazier, 1990), 20.
[44]Dreyer, *Manifestations of Grace*, 21–5.

former is present we might seek the latter. Indeed, when Dryer defines her theological anthropology of the "graced person" as "the human person fully alive," we hear echoes of Gutierrez calling liberation the pursuit of life.[45] Grace as liberation is witnessed to in the enduring, ongoing human struggle for freedom both *from* sin and *for* relationship —with God, with other persons, with creation.[46] Since we will be seeking grace within the human community of Payton, we can look for communal manifestations of grace through the framework Dreyer provides: first, by asking "who is our neighbor?"; second, by learning to be attentive to the abundant presence of grace; third, by being willing to engage in forms of solidarity, or "walking in another's shoes"; and finally, in "giving the gift of self (or receiving it from) another."[47] These questions set up the task of uncovering grace throughout the book.

Chapter 1 asks "who is our neighbor?" by looking at a brief history of how intellectual disability has been defined and treated within the United States. It covers the Parent Movement, whose demands for justice and inclusion made people with IDD visible in an unprecedented way. This chapter will also introduce Payton, born out of the Parent Movement and representing a meso-level incarnation of the macro-level social changes happening in the national disability rights movement. The changes initiated by this movement seek the flourishing of all disabled persons and, in that respect, seek grace. Chapter 2 refutes the criticisms of postliberal theologies about disability rights and their usefulness for flourishing by showing continuity between the disability rights movement and the development of the self-advocacy movement among people with IDD.

Chapter 3 explores grace with more granularity by attending to care work and dependency relationships in the everyday lives of the clients. One of the driving principles behind disability services (and arguably disability advocacy) has been "normalization." On its own, normalization is morally ambiguous. It can provide sites of grace through material and social-well-being, but it can also be restrictive and paternalistic. However, when "normalization" is viewed through the epistemic position of intellectually disabled persons in their relationships with care work and dependency, it can be molded into something more grace-filled.

Dreyer's principles indicate that the presence of sin also reveals the need for grace, so Chapter 4 addresses the tricky topic of sin, both social and personal. Sin and disability have a complex history, but the Parent Movement initiated a significant shift away from associating disability with sinfulness. The result may be an overcorrection: the narrative of the "special child" not only continues the infantilization of the IDD community but also implies

---

[45]Gutiérrez, *A Theology of Liberation*, xxxvii.
[46]Dreyer, *Manifestations of Grace*, 175–7.
[47]Dreyer, *Manifestations of Grace*, 203–4.

that intellectually disabled persons are precluded from participating in sin *because* of their disability. If we take seriously the insights of the previous chapters about the interwoven nature of agency in the IDD community, then we must also admit the agential capacity for this community to participate in sin.

The final chapter explores how faith communities can be in solidarity with the IDD community —not just through best practices for inclusion (although I do address those), but in how we can adjust our own understandings of grace and flourishing. Disability theologies waver between seeing church practices as corrupted by the ableism of the world, or as idealized communities set apart from the vagrancies of worldliness. In reality, church practices often (and rightly so) take from best practices in a range of other worldly disciplines, and then wrestle with how to implement those practices within their own set of faith commitments. Sometimes, those implementations are colored by ableism and normalcy. And sometimes, in their eagerness to be "distinctively" Christian, communities overlook opportunities to learn from places that are already saturated with grace. My hope is for this book to rectify that.

1

We Speak for Them

Payton and the Parent Movement

One of the criticisms that postliberals have expressed about the disability rights movement is that its goal, inclusion, is insufficient for responding to the needs of the IDD community. While I will address the specifics of that argument in more detail in Chapter 2, for the moment I want to explore some of the history behind inclusion—if inclusion is a potential site of grace, then it needs to have offered clear benefits for the IDD community. As we probe the history of inclusion, I am also setting up the narrative behind my fieldsite, Payton Center. To that extent, this chapter examines how Payton intersects with American disability history. Payton began as a fruit of the Parent Movement, but in the wake of the ADA, the organization has found itself at an uncertain crossroads, struggling to remain accountable to multiple agents: clients, parents/guardians, and the state regulatory powers that control funding.

Payton represents a local incarnation of the broader disability rights movement, and it is the means by which inclusion offers real material benefits to people with IDD. What I present here is an overview of the most significant moments in Payton's development and how the organization has worked toward the ever-thickening idea of inclusion. Embedded in this history is a series of tensions: segregation vs inclusion; needs and scarcity; opportunities for rehabilitation and irredeemable burdens. We can generally define inclusion as the rejection of segregation and the promotion of social integration. Yet, for Payton (and many other organizations), their noble vision of inclusion and human flourishing is often subject to a crucible of economic pressures that slows the long arc of justice.

A Note on Language

Writing historically about IDD is a troublesome, anachronistic task, since the term disability itself is a recent innovation and "intellectual and developmental disability" may be just another waystation on a road of rapidly developing definitions and terminology.[1] Many older, once-official terms have become insults over time—for example, the "Spread the Word to End the Word" campaign rightly rejects the use of "retarded," though a generation ago "mental retardation" was accepted terminology. Language once used to describe people with IDD becomes today's commonplace insults: idiot, moron, imbecile, and so on. The frequent shifts in language reject these insults, although James Trent remarks that despite new terms, "the gaze we turn on those we label mentally retarded continues to be informed by the long history of condescension, suspicion, and exclusion."[2] Therefore, throughout the chapter I will use the vocabulary that would have been employed in the era I am writing about. This is in part to reflect the fluidity of the concept "intellectual disability," but also invites the reader who is made uncomfortable by this language to reflect on that discomfort, and ask whether we use contemporary phrases to "hide from the offense [of our treatment of IDD] in ways the old terms did not permit."[3]

Defining and Describing the Feebleminded: Burden or Opportunity?

To make sense of the rights movement that dominated the last half of the twentieth century, we have to reach back into the mid-1800s, which set the stage for several patterns that appear throughout disability history. The cultural view of what would become IDD has vacillated between that of an irredeemable burden or potentially rehabilitated citizen. In debates about the possibilities of treatment and rehabilitation, two social welfare institutions emerged as the ongoing battlegrounds for control of people with IDD: schools and custodial institutions. In Payton's own history, both education and custodial care feature prominently, and these early origins show that the two strands of services are deeply interwoven with the question of what true inclusion looks like.

The first optimistic belief in rehabilitation for the feebleminded came from Edouard Seguin, who sought to make "improvable" idiots into

---

[1] Lennard Davis, *Enforcing Normalcy* (London: Verso, 1995), 23–49.
[2] James W. Trent, *Inventing the Feeble Mind: A History of Mental Retardation in the United States* (Berkeley: University of California Press, 1994), 5.
[3] Trent, *Inventing the Feeble Mind*, 5.

"productive and upright citizens" through his methods of education.[4] These early methods required "tedious, individualized training . . . the creation of a family-like environment and minute-by-minute involvement with the pupil in the classroom, at the table, in the kitchen and the bedroom."[5] In order to create such a regulated space, education for what were labeled *simple idiots* shifted from community schools or private homes into extensive, all-encompassing specialized facilities. These facilities generally did not admit adults or cases deemed particularly difficult (e.g., epileptics, or insane idiots rather than simple ones).[6] Publicized success stories made Seguin's methods more popular, and superintendents of early institutions were eager to expand their mission. However, they learned that it was almost impossible to scale up and economize that level of individualized training.[7] Furthermore, external economic pressures exacerbated the demand for institutions: in the fallout of the Civil War and the depression that began in 1873, families that were impoverished after the war (further harmed by the effect of rising inflation) sought to unload burdensome, unproductive mouths to feed. Private tuition could no longer support institutions, and pupils were no longer finding jobs once they completed their training and education. Superintendents of the once-educational institution pivoted away from temporary admission, and sought public, governmental funding that would allow them to include classes of idiot that had been previously excluded—only now as a permanent *custodial* arrangement.[8] Superintendents also decided to use the labor of educable idiots for the institution itself, and make it more economically efficient.[9] Thus, schools turned into asylums.[10]

The shift from temporary education to permanent custody was accompanied by a shift in the social perception of idiocy: the initial optimism gave way to pessimism, as idiocy moved from being a problem of training and behavior (Seguin's theory) to being a genetic pathology.[11] Now we enter the era of eugenics, a period of policy and pseudo-science that lingers as a powerful specter over disability history. Initially based on qualitative "pedigree" studies such as Richard Dugdale's *The Jukes*, eugenics used rudimentary understandings of heredity to promote not only "race purification and human perfection," but also "a solution to social problems through better human breeding."[12] The ideology behind eugenics gained momentum from the same economic and social pressures that forced the

---

[4]Trent, *Inventing the Feeble Mind*, 26.
[5]Trent, *Inventing the Feeble Mind*, 28.
[6]Trent, *Inventing the Feeble Mind*, 25–7.
[7]Trent, *Inventing the Feeble Mind*, 29.
[8]Trent, *Inventing the Feeble Mind*, 63–2.
[9]Trent, *Inventing the Feeble Mind*, 74.
[10]Trent, *Inventing the Feeble Mind*, 31–8.
[11]Carey, *On the Margins of Citizenship*, 52–3. Trent, *Inventing the Feeble Mind*, 16–23.
[12]Trent, *Inventing the Feeble Mind*, 136.

shift into asylums.[13] Eugenics did not just fixate on disability; it was deeply informed by race, gender, ethnicity, and the preservation of middle-class moral sensibilities. Eugenics was taken up to defend white, middle-class values by arguing that the members of that class were from inherently "good stock," while those who were not had been doomed by genetics.[14]

Proponents of eugenics began to classify feeblemindedness through intelligence and social adaptation. Intelligence was measured by IQ tests administered in public schools: by extension, this made the public schools one of the mechanisms for control of those deemed feebleminded. One classification system identified three levels: idiot, with a mental age below three; imbeciles, granted a mental age between three and seven years old; and finally morons, determined to be between seven and twelve years of age in development.[15] While IQ tests were often the facade for a scientific determination of feeblemindedness, social location also played a significant role. Unsurprisingly, given their racial and class biases, eugenicists documented much higher rates of feeblemindedness among immigrant populations and Black Americans.[16] A gendered version of this construction emerged in the vilification of the "feebleminded woman," targeted not so much for her achievement on an IQ test as for her moral standing. Poor women, especially women who had children out of wedlock, were blamed as one of the root causes of the problem, perpetuating the genes that caused feeblemindedness through their "lasciviousness" and lack of willpower.[17] Once the label of feebleminded was established, the feebleminded person was under near-complete medical control, with little recourse to contest the loss of their civil rights.[18] Even parents of children given this label had limited powers of control, and where the parental will conflicted with medical opinion, it was commonly ignored. Social services (sharing the medical viewpoint) also held significant powers of economic and legal suasion: they could initiate institutionalization, restrict access to services, or impose behavioral (and moralized) codes of conduct on (typically low-income) households.[19]

The legacy of eugenics is most closely associated with forced sterilizations, but that was actually a late development in the United States. Initially, the segregation of the feebleminded from society was sufficient to meet

---

[13]Trent, *Inventing the Feeble Mind*, 79.

[14]Carey, *On the Margins of Citizenship*, 53–5.

[15]Carey, *On the Margins of Citizenship*, 63; Trent, *Inventing the Feeble Mind*, 80.

[16]Trent, *Inventing the Feeble Mind*, 138–9.

[17]Carey, *On the Margins of Citizenship*, 55; Michael L. Wehmeyer, *The Story of Intellectual Disability: An Evolution of Meaning, Understanding, and Public Perception* (Baltimore: Paul H. Brookes Publishing Co, 2013), 152; Trent *Inventing the Feeble Mind*, 81–3.

[18]Carey, *On the Margins of Citizenship*, 77–9.

[19]It is worth noting that these systems of control for the feebleminded ran parallel to systems that reigned over other marginalized groups, but the significant difference was that other groups could (in theory) leave the systems by assimilating into white, middle-class values and culture.

eugenicists' goals; yet again, economic stress served as a catalyst when the United States entered the Great Depression. The physical and monetary resources of asylums fell consistently short of the demands made on them; the Great Depression simultaneously attracted more people to institutional services while shrinking institutional financial capital. Superintendents needed a valve to relieve the pressure, and the mandatory sterilization of feebleminded women and men offered an answer: those who might be able to work as productive citizens ("morons") could rejoin society, but be prevented from reproducing their faulty genes. When *Buck v. Bell* set the "three generations" precedent allowing compulsory sterilization, institutions hoped to use it to manage an exploding population crisis.[20] Sadly, just as after the Civil War, many residents of institutions who were supposed to be discharged could not find employment, and remained in custodial care: "after the 1930s, parole would wane; sterilization would not."[21]

Yet, even as mandatory sterilization picked up legal support, superintendents of the institutions were starting to resist the eugenic ideology. This was in part due to the "new psychiatry" that rose after the First World War, which "began to shift from a unit character explanation of insanity to a multicausal one." Genetic scientists had also been critical of the methods that eugenicists employed.[22] There were also important critiques from the burgeoning field of cultural anthropology, which argued in favor of "nurture" over "nature" and asserted the importance of environment in personal formation.

Finally, Carey notes that Catholic culture provided a significant site of resistance, specifically against sterilization. According to Carey:

> Unlike the scientific community, the Catholic church developed a strong grassroots campaign against pro-sterilization legislation ... more than just hard scientific evidence, the church offered an ideology that debunked the moral assumptions of eugenics, presented the danger of state intervention for democracy and faith and offered an alternative vision of justice and humanity.[23]

---

[20]Trent, *Inventing the Feeble Mind*, 198–201.

[21]Trent, *Inventing the Feeble Mind*, 203.

[22]Carey, *On the Margins of Citizenship*, 75–6. A large chunk of the research being done was through collecting oral family histories. Elizabeth Kite, a woman working for eugenicist Henry H. Goddard, is responsible for a large number of the family histories used to provide evidence of the hereditary nature of feeblemindedness. Carlson, *The Faces of Intellectual Disability*, 73–4. At the same time, this approach to the work is not as terribly far off from qualitative work as we would like to believe. The critique of "hearsay" presumes that empirical scientific research is innately superior. Rather, it would seem that the presumptions one takes into your scientific research (remember, Galton was a statistician) influences the work far more than method.

[23]Carey, *On the Margins of Citizenship*, 76.

Citing *Castii cannubi* and its clear stance against sterilization, this moment in Carey—almost an aside, an afterthought—is one of the few places in modernity where the Catholic institutional church is a visible support for people with IDD. Eugenicists in the United States sometimes targeted Catholicism because of the high birth rates of Catholic immigrants. Catholic moral thinkers honed in on the practices of sterilization, such as vasectomies, as the central moral dilemma of eugenics policy. There were some theologians who supported punitive sterilization, but for the most part it was roundly rejected, often through the language of "rights"—for example, a canon lawyer, argued that the state could not sterilize because "man's spiritual right to marry was superior to the right of society to protect itself."[24] Yet, this resistance was primarily about the problem of compulsory sterilization; the underlying premise of eugenics, to prevent hereditary degeneration (physical and mental alike) was accepted by Catholics both for and against sterilization. A few lay Catholics who wrote on the topic at the turn of the century tended to dismiss the entire eugenics movement outright, while it was Catholic clergy who supported the goals, but not the methods.[25] *Castii Cannubi* was not the origins of this resistance, but actually a culmination of the debates that finalized the position Catholics ought to take about sterilization.[26]

In this all too brief overview of what Trent calls "inventing idiocy" we see persistent tensions that manifest throughout Payton's story. There is a constant tension between who can and cannot be rehabilitated, and what to do with the latter. Economic pressure and uncertainty both create more demand for services, as communities struggle to care for the most dependent among them, and further limit the resources needed. Great successes breed optimism that then fades when budgetary belts need to be tightened. Payton's own story begins in the aftermath of the Second World War, but the problems of funding carry on even as parents and advocates hoped to rewrite the script for disability.

Disability after the Second World War

The Nazi's use of eugenics thoroughly discredited its proponents, and in the wake of the Second World War public view of the feebleminded swung back toward that of the "potentially productive citizen." Though custodial institutions would continue to grow during these decades, vocational training and employment also emerged (although participation in these was almost always predicated on the capacity to

---

[24]Christine Rosen, *Preaching Eugenics* (Oxford: Oxford University Press, 2004), 49.
[25]Rosen, *Preaching Eugenics*, 145.
[26]Rosen, *Preaching Eugenics*, 158–9.

"pass" as nondisabled—such optimism about rehabilitation never applied to profoundly intellectually disabled persons). Services for people with mental retardation were justified by a cost-benefit analysis: an investment in services such as education or vocational rehabilitation would ideally pay off when the person could become a productive member of society, pay taxes, and purchase goods.[27]

There were other cultural currents that ushered in the shift to rehabilitation. The return of veterans from the Second World War with acquired disabilities (commonly physical, but psychological traumas as well) generated both greater visibility and a stronger moral imperative toward social responsibility for people with disabilities. The services that American society felt it owed to veterans also spilled over into services for people with mental retardation. Take this telling statistic—from the mid-1950s to 1960s, funding for vocational rehabilitation in the broadest sense grew threefold; funding for vocational rehab targeted to people with mental retardation grew fifteenfold.[28] The social supports that appeared following the Second World War would have a lasting, multi-generational impact. In fact, this illustrates a common theme in the history of the disability rights movement: the heightened expectations of each successive generation. As certain supports are taken for granted, new ones are demanded; old victories become the foundation for new fights.[29] The transition ushered in by the Second World War became the cornerstone of the disability rights movement and formed a generation of parent advocates who created not only Payton itself, but the world of disability services that Payton continues to work in.

The Parent Movement

Payton's origin story begins as the fruit of what is known as the Parent Movement, a subset of the broader disability rights movement and the one most closely associated with the IDD community. Though postliberal theologians are correct when they describe how people with IDD have had limited representation in the disability rights movement, it is also important to recognize that the IDD community shares in and has benefited from many of the same goals. When bigger structures have shifted, such as access to schools or transportation, communities like Payton have benefited. Here, I focus on key events (some of them still unfolding) that have had a significant impact on Payton's development as both a community and an organization, moments which embody the ongoing tensions of integration

---

[27]Carey, *On the Margins of Citizenship*, 83–104.
[28]Carey, *On the Margins of Citizenship*, 84.
[29]Lennard Davis puts this most clearly in his discussion of the "ADA generation" at the end of his history and overview of the ADA. Davis, *Enabling Acts* (Boston: Beacon Press, 2015), 245–6.

vs segregation and the ongoing economic pressures of disability services. Payton, as a particular community, incarnates on a local level the struggles and challenges of the Parent Movement that changed the shape of how we see intellectual disabilities across the United States.

Naming and Claiming the "Special Child"

As we saw, institutions started with education in mind, and only later became the all-encompassing, custodial asylum. Taking custody of a "feebleminded" patient entailed almost a total separation from parents. Even parents who tried to stay in touch and host home visits were often discouraged from doing so, on the premise that taking a resident out of their routine caused problems upon his or her return. One such parent was the acclaimed author Pearl S. Buck: her daughter, Carol, was institutionalized in 1928 at the age of ten, on doctors' advice. Buck had originally resisted institutionalization, since she lived in China and families there kept disabled relatives in the household. Shortly after Carol's placement, Buck was able to finish *The Good Earth* and the money from its success allowed her to donate a substantial sum ($50,000) and join the board of Carol's institution, Vineland. Buck tried to keep up with visits, but "Vineland officials complained that visits to Buck's home disturbed Carol. ... Buck built a home just for Carol's stays, but eventually even her visits there ended."[30] In 1950, she published *The Child Who Never Grew*, a memoir about Carol and the long process of diagnosis and eventual placement.[31]

Buck's confessional work launched others. Another popular book was by Dale Evans Rogers (wife and performing partner of Roy Rogers), who wrote an account of her daughter Robin, who had Down Syndrome, in *Angel Unawares*.[32] What makes *Angel Unawares* particularly interesting is how Rogers framed the narrative: it is written from Robin's perspective, as if she is literally an angel in heaven following her tragic death from mumps and encephalitis. Rogers writes in her introduction: "I believe with all my heart that God sent her on a two-year mission to our household, to strengthen us spiritually and to draw us together in the knowledge and love and fellowship of God."[33]

Parents, emboldened by the solidarity expressed by such public figures as Buck and Rogers, started to reject the stigma associated with having a child with what was then called mental retardation. Where once the "feebleminded" were a curse for society to fear, the Parent Movement

---

[30]Trent, *Inventing the Feeble Mind*, 232.
[31]Pearl S. Buck, *The Child Who Never Grew* (New York: J. Day, 1950); Wehmeyer, *The Story of Intellectual Disability*, 180–2; Carey, *On the Margins of Citizenship*, 109–10.
[32]Trent, *Inventing the Feeble Mind*, 233–4.
[33]Quoted in Trent, *Inventing the Feeble Mind*, 235.

re-wrote the script, and the image of the "special child" emerged. On one hand, parent testimonies stressed the similarity of their children with IDD to any other child: "they all need love."[34] Parents insisted that their children were integral parts of their family, relying on sympathy for the middle-class "family values" that were emerging at the time. On the other hand, they played up the innocence of their children and rejected the cost-benefit analysis that had driven earlier calls for services. Parents made claims based on their children's needs, not their potential contribution.[35] The efficacy of the "special child" would arguably prove to be a double-edged sword. Playing upon the "eternal child" stereotype of people with IDD may have been an effective tactic on a certain level, to seek sympathy (or perhaps pity) on their children's behalf. Yet, in stressing thir innocent, joyful natures, these parents may have inadvertently been putting forward another variation on the narrative of the "deserving poor."

This need-based narrative for rights that parents now offered was made possible by the growing cultural acceptance of social welfare and post-war language of human rights.[36] First, they claimed parents' rights: to determine the best for their children and to actively parent their children, whether that child lived in their home or in an institution. By the late 1950s, parents came to claim rights on their children's behalf, as well, which included (per Carey): community clinics; access to regular medical exams; community-based parent education programs; vocational training; integration within community organizations and programs; day care and respite programs; guardianship legislation; public support for research; improved quality of residential centers; and standardization of training requirements for professional care and service providers. Yet, as Carey notes, at this time rights actually had very limited legal suasion. While examples such as "The Bill of Rights for Retarded Children" (1959) show some embrace of the term (and pose rights as a result of intrinsic human worth), the actual regulatory power of such legislation was extremely limited.[37]

In this respect, one of the greatest boons for parents came from one of the United States' legacy families, who were laden with capital in every sense of the word: the Kennedys. In the 1960s, Eunice Kennedy Shriver started writing publicly about her older sister, Rosemary Kennedy. Rosemary was the third child born to Joe Kennedy Sr. and Rose Fitzgerald, a year younger than the eventual president, John F. Kennedy. Though diagnosed with mental retardation at a young age, Rosemary lived with her parents for the first part of her life. As she matured and went through adolescence,

---

[34]Wehmeyer, *The Story of Intellectual Disability*, 191; Carey, *On the Margins of Citizenship*, 110–20; Trent, *Inventing the Feeble Mind*, 230–7.
[35]Carey, *On the Margins of Citizenship*, 119.
[36]Carey, *On the Margins of Citizenship*, 117–22.
[37]Carey, *On the Margins of Citizenship*, 120–1.

Rosemary became rebellious, and some report she had severe, uncontrolled moodswings. Other reports discuss her desire for sexual relationships with men as contributing factors to her increasingly "troublesome" behavior.[38] In 1941 she attacked her maternal grandfather, and Joe Kennedy sent his daughter for a lobotomy. At the time, these were new procedures believed to cure those who suffered from behavioral problems or severe mood swings.[39] Instead, the lobotomy severely diminished the capacities that Rosemary had previously displayed. At that point, she was institutionalized, and the Kennedys hid the truth of her condition ("as much because of Rosemary's lobotomy as because of her retardation") until John was elected in 1961.[40] After her brother's election to the presidency, Shriver seized the opportunity that his position and her own family's social capital gave her, and wrote publicly about Rosemary's condition in a letter for the *Saturday Evening Post*—"that she had reviewed carefully with the White House."[41]

From that point forward, the Kennedys became powerful public allies for parent advocates, investing both social and financial capital in supporting the goals of the Parent Movement. In the public sector, Kennedy established the "President's Committee on Mental Retardation"; a key member was Elizabeth Boggs, a well-known leader in the Parent Movement. Furthermore, shortly before Kennedy's death, he signed a massive public funding bill, "Community Mental Health Centers Construction Act of 1963," designed to expand rehabilitative services. For her part, Shriver would do a great deal of advocacy work for the IDD community in the private sector, writing against the abuses found within custodial institutions, and eventually founding the Special Olympics.

Rita Jo's Parents and a New School

In 1950, Payton Center was founded by a concerned group of parents. As the story goes, a Jewish grocer and his wife living in northwest Indiana had a daughter, Rita Jo—but her delivery was troubled. Forceps were used, there was an accident, and severe bleeding left Rita Jo with significant disabilities for the rest of her life. Rita Jo's parents flatly refused the recommendation of institutionalization. Her mother sought other mothers facing the challenges of raising a child with a disability, and shortly thereafter, the "Retarded Children's Committee" was founded in March 1950, with Rita Jo's father as president.[42] The origin story of Payton begins with this collection of

---

[38]Wehmeyer, *The Story of Intellectual Disability*, 199–200.
[39]Trent, *Inventing the Feeble Mind*, 247–8.
[40]Trent, *Inventing the Feeble Mind*, 248.
[41]Trent, *Inventing the Feeble Mind*, 248.
[42]The original name for Payton has been changed in order to preserve privacy.

parents who came together to figure out how to serve their children. On its website, Payton writes: "When a handful of families from every corner of the community, rich and poor, decided they'd no longer allow their children to be sent away to institutions, they started their own school on [Payton] Street." Starting with bake sales to fundraise, they secured a dilapidated building that the school system was no longer using. Together, the parents performed the cleaning and painting for this building with their own hands to turn it into a school for children with intellectual disabilities: "The Payton School for Retarded Children."

Two points of this origin story are repeated throughout Payton's internal documents (including a kind of oral history written by a journalist for its fiftieth anniversary): first, the community of parents that come together; second, the lack of money. Notably, the original name—Retarded Children's Committee—is often absent. The way Payton tells its story paints a portrait of risk-takers who stumbled upon a way to offer hope to fellow parents, fellow citizens.

However, newspapers from the time tell a more complex story. In 1949, the city already had three community groups concerned for people with mental retardation: the Christian Family Movement, the Citizen's Society for Mental Health, and a parent group, Parents for Children with Cerebral Palsy. At least one public address is on record as advocating for "mentally ill children."[43] The rehabilitation and education model is evident: in the public address, a local priest and professor argued that people with disabilities can be taught, and trained to integrate with the workforce. Given these preexisting groups and public conversations, it is possible to see the founding of the Committee (Payton), as the result of a movement already in motion, both locally and nationally.

The early emphasis on education by the Committee mimics the priorities of the Parent Movement, especially the National Associated for Retarded Children (NARC, the predecessor to the organization now known as the ARC, today). Although they advocated for a variety of services, "the need for educational services was often *the* driving motivation for [parent] organizing."[44] While institutions and asylums had become the primary context for disability services, the was never sufficient room for the need, so there were still many children with mental retardation living at home. Associations like NARC were not opposed to custodial institutions, but they did have doubts about them.[45] Furthermore, over eighty-six thousand students with mental retardation were not in custodial institutions, but in local schools (as of 1948).[46] Often segregated from the nondisabled

---

[43]"Mentally Ill Children to Receive Aid," *South Bend Tribune*, November 16, 1949.
[44]Carey, *On the Margins of Citizenship*, 122, emphasis original.
[45]Trent, *Inventing the Feeble Mind*, 242.
[46]Trent, *Inventing the Feeble Mind*, 238.

students, these "special education classes and schools, when they existed at all, had become the dumping grounds for many 'problem' children"—not just those with mental retardation, but also physical disabilities, juvenile delinquents, and those with mental illnesses.[47] Local associations, like the Committee, focused on improving the services immediately available in their community—in this case, that meant schools and "*specialized* education," or the belief that mental retardation deserved particular attention apart from the other groups of students who had previously been grouped together.[48]

So when the Committee was established, education was its primary mission: although initially Payton was described as an "occupational center" rather than a school, eventually that language drops out and the school language dominates.[49] The organizers may have run bake sales, but they also received capital in multiple forms: money, building space, and donated labor. After being founded in March, by June the Committee had secured the location of the school building.[50] Articles appear regularly in the local paper to describe the progress of the school through 1950–1951. Most of these are about money, but they also frequently describe the kinds of volunteer labor given to fix up the building (including professional painters, alongside parents).[51] The initial cost of the school was projected to be $15,000.[52] Substantial capital came from courting major donors. In August, before the school opening, a major car company gave a $2,400 donation to pay the salary of one teacher.[53] The company then ran an ad in November 1950 advertising for both itself and Payton, speaking of a waitlist of children to attend the school.[54]

Despite the initial success in opening the school, by February 1952 the Committee felt the same resource pinch as the early custodial institutions, and they began to advocate for increased funding through the public school system. As Payton School became a recognizable part of the community, articles throughout the 1950s and 1960s focus on this debate: can their school receive public funds? Public funding presented a stability for Payton that rummage sales and ad hoc corporate donations could not. The tug-of-war that appears in these first few years of Payton's history maps onto

---

[47]Trent, *Inventing the Feeble Mind*, 239.

[48]Trent, *Inventing the Feeble Mind*, 242–3, emphasis original.

[49]"Retarded Pupil Center Planned," *South Bend Tribune*, May 22, 1950.

[50]"Society Rents School Site, Mentally Retarded Children to be Trained," *South Bend Tribune*, June 15, 1950.

[51]"School Plan Receives Help, Retarded Children to Get Special Training," *South Bend Tribune*, June 25, 1950.

[52]Approximately $181,926.97 in 2022.

[53]$29,108.32 for today, a low number even given the overall stagnation of teaching salaries. "Retarded Child Project Aided, [Company] Local to Pay Teacher for One Year," *South Bend Tribune*, August 2, 1950.

[54]"These Our Children: [Company] People Help Start School for Retarded Boys and Girls," *South Bend Tribune*, Slide Spotlight, November 1950.

later debates about integration within the public school system. At first, segregation for retarded children was simply accepted, in part because of a return to Seguin's turn-of-the-century optimism that specialized structures—whether schools or custodial institutions—would be the best option for children with mental retardation. Nonetheless, by 1952, the local factory union (already supporting Payton financially and publicly) sponsored a motion that accused the school board of neglect, because it was failing to offer state-sponsored special education.[55] Reports about public funding for Payton specifically, and special education generally, distinguished between the "educatable" and the "trainable" students—employing old classifications that first appeared among custodial institutions. The *educatable* were argued to be eligible for school integration, while the *trainable* belong to segregated places like Payton.[56] Hence, integration was supported only on the basis of how likely the candidate was to be a potentially productive (i.e., wage-earning) citizen as an adult.

In 1954, the city superintendent of schools argued in favor of supporting Payton School as a separate institution, but also offering government money:

[Payton] has helped "to glamourize" the problems of retarded children by setting an example of the achievements these children are capable of if given proper instruction. He said the children were taught in special classes in public schools, these classes would become "just another institution for the retarded" in which the public would soon lose interest.[57]

The argument here is a fascinating twist on what we might expect—Payton School is seen as doing something different, something that grabs the public attention more than if the education of people with IDD were integrated into standard, expected institutions. The superintendent sees this as worth supporting with public money, but not at the cost of Payton's distinctive identity within the community.

Then, in the 1960s, Committee begins to build a new facility with the help of a federal grant—likely the very grant that Kennedy signed into being. The new location for the Payton School was next to the State Children's Hospital, one of the largest custodial institutions in Indiana. The massive building project brought new visibility to Payton, and offered a more strategic location, being literally, geographically sandwiched between the state hospital and the local university. However, the grant held a fatal flaw: it allotted a great deal of money to new construction, but very little for maintenance and operations. Payton learned this the hard way in 1969,

---

[55]"School Board Denies Neglect, Complainants' Aid asked in Retarded Child Program," *South Bend Tribune*, May 13, 1952.
[56]"Retarded Child Needs New Aid," *South Bend Tribune*, November 19, 1953.
[57]"Allen Opposes Integration of [Payton] School," *South Bend Tribune*, January 28, 1954.

when the City Council cut funding to the school by over 25 percent, and Payton was unable to cover the rising costs of operating the new building.[58] The new financial crisis prompted Payton to make a petition to the school board for emergency funds to stay open.[59]

While Payton made desperate appeals for funding, the parent-driven Pennsylvania Association for Retarded Children (PARC) was launching a groundbreaking civil suit against their state education system.[60] In 1971, taking *Brown vs. the Board of Education* as inspiration, PARC challenged the school system to provide access to the education to which they felt their children had a right. Since the constitution does not actually guarantee an education to every child, the case was made through the fourteenth amendment, that is, "equal protection under the law." A similar suit in 1972, *Mills vs. Board of Education* made a similar ruling for Washington, D.C. The call for mainstreaming—special education that was integrated into public schools—was now gaining momentum, and in 1975 the Education for Handicapped Children Act was passed. This was the legal predecessor to the IDEA Act, which today ensures free public education for all children, regardless of ability status.[61] These court cases set the trajectory of "special education" as it became increasingly committed to the inclusion and integration of people with disabilities.

The Progression of Inclusion

From Special to Mainstream

In the decades that followed the 1975 Education for all Handicapped Children Act, the functions of the Payton School would be slowly but steadily absorbed into the public school system. As a result, Payton's mission had to shift away from schools to other community supports, especially for adults who aged out of the school system. There were clear benefits for bringing education for children with IDD into the public school system: after all, like the early institutions, Payton could never take in all the students who wanted to attend and the school had to charge some level of tuition, even if it was heavily subsidized. Forcing the hand of the public schools

---

[58]Patricia Koval, "Untitled," *South Bend Tribune*, September 10, 1969.
[59]"Untitled," *South Bend Tribune*, September 23, 1969.
[60]Doris Zames Fleisher and Frieda Zames, *The Disability Rights Movement: From Charity to Confrontation* (Philadelphia: Temple University Press, 2011), 184–5.
[61]Fred Pelka, *What We Have Done: An Oral History of the Disability Rights Movement* (Amherst: University of Massachusetts Press, 2012), 135–41. Fleisher and Zames give a comprehensive overview of the juridical development of special education following *PARC vs. PA*, in Fleisher and Zames, *The Disability Rights Movement*, 185–96.

guaranteed education without waiting lists and without tuition. Still, the transition was an imperfect process. In some states, like Mississippi, only Black children were placed in special education classes; in other places like New York, students were placed in special education if English was not their first language.[62] Fleischer and Zames note that the educational ideal laid out in the 1975 law required other class action lawsuits to enforce.[63] But even winning a suit, like the Brooklyn-based *Jose P. vs Board of Education* (1979), would leave school systems scrambling to evaluate and create Individual Education Plans (IEPs) for an estimated thirty thousand students within a year, without nearly enough trained personnel.[64]

For its part, Payton continued to advocate for students and employ its social capital when it could. One example: for a while Payton rented its original school building back to the public school system, which needed the space as it took in a greater number of students for special education. However, frustrated by the continued segregation of disabled children, Payton eventually threatened to revoke the school's access to the space unless the public school moved forward with the integration of special education.[65] Payton also remained active in childhood education by structuring its services around the gaps in the school system. First, Payton offered a Pre-K for young children (three to five years old) with IDD. And then the state made public Pre-K mandatory, and Payton stopped. Then, Payton tried to offer playgroups for these young children that could prep them with necessary skills for socializing and schooling, but then the state decided that all therapies for children with IDD needed to take place in a "natural" (i.e., non-segregated) environment. The playgroups, being exclusive to those with IDD, failed to meet the criteria.

The progression of Payton's child services reflects the impact that the principle of "normalization" began to have on both rehabilitation and education for disabled children. Established by Wolf Wolfensberger, normalization (which he would later rename social role valorization, discussed in more detail in the following chapters), emphasized "culturally normative settings" for disability services and education. This is reflected by the IDEA Act, which establishes the principle of "least restrictive environment," a part of the law that "stipulates . . . whenever feasible, the child with a disability should be educated with nondisabled children to the maximum extent appropriate."[66] The terminology of "natural environments" is an outgrowth of this principle and the increasing moral imperative to integration.

---

[62]Fleisher and Zames, *The Disability Rights Movement*, 186.
[63]Fleisher and Zames, *The Disability Rights Movement*, 186.
[64]Fleisher and Zames, *The Disability Rights Movement*, 186.
[65]Protective Services Caseworker, Personal Interview, July 17, 2015.
[66]Fleisher and Zames, *The Disability Rights Movement*, 187.

As much as integration benefits children—both with and without disabilities—this trend also came with a loss, at least for parents who had built networks and communities of solidarity by being able to meet other parents of children with IDD in these specialized settings. One of the administrators for Payton's Children's Services noted this tension and the loss of choice it entails:

The idea of helping them [children] integrate into a regular classroom and stuff is great, but if we don't have the resources to teach, really teach them at their level in the classroom while they're there, is that a service or a disservice to the child? They may be around their peers, I don't know if they're integrating with their peers, you know their age peers? Are they being taught at the same quality of service level and their peers are being taught? So, uh, you really have to look at the overall thing. It's great that they're there, but are we doing the best service we should for that child?

. . . it was a slow transition [out of Payton's school services]. When I came into children's services, we did have the preschools, 3 to 5-year-old pre-school at the time. And, uhm, we also had a small playgroup, for 2–3 year olds . . . what we found that helped with the parents was that, when they came to pick up and drop off their child, at our 2–3-year old [group]—the parents would talk, you know, they'd be waiting out there maybe 15–20 minutes early, and they'd have a chance to talk. Oh, isn't this—I can't figure out how to do this. Oh, you know there's this resource here, try that, you know? There was that family connection, family to family, that you can't find in any other scenario.

Then when we lost the classrooms, the 3–5-year-old classrooms to the school system, we still continued to have the little groups, and we still continued to have that, which was great. And we also, we had the ability to, uhm, transition. They transitioned easier from our little playgroups to preschool, because they learned to sit at a table, they learned how to sit in those little story groups, they learned how to transition from the classroom to the snack time, or eating, they learned how to transition to swimming. All these transition experiences they got. And then the federal government said—okay, now we're into this early childhood thing, but we want it to be in natural environments. So that eliminated Payton as a possibility of being a natural environment, because they saw Payton as a D-[evelopmental] D-[isabilities] agency where only special needs people went.

. . . One school system doesn't have total integration, and so they don't have a choice, and the other school system has total integration, but they still don't have a choice. What if I want my child, especially if it's a class-room where they're only addressing their special needs, as opposed to where there's an actual teacher, who's taught how to work with special needs kids, as opposed to a pair of professionals who've never worked with a special needs child and then is assigned. But I think choice is probably the best thing ever, you know. Looking at the child, what is this child's—where will this child do the best, according to skill level, according to his emotional level, and everything else. . . . As a parent I don't know what choice I would make.[67]

Today's parents are still essential advocates for people with IDD and still a powerful political force that continues to build on prior victories. The presume a place in the public education system. They fight battles for their children within that institutional structure, rather than with custodial institutions. They are able to focus on IEPs, rather than just trying to get a proverbial foot in the door. As agitators and consumers, parents made significant changes in the shape of public education, but that may have come at the cost of the very choice that Rita Jo's parents and friends first sought in establishing Payton School.

Furthermore, public education does come to an end. While some programs will keep students until their twenties, children do eventually age out of school. The parents that have become accustomed to early intervention and education for children are startled to find how few options exist for their adult children once they graduate. Access to things like independent living, intimate relationships, and marriage presents the next horizons for battle.

Deinstitutionalization

Although institutions loom large in the history of disability, in practical numbers they only served a minority of the "feebleminded." There were also significant differences in the rate of institutionalization along racial and class divides. For example, according to a 1923 census, 7.4 per 100,000 white individuals had been placed in institutional care, while only 2.5 per 100,000 African Americans had been admitted.[68] Public institutions had long waitlists, and private custodial institutions (such as where Buck placed her daughter) were often expensive; despite sliding scale tuitions, cost could be prohibitive for families.[69] How to interpret the impact of these differences depends on whether institutions were seen as positives (access to treatment) or negatives (system of control). The moral ambivalence toward custodial institutions is reflected in the early Parent Movement, which both challenged and collaborated with institutions. Although Payton today has small, community-based residences for clients, it was never involved in the large-scale kind of custodial care that marked early institutions and

---

[67]Director of Children's Services, Personal Interview, March 10, 2016.
[68]Carey, *On the Margins of Citizenship*, 80–2.
[69]See Trent, *Inventing the Feeble Mind*, 142–4; 185–7.

asylums; nonetheless, the legacy of custodial institutions left its own mark on Payton's history and development.

Custodial institutions were typically restrictive, isolating experiences for most people with disabilities, regardless of whether their impairments were physical or intellectual. We've seen that these institutions started with educational goals in mind, but the expansion and subsequent reduction of resources led to "total institutionalization," or a system that would "take feeble minds who were not productive out of society, where they were 'not conducive to the national prosperity.'"[70] Wolfensberger famously described the trajectory of custodial institutions as "isolation, enlargement, and economization." His phrasing maps onto the economic pressures and patterns described in the late nineteenth and early twentieth century, which in turn lead to declining standards of care.[71] These problems were well known within the Parent Movement, and yet between 1950 and 1970 "state authorities built, refurbished, and added to more public facilities than in any other period of their American history."[72] Despite the initial momentum to name and claim their special children, it was clear that institutional placement remained in high demand well into the maturity of the Parent Movement.

Gunnar Dybwad (leader in the Parent Movement and president of ARC) pushed early for the deinstitutionalization of the IDD community.[73] Dybwad criticized the chaotic structure of not only the custodial institutions, but the governing structures behind them:

These mental deficiency institutions were, in most states, completely isolated. You have to understand that you didn't have departments of mental health with institutions carefully separated between juveniles and adults, and between mentally retarded—they would say mental defectives—and people with epilepsy, and those [with other disabilities]. Nobody cared about such differences. . . . You must not try to look too much for any, quote, system, unquote. Each state worked out its own system . . . you would search in vain for any kind of standards. You'd say, "What about the state department [of mental retardation]?" Hell! There was no state department. In general these people got an institution to run, whether through political influence, or not, makes no difference. They were to run these institutions as cheaply as possible, and as long as they didn't cause any trouble, nobody interfered.[74]

---

[70]Trent, *Inventing the Feeble Mind*, 143.
[71]Cited in Wehmeyer, *The Story of Intellectual Disability*, 137.
[72]Trent, *Inventing the Feeble Mind*, 250.
[73]Pelka, *What We Have Done*, 50–6.
[74]Pelka, *What We Have Done*, 51–2.

Even more important is the testimony of Terry Schwartz, a man with IDD who would eventually become the second president of People First, a self-advocacy organization:

> We didn't have no freedom, we didn't have rights at all. They decided when we go to bed. We weren't allowed to take naps. We couldn't go lie down on your own bed if you wanted to relax or take a little nap or something. They controlled everything we did. We're not allowed to have money. Or, we're not allowed to do this, we're not allowed to do that.[75]

Today, advocates refer to the "burrito test" when establishing whether an organization serving the IDD community is an institution: can you get up in the middle of night and heat up a burrito, if you so choose? If not, then it is an institution much like the one Schwartz described. Stories of positive experiences in custodial care are few and far between.[76]

Still, the question of deinstitutionalization for people with IDD was a deeply polarizing one at the beginning of the Parent Movement. A divide emerged between parents who willingly placed their children in institutions, and the parents who unwillingly placed their children, were unable to place their children, or simply refused to place their children in a custodial institution. Parents who supported institutions argued that they lacked the (physical, emotional, monetary) capacities to properly care for their children, and needed the services of an institution. They offered stories of children being happy in their placements, eager to return after visits home. Those parents who disagreed accused institutional supporters of being bad parents who rejected their children and refused the responsibilities that came with having a child with IDD. In a newsletter published by ARC, a parent opposed to institutionalization questions: "where are the parents of these children? Aren't too many parents asking the state to do what they themselves will

---

[75]Pelka, *What We Have Done*, 56.

[76]Fred Fay, a disability advocate who was particularly active in the Democratic Party while trying to get the ADA passed, attended the facility where FDR had been treated following polio: Warm Springs, GA. There, Fay describes finding hope for the first time since he broke his neck from a trapeze accident: "The second day I was there, I realized that some of the teachers were in wheelchairs: my English teacher, my physics teacher, and my German teacher. That had an impact: There was a lot of stuff you could do from a wheelchair" (Pelka, *What We Have Done*, 88). Fay benefited tremendously from peer counseling over the course of his stay, which was not commonly available in 1962. And yet, Fay notes that, even then the facility still practiced Jim Crow segregation. Marilyn Saviola, an activist with Huemann's group, Disability in Action, speaks of choosing to move into an institution as a teenager, seeing the accessible space and peer group in her long-term rehab facility as giving her greater independence than her inaccessible house and pitying neighborhood peers offered (Pelka, *What We Have Done*, 92–3). It is perhaps significant here that both the institutions with positive stories embraced the agency of people with disabilities, whether in Fay's peer counseling or Saviola's capacity to build peer relationships and get out and about easier than in her parents' home. For people with IDD, these options were rarely available in their institutional settings.

not do—that is, accept the retarded as human beings?" Polemics were harsh, and emotions clearly ran high.[77]

By the 1980s the moral momentum had turned against custodial institutions, largely from several significant exposés.[78] The most famous of these was Willowbrook State School. Investigated in a televised report by Geraldo Rivera in 1972, he offered a visceral shock to the public with the degrading treatment of residents, including some who were naked, and lying in their own feces.[79] In the public imagination, Willowbrook issued a moral indictment of an institutional system that had become over-populated and understaffed, neglecting some of the most vulnerable members of the community. That being said, despite the scandal of Willowbrook (and other institutions), there were many parent advocates who spoke up in support of custodial institutions, dependent on them because they could not provide care on their own. Payton's own story is tied up in the deinstitutionalization movement not because of its residential system, but because of its neighbor: the State Children's Hospital.

The State Children's Hospital

In the original plans, the State Children's Hospital would be a temporary care facility for children with life-threatening infectious diseases, such as polio or tuberculosis. Ground was broken in 1947, on land that the local university had purchased and donated, just south of the school's boundaries.[80] The hospital opened in March of 1950, and the layout was celebrated as state of the art: articles highlight the full-length windows that allowed in plenty of natural light and gave the patients who may have had outdoor activity restricted a full view of the area surrounding them.[81]

Yet, as this new facility opened, the polio vaccine lingered just around the corner, waiting to render its raison d'etre obsolete. When the hospital deficit started to run high, and beds started to empty, politicians began suggesting alternatives for the space. By 1957, the first murmurings surfaced about bringing in patients diagnosed with mental retardation. At the time, Indiana

---

[77]Carey, *On the Margins of Citizenship*, 122–3.
[78]One example being Robert Kennedy's scathing report following his visit, after inmates had been infected with hepatitis in order to test a vaccine, without consent. Kennedy's report led to a 1965 photo essay titled "Christmas in Purgatory" by disability scholar Burton Blatt and photographer Fred Kaplan. Wehmeyer, *The Story of Intellectual Disability*, 222–3.
[79]The report was eventually published as a book: Geraldo Rivera, *Willowbrook: A Report On How It Is And Why It Doesn't Have To Be That Way* (New York: Vintage Books, 1972).
[80]"Directors in Meeting Vote Unanimously," *South Bend Tribune*, August 16, 1946; "Presentation Made to Gates by Kiwanians," *South Bend Tribune*, November 29, 1946.
[81]"Northern Indiana Children's Hospital Opens Doors Today," *South Bend Tribune*, March 15, 1950.

had an overcrowded state institution in Muscatatuck, with a reported waitlist "between 100 and 200 children"—a situation that was fairly typical of the institutional system at the time.[82] The proposal to use the hospital for the "mentally deficient" garnered resistance, but both the city and the state hospital soon found themselves caught up in the broader social dynamics at the time. Despite whatever resistance the city may have had, Indiana's state government made the executive decision to move patients from Muscatatuck into the children's hospital in 1958, though at first it was for just 20 out of 100 beds.[83] By 1960, sixty-nine patients had been transferred to the local hospital, and room was being requested for eighty.[84] The final conversion into a custodial institution occurred in 1961.[85] From this point forward, the trajectory of the institution seems to at least roughly align with Wolfensberger's "isolation, enlargement, and economization." The physical capacity of the site expanded from 100 beds to 200, to 300: triple what the original hospital had been designed to hold.[86] Reports appear in the papers about lay-offs in 1969, an indication of the slow tightening of money belts that marked a great deal of the problems with institutional abuse, overcrowding, and neglect.[87]

Meanwhile, Payton had moved out of the school building where it started, and built a new facility that opened in 1968, right next to what was now colloquially known as the "state school." The strategic location for Payton was a harbinger of social changes to come. The 1970s brought a rapid change of fortunes for the state school. By 1972, the year that Rivera's expose of Willowbrook aired, people began to talk of closing the state school.[88] An extensive, three-part feature in the local paper discussed the "disappearing waitlists" for institutional placement, shifts in cultural attitudes, and the increasing availability of community services—in places such as Payton itself. The thematic image that runs through this reporting are the "broken windows" of the state school. Despite the rapid increase in patient population, funds had been increasingly restricted: as the once celebrated, floor-length windows broke, they were boarded up and left in disrepair. Slowly, the children in the state school were being condemned to live in the dark, hidden from sight.

---

[82]"No Decision on Retarded at Children's Hospital and State Deny Muscatatuck Transfer," *South Bend Tribune*, September 13, 1957.

[83]"Begin Shift of Patients: Retarded Children Move Begins to South Bend," *South Bend Tribune*, March 3, 1958.

[84]"Plan Increase at Hospital: Retarded Children Figure Will Rise to 80," *South Bend Tribune*, March 16, 1960.

[85]"61 Assembly May Convert Institution: Children's Hospital Would Be Solely For Retarded," *South Bend Tribune*, January 1, 1961.

[86]"Cost of Expansion Estimated at $782,000," *South Bend Tribune*, June 29, 1962; "Ask $462,000 for Hospital," *South Bend Tribune*, June 24, 1964.

[87]Patricia Koval, "Untitled," *South Bend Tribune*, April 24, 1969.

[88]"First of Three Articles," *South Bend Tribune*, May 28, 1972.

But the children who lived in the state school were hardly broken, and this was one of the driving beliefs behind Payton's forays into advocacy work concerning the institutional system. In November 1972, Payton filed a formal complaint charging the state school with inadequate care.[89] The list of violations put forward was lengthy: the broken windows, odors and lack of ventilation, deteriorating ceilings and floors, use of cribs rather than "normal" beds, inadequate programming, lack of privacy for residents, and inappropriate use of medical isolation. Parents demanded training and education, not just custodial care. A second parents' organization joined Payton's formal complaint. The state school responded to the complaint by arguing that the changes which needed to be made would take a drastic increase in staff—the director notes that "a major problem . . . is keeping employees who make $80-$90 a week and have to care for up to a dozen patients."[90] Nonetheless, by the end of January the complaint was settled and money was dedicated to the needed repairs on the physical building. "Some of the windows had been boarded up since 1963," notes the article; it is perhaps significant that this, the earliest given date for the building's disrepair, came only after the official changeover from hospital to state school and custodial institution.[91]

Money troubles continued to plague the state school, but the local government kept pulling through at the last minute to save it during repeated budget crises.[92] There was also evidence of parent groups that functioned as institutional allies continuing to provide assistance: for example, parents contributed new furniture following a salmonella outbreak in 1972.[93] The institution then made changes in order to become more of a rehabilitation facility than a custodial facility, trying to make the stays of people with IDD shorter. Payton continued collaborating with the state school during this period, but deinstitutionalization generated a new set of problems. Since the state school was designated as a juvenile facility, it only had a legal responsibility to residents until they turned eighteen. Past eighteen, the state school tried to send residents to a "community placement," but the resources to house them outside of institutions were slow to develop (and still are, many advocates argue). One of Payton's caseworkers recalls that "for many, many years a community setting for folks with IDD was a nursing home," which was rarely different than an institution (and in most cases fails the

---

[89]Dolores Liebeler, "Untitled," *South Bend Tribune*, November 26, 1972.
[90]Liebeler, "Untitled"; John Nichols, "Hospital Windows Symbolic," *South Bend Tribune*, January 25, 1973. The salary of $80–90/week would be the equivalents to $460–$515/week today, or a yearly salary of $24,000–$26,700.
[91]Nancy Sulok, "Untitled," *South Bend Tribune*, March 15, 1973.
[92]Newspaper records indicate that State School had to make appeals to the city on at least three occasions: in 1973, 1978, and 1992.
[93]"Untitled," *South Bend Tribune*, August 22 1972.

burrito test).[94] At this point, Payton did offer a group home option, but it was designed for higher-functioning individuals than those who were placed in nursing homes. Most significantly, at this point (the 1980s) Payton was unable to serve people who used wheelchairs; so people with significant mobility impairments were frequently consigned to nursing homes.[95]

Eastside Center

In 1974, a handful of families grew concerned about what would happen to their now-grown children with IDD once the parents had passed on.[96] This was the impetus for developing the Protective Services Board (PSB), a guardianship service and one of Payton's more unique components. Modeled after the kind of care that families might provide, caseworkers on the PSB are involved with every and any detail of a client's day-to-day life that you can think of: shopping, budgets, household cleanliness, meetings, medical needs, even those occasions when someone locks themselves out of an apartment. The union of guardianship with service provider is uncommon, and raises potential conflicts of interest around reporting and accountability to state regulations. To accommodate that, Payton created a distinct board for oversight of the PSB, one which has independent finances and is not accountable to Payton Center's own board. Nonetheless, caseworkers for PSB work in the same office space as the rest of the Payton administrators. This can create understandable awkwardness and tension when a caseworker may have to advocate for a client who they feel is not being adequately served by another of Payton's programs. For many of the long-time members of Payton however, the PSB seems to be the identifying mark of Payton as a whole, and what sets it apart from other strictly service-oriented organizations. It is integral to how Payton sees itself as an advocate, as the story of Eastside Center reveals.

By 1978, the PSB had assumed guardianship of ten clients; meanwhile, caseworkers were aware that one particular nursing home, Eastside Center, was becoming a problem.[97] In 1978, a large blizzard prevented Eastside's staff from reaching their residents, and Payton had to step in to provide help. Although aware of problems, Payton's staff were upset by the level

---

[94]Protective Services Caseworker, Personal Interview, July 17, 2015.
[95]Granted, at this time Payton was not the only service organization offering residential services. There were a handful of other local organizations, and at least one employee the aforementioned caseworker before she got a job at Payton. However, she describe the other organization as focused on respite care (and not Medicaid certified), which would have narrowed the potential population it served. Personal Interview, July 17, 2015.
[96] Protective Services Caseworker, Personal Interview, July 17, 2015.
[97]Protective Services Caseworker, Personal Interview, July 17, 2015—name of the nursing home changed for privacy.

of neglect they discovered. Soon, they involved the city prosecutor and the police department in an investigation. On Halloween 1981, official charges were filed and the nursing home was shut down. One of the caseworkers present for the event described the impact of this event at some length:

So [former residents of the state school] were placed into a local nursing home called [Eastside] Center, and um, initially uh the state hospital sent out different staff, specialists, therapists to work with these individuals in that setting. After a while those folks pulled out, and uh, the nursing home was left to, to its own devices to care for these very needy individuals.

... So when I came on board [in 1981] we were guardians to these ten individuals. And we were aware that there were still issues with this nursing home, that, that folks' needs were not being met. And I think within a month of my starting this job, we got a call saying that the prosecutor was, ah, there had been an undercover police at that nursing home trying to discover what was going on. And the prosecutor ... was actually pressing charges against the corporation. And they had uncovered and witnessed many incidents of physical abuse, and lots of incidences of neglect. So in October—I started in maybe August, or September—in October we became guardian to twenty-seven individuals from that nursing home in one day.

... We went to court and became emergency guardians for twenty-seven in one day, we went into the nursing home to try and meet the folks and find out about them. That was a very specific, and very significant change in the direction of the PSB was going. For as we were taking care earlier of people that the families were no longer able to do it, we then moved into taking care of individuals who had been institutionalized most of their life, and were very needy of all kinds of services, were medically neglected. We were able to find other nursing home placements for them, most of them that didn't have significant medical needs went to a local nursing home on the west side of town, ah, and we became very involved in their life.

... We got very involved with medical, we spent most of our time trying to help these folks with their medical needs, helping them go to doctor's appointments, advocating. Many of them were very, very uh, very overusing psychiatric medications for behavioral problems. So, we were starting our long, and never ending advocacy for appropriate treatment for folks with behaviors.[98]

The closing of Eastside Center comes up again and again in interviews with staff who have a long enough history with Payton. It is a point of pride, that

---

[98]Protective Services Caseworker, Personal Interview, July 17, 2015.

the organization stepped in so quickly, so willingly, despite limitations on resources. This moment was Payton's Willowbrook, when deep, systemic violence and injustice became visible and demanded a moral response.

As significant as the closing of Eastside Center was for Payton's own conscience, it would take much longer for real systemic change to occur. In 2004, well after the passage of the ADA and the Olmstead ruling, Payton saw that Indiana was still putting people with IDD into nursing homes rather than more appropriate community placements.[99] They filed another lawsuit against the state in 2004; when I was conducting interviews in 2015, it was just reaching a settlement.

The Special Olympics: Does Inclusion Require Integration?

For both schools and institutions, the history of disability begins with segregated, disability-only spaces, only to demand more inclusion and community-based services as advocacy evolved. We saw this pattern with Payton School and the shift to natural supports in public education. Deinstitutionalization also displays reflects this moral instinct. Yet, tensions around integration remain. What is asserted in principle (inclusion) struggles to be met in practice. One of the ongoing challenges that Payton (and many other disability service providers) will have to navigate is how to promote inclusion when their historical models (schools and institutions) have required specialized, segregated spaces. This applies not only to education and rehabilitation, but also to social spaces, as well—and one contested site of inclusion has been the Special Olympics.

One of the most important moments in the formation of Payton's identity came when the organization won the bid to host the International Special Olympics. Founded by Eunice Shriver in 1968, the Special Olympics were a way to promote health in the IDD community through greater physical activity. As the games and organization developed, they became a unique opportunity for people with a range of disabilities to come together to experience collaboration, teamwork, and community. On both local and international levels, the games became a place where people with IDD were visible and visibly celebrated. Eager to offer positive reinforcement to a community that rarely received it, organizers of the Special Olympics

---

[99]*Olmstead vs. LC* was an important case for jurisprudence and interpretation of the ADA, particularly as it refers to people with mental illness or intellectual disabilities. The precedent set by Olmstead says that people with disabilities are to live in the "least restricted environment" possible; hence the state of Indiana, by continuing make placements in nursing homes for clients that could live in a less restrictive environment, is in violation of the ADA. More on Olmstead is given in Chapter 2.

created multiple systems to facilitate participation regardless of ability, amassed corporate fundraising, and assembled a vast array of volunteer coaches and assistants. To this day, the Special Olympics first and foremost understands itself as a source of empowerment through building community, relationships, and offering what they believe is a visible site of dignity and joy for the IDD community. Winning the bid to host the international games (alongside the local university) allowed Payton to transition from a small nonprofit struggling for resources to an established force within the community.

Yet, around the time that Payton was hosting, the Special Olympics were coming under criticism over the de facto segregation required for the "Special" Olympics. Journalist Joseph Shapiro describes these tensions during the 1991 International Special Olympics in Minneapolis, which "was having trouble keeping up with the new militancy of younger parents demanding full integration."[100] Barbara Gill, mother of Amar (who has IDD), spoke to Shapiro about her boycott of the 1991 Special Olympics:

> "We have separated people with disabilities into a shadow world . . . it's an imitation world and it can never be as rich or meaningful as the real world." The Special Olympics, she argued, was just one more separate but unequal place in the shadows. The week before . . . Amar Gill, who is retarded, and five other twelve-year-olds won medals in the Milk Carton Boat Race at the Minneapolis Aquatennial Festival, a yearly celebration of the city's lakes. Amar helped his friends, none of whom were disabled, build the fifteen-foot long boat of plastic milk cartons and wood, painted green and shaped like a dragon. He paddled, too, along with the others. To Barbara Gill it was an important moment because "he felt accepted. He felt part of a team."[101]

Amar's story encapsulates the ongoing tensions about integration and inclusion: what serves the IDD community best? Amar's mother believes that total integration, full stop, is the answer. But one has to wonder if Amar would have been accepted so easily by his peers if he were unable to fulfill the basic tasks described: if he used a wheelchair and could not paddle, or lacked the fine motor skills to assist with building the boat. Amar's participation in the Aquatennial relied on the ways in which he passes for normal, not the ways in which he is disabled.

Wolfensberger wrote a critique of the Special Olympics in 1995, which nuances the complaint that the Special Olympics result in "social

---

[100]Joseph P. Shapiro, *No Pity: People with Disabilities Forging a New Civil Rights Movement* (New York: Times Books, 1993), 177.
[101]Shapiro, *No Pity*, 177.

segregation"; given that the Special Olympics necessarily integrates a large number of nondisabled coaches and volunteers within the event, it was not segregated in a practical sense. Rather, Wolfensberger finds the cultural symbolism around the program to be problematic: "both children and adults competed . . . there were [sic] a 'flame of hope' and 'escort huggers,' and like so many other Special Olympics events, the Syracuse games have crawled with clowns and clownery motifs, which reinforce the cultural tendency to see retarded people as clowns and other objects of ridicule."[102] A decade later Keith Storey built on Wolfensberger's criticisms with a longer list of complaints, including the promotion of negative stereotypes rooted in pity; ongoing paternalism in the organizational structure; the power differential between the nondisabled coach and the participants with disabilities negating the development of genuine relationships; the lack of age appropriateness among the activities; a lack of "functional" skills training; a lack of empirical evidence that the Special Olympics improves outcomes for quality of life; and finally, concerns about the financial structure of the organization, citing both internal salaries and the money that corporations spend on self-promotion (as opposed to changing hiring practices for better supporting people with disabilities).[103]

While I am sympathetic to many of the structural criticisms offered by Storey and Wolfensberger, some implicit strands of ableism run through them. First, that social integration is framed by the presence of nondisabled people. Socialization among people with IDD is not considered or seen as valuable. Second, Storey's critiques place value on only certain kinds of benefits. For example, the complaint about "functional skills training" is that "functionality is whether an individual who does not learn to perform a particular activity needs to have someone else do it for him or her. If the answer is yes, the activity is likely to be functional. Many of the Special Olympics events are of doubtful functional value. . . . In the Special Olympics, there is a lack of skill acquisition, and much precious teaching time of functional activities is lost."[104] To say that engaging in regular physical activity and socializing with friends lacks function simply because it does not relate directly to a required life activity is to construe a fairly narrow definition of what benefits the IDD community. The claim that the activities of the Special Olympics detract from time to teach functional skills seems to directly contradict the assertion that Storey begins with, that "people with developmental disabilities often have an abundance of unstructured

[102]Wolf Wolfensberger, "Of 'Normalization,' Lifestyles, the Special Olympics, Deinstitutionalization, Mainstreaming, Integration, and Cabbages and Kings," *Mental Retardation* 33, no. 2 (1995): 128.
[103]Keith Storey, "The Case Against the Special Olympics," *Journal of Disability Policy Studies* 15, no. 1 (2004): 35–42.
[104]Storey, *No Pity*, 36.

free time."[105] While some structural questions about the Special Olympics are justified, particularly concerning the images that the media promotes and the sense of paternalism, on the ground the experiences of the Special Olympics are more complicated.

Payton, at least, believes that their experience with the Special Olympics was ultimately a benefit to the clients and the community, both disabled and nondisabled. From Payton's viewpoint, the Special Olympics promoted inclusion precisely because it brought together the entire community. From the money and volunteer labor that the Special Olympics provided, Payton was able to forge a new sense of stability and standing within the community. It established the Payton Foundation for fundraising, and hired a full-time volunteer coordinator (previously they relied on students and other part-time volunteers). At the time of interviews, the volunteer coordinator held close ties to the marketing department: the current director of marketing started as the director of volunteers until the former, and first, marketing director retired.

There is another angle from which the question of inclusion needs to be seen, and that is the view of the IDD community itself—a view not well documented in histories written from the perspective of caregivers and nondisabled advocates. Many clients who participated in my work attend the local Special Olympics every year, with great excitement. They speak eagerly about going to practice each week leading up to the games, practice where they see friends who live in other parts of the county. It seems to me that criticisms about segregated disability services need to take that perspective into account. "Natural environments" may be the clear moral trajectory of inclusion in disability services and advocacy, but the claim of "we speak for them" should be sure they actually understand what the people they speak for want and desire.

The Future of Parent Advocacy

I noticed in the interviews done with staff and administration at Payton that the events mentioned (the school, Eastside Center, the Special Olympics) all occurred before the passing of the Americans with Disabilities Act in 1990. This was seen as the civil rights victory of the disability rights movement, and the Parent Movement did play a role in it—the ADA was not just a victory for physical disabilities. Payton has benefited from the ADA, through the expansions made to Medicaid and the increased emphasis on the kinds of community-based services they offer. The ADA also means that the version of inclusion visible in the push to integrate schools and deinstitutionalize

---

[105]Storey, *No Pity*, 35.

housing has started to expand to other areas of disability services, revealing ways that Payton's infrastructure has potentially fallen behind the curve.

According to a former CEO of Payton, the industry is increasing its insistence on the "least restrictive setting," moving away from any kind of "facility-based services" and instead toward building up "home and community-based services" (HCBS):

> It's challenging states to put a transition plan together, focusing on home and community-based services. And that's where, you know, segregated, you know, workshops come into play, it's even what we're doing with our facility-based programs where, you know, people are coming into a facility-based setting during the day, and, you know, the—that particular rule is saying we want folks in the community, the majority of the day, out in the community.
>
> . . . You know it's, what's interesting about it is they've made this a big subject, but in reality over the last ten years we've been kinda going that way. The, I would say the state of Indiana, at least in my experience, we've done a relatively good job of making sure that our services fall into those categories. But now the federal government has, you know, put all this stuff in writing and so, it's, it's becoming uh, something that the state is really focusing on and working with providers. And I think over the next couple of years, um, you know we're, we're gonna be scrutinized as providers that if you're not doing these things, you're gonna have to. And so on the residential side of things, I'm not worried, from what we're [Payton] doing. You know, even our group homes, they're all in neighborhoods. . . . [T]his rule, from our standpoint, really affects what we're doing during the day, with people coming into our facilities and participating in classroom settings, I don't know if that's going to fly under this home and community based rule. And the workshop is another setting we're concerned about.[106]

The CEO expressed general optimism about Payton's future—their community residences, for example, do seem to meet "the burrito test" and are integrated with their neighborhoods. Nonetheless, he does name the issue that many of their services rely on facilities that house only disability-specific services: not only the sheltered workshop, but also some of the recreation events and day programs.

Indiana's funding priorities reflect the trajectory that the CEO discussed. A long-term Payton volunteer, Protective Services Board member, and father of a son with Down Syndrome told me about a shift concerning Indiana's Medicaid waiver: at one point Indiana offered a comprehensive waiver

---

[106]Former CEO, Personal Interview, July 29, 2015.

that covered a multitude of things: housing, direct support professionals, therapies, etc. It met "90% of the need for the few who had it."[107] Then, around 2010 (it is worth noting this is around the time when the Affordable Care Act was passed, though the father did not bring that up in the interview) Indiana surveyed families and caretakers of people with IDD, and changed how the waiver worked. They made it more accessible, but covered far less of the needs that consumers had. Thinking of his son, this father "pressed the office for an answer, and they swear it's because in the survey, most parents wanted to keep their children at home. But I know what it's really about, it's about the fact that expecting kids with IDD to stay in their home means it will be cheaper for the state."[108] He and his spouse want to give their son the option of living independently. Although they are financially comfortable and could afford to subsidize his living, they also know that's not a position that every family might have. While his account of the change is hearsay, it does at least reflect the belief that even if inclusion (in the sense of community placements) is the state's goal, the pathway to that inclusion will be shaped by the bottom line.

New Opportunities, Similar Limitations

Despite the questionable future of facility-based services, there is one area where Payton has experienced a great deal of growth in the past decade, and that is Autism services. Another instantiation of parent advocacy, there has been an explosion of financial support for diagnosis, treatment, and therapies for autistic children—to the extent that in some states there is a separate "Autism waiver" (in addition to other HCBS waivers) to provide funding for these services (12 as of 2018).[109] As a result, Payton has experienced unprecedented expansion: in 2011 there were three employees under Autism services, but by 2015 there were over 100. In the city in 2011 there had been no centers dedicated only to Autism; by 2015 there were four—Payton plus three for-profit service providers. And this growth is not limited to Payton— it is being seen on a national scale.

"Something about the Autism awareness program has been so successful that it's made Autism different."[110] This observation, from Payton's Chief Strategy Officer for Autism Services (who I will call Jim), reveals how Autism advocacy has experienced the same kinds of successes as the early Parent Movement, but more rapidly and on an even greater scale than the

---

[107]Payton volunteer and parent, Personal Interview, October 2, 2015.
[108]Payton volunteer and parent, Personal Interview, October 2, 2015.
[109]National Congress of State Legislators, "Autism and Insurance Coverage: State Laws," available online: https://www.ncsl.org/research/health/autism-and-insurance-coverage-state-laws.aspx (accessed June 29, 2020).
[110]Chief Strategy Officer for Autism Services, Personal Interview, August 11, 2015.

decades-long disability rights movement. In fact, that was something that Jim rather bemoaned: "it's really kind of a travesty that all this funding has come into providing Autism services, and it hasn't been spread into other developmental disabilities."[111] Instead, Autism has been siloed off from Payton's other children's services—sometimes to the great frustration of parents who knew that the behavioral, occupational, and speech therapies offered would benefit their non-autistic children. In fact, because of the broadening of the diagnostic criteria, that makes it possible that a family with a different diagnosis, such as Down Syndrome, may pursue an Autism diagnosis as well in order to gain access to these well-funded services. "Whether or not that's right or wrong, that's the way it is right now," Jim told me, sympathetic to the plight of these families.[112]

There are a lot of parallels to be drawn between parent advocates for Autism and the origins of the Parent Movement. While Autism is closely associated with IDD, it is not itself an intellectual disability—because it is a spectrum, it has a wide range of expression, not all of which are inherently disabling. The growth of Autism services could be connected to this wider range of diversity, in that a larger number of autistic people can become the "potentially productive citizen" as hoped for by early rehabilitation attempts. Furthermore, because of its broadened diagnostic criteria, it's arguable that Autism has created a larger sense of group cohesion across parents:

> Families with autism banded together and fought for this. Autism is more common than Down Syndrome, it's more common than Fragile X. . . . it's actually more common than most of the other diagnoses combined, because a lot of what we're talking about with these other diagnoses is we're talking about these rare genetic conditions that what binds them together is that there's an intellectual disability. And often their parent groups are separate . . . and so it's harder to have that kind of advocacy.[113]

Autism seems to be benefiting from the sense of solidarity that marked the initiation of the early Parent Movement.[114]

Yet, we must question how far this solidarity goes: as Isasi-Díaz taught us, solidarity cannot sacrifice one oppressed group for another. This problem is exacerbated by a problem both Jim and Trent identify: the increasing emphasis on a "particularistic" approach to IDD, or "the tendency to

[111]Chief Strategy Officer for Autism Services, Personal Interview, August 11, 2015.
[112]Chief Strategy Officer for Autism Services, Personal Interview, August 11, 2015.
[113]Chief Strategy Officer for Autism Services, Personal Interview, August 11, 2015
[114]K. Boshoff, D. Gibbs, R. L. Phillips, L. Wiles, and L. Porter, "Parents' Voices: 'Our Process of Advocating for Our Child with Autism.' A Meta-Synthesis of Parents' Perspectives," *Child: Care, Health & Development* 44, no. 1 (January 2018): 147–60. https://doi.org/10.1111/cch .12504.

analyze the problem of mental retardation into ever smaller pieces that can be more easily isolated and manipulated."[115] The increasing emphasis on distinct diagnoses divides groups, rather than uniting them under the catch-all heading of "mental retardation" where many of these conditions once fell. It is not a problem, per se, to learn the genetic and medical origins of developmental delays, though it could be argued that this reveals an ongoing preference for cures over treatment (more on that in Chapter 3). We might also question whether this diagnostic emphasis loses some sense of community-building and solidarity.

While Payton has jumped into Autism services, Jim is hoping to avoid some of the pitfalls that Payton had encountered earlier. For example—Jim seems to be well aware of the ebb and flow of funding and knows that in all likelihood this boom for Autism services is only temporary. One of his key goals for growing Autism services is sustainability:

> We absolutely know that there's an opportunity right now to provide Autism services at rates that are profitable. That's the reason why there are for-profit organizations . . . you can make money off of that. Those organizations are going to disappear when the profits disappear. Payton's been here through the good times and the bad times, so what we have to do as an organization, we have to think about ways of making our services sustainable.[116]

While Autism is giving Payton a foothold in the states and counties bordering its city of origin, Jim believes the invitation is not restricted to Autism—rather, these places want "all of Payton," residential, recreational, vocational rehab, and so on. But this must be done in a way that can continue on when the inevitable budget tightening occurs. For Payton to survive as an institution, it has to find new ways to adapt to new demands; for Payton to survive with the integrity of its mission, it needs to make sure it can do so without abandoning any of the clients that ought to be their priority.

As I write this in 2022, seven years after speaking with Jim, I know that Payton struggled in the midst of the mass quarantines and workplace shutdowns that occurred because of the Covid-19 epidemic. Personal protective equipment, already in short supply for hospitals and emergency rooms, was even more difficult to come by for the essential workers in Payton's community residences. The sheltered workshop was shut down, as was the face-to-face work of the Autism centers. Beyond Payton, many of the hard-won victories for special education in the public schools—IEPs, classroom assistants—proved almost impossible to implement in the context

---

[115]Trent, *Inventing the Feeble Mind*, 274.
[116]Chief Strategy Officer for Autism Services, Personal Interview, August 11, 2015.

of remote instruction as schools shut down.[117] Nursing homes persist as residences for people with profound IDD, and Covid-19 has spread through them like wildfire.[118] These present clear material challenges not only to Payton, but the project of inclusion as a whole.

The Parent Movement changed the script about IDD, rejecting the eugenics and demanding a place for their children in their homes and communities. They built out the work of inclusion first started by the optimism of Seguin, but have run into many of the same obstacles: financial precarity, debates about integration, promises of support made by governments and leaders that have gone unfulfilled. In this story, both parents and Payton have learned to adapt, driven by a claim to justice, by a claim that "we speak for them."

That has been a noble mission, but the problem with nondisabled voices doing the talking is that it does not fully disrupt the problem of normalcy. On the contrary, Trent rightly notes that "policy formations have almost always placed the burden of change on the retarded person."[119] While aspects of the Parent Movement did work to alter society itself, especially with deinstitutionalization and the integration of schools, it is also the case that this work views inclusion as the closest possible proximity to normal: "least restrictive setting" or "natural environments." Is it possible to pursue normal without normalcy? To seek normal not as a parent wishes, but through the things for which people with IDD desire and dream? That is the self-advocacy movement, an often understated but nonetheless critical player in the history of IDD.

---

[117]Faith Hill, "The Pandemic is a Crisis for Students with Special Needs," *The Atlantic*, April 18, 2020, available online: https://www.theatlantic.com/education/archive/2020/04/special-education-goes-remote-covid-19-pandemic/610231/.

[118]"COVID-19 Cases at Group Homes, Institutions Going Untracked," *Disability Scoop*, May 11, 2020, available online: https://www.disabilityscoop.com/2020/05/11/covid-19-cases-at-group-homes-institutions-going-untracked/28313/.

[119]Trent, *Inventing the Feeble Mind*, 274.

2

We Speak for Ourselves

Self-Advocacy, Autonomy, and Flourishing

Danny is a man of few words, pithy, and dignified. He stands about five and a half feet tall, with a medium build, and looks to be in his mid- to late forties (though my experience in the field has revealed that I am terrible at estimating ages). His hair is straight and brown, laying flat against his forehead, and his face is craggy with acne scars and unevenly shaved stubble. He looks at you through small, wire-rimmed glasses, skepticism indicated through a heavy, half-lidded gaze (though, this kind of look is partially explained by Danny's epithelial fold, common among people with Down Syndrome). Ask him a question and he answers in as few words as possible: *yes, no, good, sure, ok*. Much longer than that, and (Danny seems to have figured out) staff and volunteers have a hard time understanding him; he has a pronounced speech delay, speaking in saturated vowels with an inadequate number of consonants.

As Payton clients go, Danny is relatively self-sufficient, though I supposed he is not accurately called independent. He works well when he has routine and guidance established by a safety net of relationships: staff, volunteers, coworkers, and friends. Yet Danny's reliability within this system of relationships is valued. He takes direction well, though he also takes time to learn things completely. But when his schedule is thrown, he is agitated. One afternoon he was delayed in leaving Payton for "community hab"—Payton's term for community service. This is one of the few times that Danny sought me out, waving me over to say, "No one has come today." Arms crossed over his chest, glasses slid halfway down his nose, he looked irritable and frustrated, and he wanted everyone, even me, to know.

My first encounters with Danny had come in rehearsals for the annual summer play put on by Payton's recreational program. Danny was one of the few clients that could memorize stage directions. He did not read well or memorize a script, but his performance was guided by a volunteer who worked with him onstage, initiating the lines that Danny would then repeat or finish. Repeated through enough rehearsals, and Danny was able to work on cue. The second year I volunteered, Danny played the titular Lorax in Payton's adaptation of the Dr. Seuss story. He was not the only Lorax, but one of two—the other played by a volunteer—who always appeared onstage together. His lines were echoes and confirmations of the longer lines given by the other Lorax, though sometimes he gave independent information. But they worked in tandem onstage, a singular unit of two.

When that doubled-Lorax appeared onstage, the famous line from the book changed: "We are the Lorax. We speak for the trees." Danny only spoke half this line from his own lips, but in the context of the play, it doesn't matter: both lines belong to him. He is still a part of the subject—he is also a *we*, a *we* that speaks for those who cannot.

Parents also made the claim that "we speak for them," but the rise of self-advocacy among the IDD shifts to "we speak for ourselves." If we follow Wehmeyer's description of three waves of the disability rights movement, the first began where the previous chapter did: with professionals like Seguin seeking treatment and correction that can make disabled people "productive citizens." This gave way to both the second wave, which was encapsulated by the Parent Movement, and the third wave, which contained the self-advocacy movement. Although Wehmeyer identifies the self-advocacy movement for the IDD community from the 1970s to the 1990s, its roots are connected to other civil rights movements of the 1960s, and aspects of self-advocacy developed in parallel with the Parent Movement. The rights for which parents lobbied in the name of inclusion were taken up by self-advocates—and also, as with any process of maturation, this came with challenges to parental authority.

Now, the self-advocacy movement is not a large part of Payton's parent-driven history, so taking up the topic presents something of an ethnographic challenge: I am writing about a gap, or a lack in Payton's services. However, even if Payton is not structured like People First, the impact of the self-advocacy movement on Payton can be seen in both structural and material ways. So we set up the following ethnographic tasks for this chapter: first, to attend to how the macro-level shifts in the disability rights movement made the self-advocacy of people with IDD possible. Second, we examine the material impacts those macro-level changes have had on Payton—this is best seen in the interwoven history of self-advocacy and the concept of normalization in disability services. Finally, we zoom in on the micro and ask how self-advocacy and normalization affect the day-to-day lives of current Payton clients like Danny. In the course of these ethnographic tasks, we will also be revisiting postliberal criticisms concerning rights language and the

ADA. Their claim of "insufficiency" presumes that the goal of the disability rights movement was autonomy and independence—something that seems impossible for many, like Danny, within the IDD community. However, I contend that this critique lacks a robust understanding of "disability justice," as developed by disabled self-advocates. Rather, the disability advocates have always recognized how agencies are linked together—how the doubled-Lorax needs both halves. The arc of the disability rights movement bends toward inclusion, but inclusion (and normalization) *without* disability justice is what results in the "thinness" of rights language which postliberals criticize.

Setting the Groundwork: Shared Advocacy and Goals

One thread that unites the Parent Movement with self-advocacy is that many self-advocates with physical disabilities benefited from having a parent advocate, first. Before there was Ed Roberts, there was his mother, Zona. Roberts became disabled when he survived polio at the age of fourteen, in 1953. The majority of his muscles were paralyzed, and he spent his first year following the infection in an iron lung: "yellow, alien looking, and as big as a telephone booth."[1] This was a difficult transition from being a typically abled teenage boy to one now reliant on various kinds of technology for his most basic life-sustaining actions—not the least because even his doctors thought it would have been better if Roberts had died, rather than live as a "vegetable."[2] Through struggles with depression and suicidal feelings, Roberts gradually came to integrate his disability into his identity. He threw himself into his education, seeing that as his best means of empowerment.

As determined as Roberts was, there were many obstacles ahead, and as a child he needed help. So, Zona Roberts jumped into the fray, drawing on skills she learned through labor organizing. One major fight was Ed's graduation requirements from high school. Despite completing all his academic requirements, Ed was refused a diploma because he had not completed gym and driver's education credits—requirements which seemed rightly absurd in light of his disability. Zona brokered the final compromise: the district would drop the driver's education requirement and her son's physical therapy counted for physical education. Roberts speaks to the impact of his mother's advocacy: "'parents willing to fight for you and include you in the fight' is 'the most important skill you can learn to be successful.'"[3] From

---

[1] Shapiro, *No Pity*, 42.
[2] Shapiro, *No Pity*, 42.
[3] Shapiro, *No Pity*, 44.

Zona, Ed Roberts learned the patterns of organizing that would later make him successful in starting the Centers for Independent Living.

This pattern holds for another major activist, Judith Heumann. Unlike Roberts, Heumann's infection with polio came young, at eighteen months old. Like Roberts, the first major battle that Heumann and her mother Ilsa fought was in the school system, arguing against policies that kept Heumann out of classrooms with her peers: "Ilsa Heumann became a battler, emboldened by small victories," and her daughter followed this fighting spirit.[4] Seeking a job as a public school teacher, Heumann was initially denied the required certification (despite passing written and oral exams) on the basis of her medical exam. District officials claimed she could not use the bathroom, or help either children or herself exit the building in an emergency. She responded with a lawsuit against the New York Board of Education for discrimination, which eventually settled out of court and granted Heumann her teaching certificate.[5]

Critics of the disability rights movement often divide the self-advocacy of people with physical disabilities from the advocacy needed for the IDD community. Yet, these two examples show us how advocacy by others and advocacy for oneself are deeply intertwined. It is true that for many people with physical disabilities, their parental encouragement gave way to their own self-advocacy more easily and earlier than for people with IDD. The emphasis on self-representation among physically disabled advocates does not create an unbreachable partition between the IDD community and the broader rights movement. Furthermore, much of what early advocates fought for on the way to passing the ADA continues to have tremendous benefits for the IDD community.

Deinstitutionalization is a prime example of this: not only was it a goal for the Parent Movement, but it also motivated Roberts to start the Centers for Independent Living (CILs). He started the first CIL at UC Berkeley when he enrolled there as an undergraduate. The only place on campus that could hold the heavy iron lung that Roberts still needed to use was a hospital wing—so he moved in there with his personal care support person. Soon, other students with significant physical disabilities moved in with him, and they become a community of advocates. Today, CILs are "consumer-led"—meaning that, unlike institutions, disabled people retain control of the community, rather than service providers.

Although CILs claimed a "cross-disabilities" approach, the first ones admittedly centered on the needs of physically disabled persons and had some rough edges concerning intersectional needs and experiences.

---

[4]Shapiro, *No Pity*, 56.
[5]Even once Heumann had jumped this hurdle, she found that no schools in the New York City area were willing to hire her, until the elementary school she had attended in Brooklyn gave her a position. Shapiro, *No Pity*, 57.

Donald Galloway, a blind Black man who joined the CIL movement, was frustrated by how the rhetoric of "we're all one" was often used to block his attempts to specifically engage the Black disabled community. He felt that "people in wheelchairs, the people that were physically disabled, basically ran the joint."[6] Nonetheless, CILs set precedents that proved to be highly beneficial for people with IDD, as well. The clearest example comes from the role of personal care assistants—predecessors to today's direct support professionals. These assistants help with eating, personal grooming, toileting, and more; the importance of these assistants undermines the claim that disability advocates privilege independence and individuality. In fact, personal assistants were not only a critical component of the CILs, but they also often become advocates themselves. In this respect, CILs may not be very different in practice from the integrated role that an organization like L'Arche claims for its assistants, vis-a-vis the core members.[7]

Some advocates did see their relationship with assistants more as a tool than a partner: "An attendant is not a caretaker . . . but should be a neutral extension of the disabled person. In this way, an attendant is best compared to a piece of assistive technology."[8] This description poses a fascinating paradox: on the one hand, personal assistants are necessary extensions of the person with a disability, likened to something like speech-to-text computers. This suggests that the agency of the care assistant or direct support professional is meant to be hidden and on hold for as long as they are in the position of caring. The moral problems this poses will be discussed in greater detail as a part of care work in the following chapter, but for the moment it is sufficient to say that access to these assistants is an integral structural support to community placements for the IDD community, and self-advocates are to thank for that. This is but one example of how, from the beginning, the rights movement in the United States created structures that benefited everyone in disability's big tent.

The ADA—No One Left Behind

The previous chapter illustrated how events on the national stage impacted Payton and its surrounding area: for example, the 1964 funding bill signed by President Kennedy helped Payton to build its new facilities. That is why Payton's silence around the Americans with Disabilities Act (at least in my

---

[6]Pelka, *What We Have Done*, 184, 220.
[7]Shapiro, *No Pity*, 251. After the ADA was passed, personal care assistants became the new frontier for the rights movement, to the extent that ADAPT, the major organizers around accessible public transportation, changed the acronym behind their name to "American Disabled for Attendant Programs Today."
[8]Shapiro, *No Pity*, 255.

interviews and their own oral history) makes for a strange gap, given the bill's significance. The ADA frequently serves as the climactic finale to most narratives about the movement (even if activists would insist it was only the start, not the end of their work). This could be taken as evidence in favor of Swinton or Reinders's claims that rights language, and the ADA broadly, are irrelevant to the needs of people with IDD; yet, close attention to the story of the ADA reveals that the IDD community and allies were part of its creation. Paul Marchand, of ARC, was a major actor in writing the early drafts of the ADA. Elizabeth Boggs, a leader of the Parent Movement, and Connie Martinez, a self-advocate, were both members of the Congressional Task Force on the Rights and Empowerment of Americans with Disabilities.[9] The history behind the legislation shows that the writers and supporters of the ADA went out of their way to ensure "no one was thrown under the bus."[10]

The first draft of the bill that would become the ADA was written in 1988 by Bob Burgdorf, a lawyer for the National Council on Disability. In its original form, the ADA took a "flat earth" approach: "the legislation would flatten the playing field for people with disabilities by eliminating all barriers and doing so immediately . . . all buildings, new and old, would be transformed. All transportation would become accessible. The proposed legislation was about as radical a piece of civil rights legislation one could imagine."[11] Sadly, albeit unsurprisingly, the flat earth version of the bill was not the version that eventually passed, and there were several battles over the "carve-outs" that Hill legislators started to work into the bill. One of these was the "local option" regarding transportation: this carve-out allowed for local municipalities to avoid making all buses and public transportation accessible, so long as they could offer comparable alternative services.[12]

The local option gave birth to paratransit, which is what the city where Payton is located uses. Many of Danny's coworkers at Payton use paratransit, arriving at the workshop in a special bus equipped for wheelchairs (though not all the clients who use this have a mobility impairment). However, paratransit runs into the same separate-but-unequal problem that education had in the previous chapter. Here is what paratransit entails: according to the city's public transportation website, each bus trip costs twice as much as a trip on the regular local bus (a $2 fare to a $1 fare), and clients have to request a pickup twenty-four hours in advance, and even then, they are told that their pickup times may be moved up to an hour before or after the requested time. When the pickup time is confirmed, clients must be

---

[9]Carey, *On the Margins of Citizenship*, 196–7.
[10]Davis, *Enabling Acts*, 114.
[11]Davis, *Enabling Acts*, 84.
[12]This particular carve-out pre-existed the ADA, as it was used in 1981 to revise the implementations of guidelines for Section 504 (after heavy lobbying by the American Public Transit Association). Davis, *Enabling Acts*, 76.

ready for the bus anytime within a thirty-minute window, fifteen before and fifteen after the pickup time. So a request for a 2:00 pm pickup could be rescheduled to 1:00 pm, and then could actually happen between 12:45 pm and 1:15 pm. Once the bus shows up, it waits only five minutes. A bus that arrives at 12:45 pm would leave by 12:50 pm, a full seventy minutes before the original desired pickup time (there is an exception to this for medical appointments, where the bus will wait longer). Furthermore, the site includes a lengthy warning about no-shows and the potential suspension of service: if a client does not show up for the bus, does not cancel an unneeded bus at least sixty minutes in advance, or is more than five minutes late he or she might be liable to lose access to the paratransit system. This only has to happen three times (out of a minimum of four trips) in thirty days for the client to receive a written warning. After that warning, if more than 12 percent of scheduled trips are "no-shows," the client can lose access for up to thirty days. The city's public bus system is hardly extensive, but the paratransit system is even more cumbersome and places a greater burden on people with disabilities. This setup reflects the fear that activists had: carve-outs end up placing a greater burden on disabled people, preventing the equity that a flat earth approach was supposed to establish. This also serves as a good example of the kind of "independence" that disabled advocates sought: buses are hardly an autonomous form of transportation. They rely on drivers and strong city infrastructure, offering independence through interdependence.

Yet, activists did win one struggle over the bill, a struggle which affirmed the activists' core principle (as expressed by Marchand from ARC): "we all had to stick together."[13] The ADA's definition of disability embraces the social model. The protections of the bill include persons who are currently disabled, persons with a record of previous disabilities, and importantly, persons who may not have a disability but are *perceived* as having one. The expansive nature of this definition meant that people with HIV/AIDS would be covered as a part of the ADA's protected class—an incendiary question at the height of the AIDS panic.[14] When the restaurant lobby tried to remove HIV+people from the ADA's protection, disability activists threatened to walk on the bill altogether. This was their commitment to leaving no group behind: they were prepared to leave years of work rather than exclude a stigmatized community. It was republican Orrin Hatch who brokered a

---

[13]Quoted in Davis, *Enabling Acts*, 114.
[14]Davis, *Enabling Acts*, 178–9: This debate caused explosive conflicts in both the Senate and the House. This battle came to a head in early July 1990 over the Chapman Amendment, an attempt to carve out HIV positive employees from employment discrimination—an amendment specifically generated by restaurant owners, fearful of that would happen to their businesses if the broader public learned that someone who was HIV positive was handling their food in the back of the house. Disability activists and restaurant owners both lobbied intensely, to remove and the keep the amendment respectively.

workable compromise, preserving the "all for one and one for all" strategy; the ADA was then signed by George H. Bush on July 27, 1990.[15]

The broad reach of the ADA, despite carve-outs, has affected at least one critical case with a direct impact on Payton and the kinds of services it provides: *Olmstead vs. LC* in 1999. The Olmstead case was led by two women with developmental and psychiatric disabilities, Lois Curtis and Elaine Wilson, who filed suit against the state of Georgia over the waitlist for community housing. Both had been classified as "high functioning," and capable of being placed into a community residence (like the one Danny lives in); however, they had been stuck in their institution because of Georgia's reluctance to pay for the increased cost of care entailed by community placements. As we have seen time and again in disability history, funding dictates policy. Georgia's Medicaid program had a "home and community-based waiver" for people like Curtis and Wilson; but despite the availability of over 2,100 spots according to the *federal* waiver, Georgia's *state* legislature only provided the funds for 700 spots.[16] The other two-thirds of the positions would be left without sufficient state funding, so people like Curtis and Wilson were placed on a years-long waitlist.

After a lower court upheld Curtis and Wilson's rights to community-based care, Georgia's director of social services, Thomas Olmstead, tried to appeal the decision through the Supreme Court, making his case based on the expense of such community-based care. The Supreme Court upheld the lower court's decision, calling for state programs to provide a "comprehensive, effectively working plan for placing qualified persons . . . in less restrictive settings and a waiting list that moved at a reasonable pace not controlled by the state's endeavors to keep the institutions fully populated."[17] Here, too, we see the principle of "least restrictive setting"—recognizable from public school integration and a key driver of disability services today. Now, "least restrictive setting" could be taken as a move toward the autonomy and independence that is often criticized by postliberals. After all, the kind of community placement sought by Curtis and Wilson is not what people with profound intellectual disabilities seem to need for their well-being. Still, the story of Olmstead, of the ADA, and of the self-advocacy movement is a story of imagination, a story of understanding and deepening inclusion through justly ordered interdependence.

---

[15]Davis, *Enabling Acts*, 211. The compromise consisted of the following: the secretary of health and human services would annually release a list of communicable diseases and how they were spread. A restaurant employee with one of these diseases could not be fired, but could be moved away from food-handling positions "with no negative financial consequences."

[16]Joel Teitelbaum, Taylor Burke, and Sara Rosenbaum, "Olmstead V. L. C. and the Americans with Disabilities Act: Implications for Public Health Policy and Practice," *Public Health Reports (1974–)* 119, no. 3 (2004): 371.

[17]Teitelbaum et al., "Olmstead V. L. C. and the Americans with Disabilities Act," 372.

Putting Rights to Good Use: People First and Self-Advocacy

Parents may have been the primary activists for people with IDD throughout the 1960s and 1970s, but the self-advocacy movement officially arrived in the United States with the founding of People First.[18] This was spurred on by deinstitutionalization, as well as increased access to education and rehabilitation services. The earliest start of the self-advocacy movement for people with IDD is traced back to Sweden in about 1968 when Bengt Nirje organized the first groups. He argued that people with IDD knew their own desires, maybe even better than the professionals in charge of decisions concerning the quality of life.[19] The start of this movement resonates with the broader rights coalition. For example, like CILs there are interwoven threads of agency at work: just as personal care assistants played a role in advocacy alongside disabled CIL residents, in self-advocacy, a nondisabled professional used his privilege and social capital to create the space where people with IDD could exert their own agency. Like Danny's Lorax, Nirje started the script and the IDD community finished it.

In 1973, there was a conference in Vancouver organized around "normalization"—this was a concept that Nirje used alongside self-advocacy, though in the United States the development of normalization was more influenced by Wolf Wolfensberger (to be discussed, later). Unfortunately, this conference was marked by the paternalism that future self-advocates would struggle against. As Dennis Heath, a field worker for a custodial institution, described the Vancouver conference:

> I got in a group, and each of my people go into a group. They introduced me . . . And I asked, "How come none of you have gotten up and said anything?"

> The room was just quiet. There were twenty people in the room. And I said, "I read the brochure and it said people from group homes, and wherever you were from, were going to run this convention." And this one guy laughed and he said, "Well, you can see how much we're running it." And since it was billed as from the Association for Retarded Citizens, I said, "What do you all thinking of the name 'retarded'?" And there was like a unison of people who said, "We hate that name! We hate that!" And I said, "Have you ever told anybody? Have you ever said anything?" "Well, nobody will listen to us." . . .

---

[18]Wehmeyer, *The Story of Intellectual Disability*, 238, 240.
[19]Shapiro, *No Pity*, 195–9.

So when that session was over the people went out into the general meeting. And a teacher said, "Well, I'll summarize" what happened in our
little group, and I said, "Why don't we let this gentleman here, who's got
some strong feelings, summarize?" I tried to get one person up there who
wasn't a teacher, or a parent, or from the Association for Retarded Citizens. And he said, "You know, we were kind of wondering in our group
why none of us have said anything yet." And then he said, "We also said
that we don't like the word 'retarded,' as we think the Association for
Retarded Citizens should change its name." Ooooh, did that ever—they
really got pissed at me then . . .

This was my first look outside of Salem, looking at what other people did,
and I thought, if that's what's being done—so I said, "Larry, we need to
get some people together from both the institution and the community,
and talk about this. Let's have something here in this state where people
that have lived in institutions can get together and have a real convention
where *they* are in control, and *they* do the talking, and have the microphone." . . . Because who has the microphone has the power.[20]

There is, of course, a certain irony in the fact that we only have this account
of the Vancouver conference through the voice of a nondisabled field worker,
and that the turning point in self-expression for people with IDD—at least in
his version of the narrative—comes only through his encouragement. In fact,
this represents the quintessential struggle of the self-advocacy movement:
even if the whole point of the movement is "to speak for ourselves," the
means and methods by which these voices are heard rely on scaffolding
performed by people who are not intellectually disabled.

As Heath wanted, another conference was held in Oregon the following
year, which allowed people with IDD to "hold the mic." Famously, a
participant at this gathering issued the line: "I'm a person, first"—and so
the name People First was born.[21] These early stirrings of the movement
spread slowly. As Shapiro notes, deinstitutionalization was just gaining
ground in the mid-1970s, and many people with IDD had spent their entire
lives within institutional structures, where choice was never an option.[22]
Nonetheless, today People First has twenty-nine chapters in the United
States, as well as chapters in the United Kingdom, Canada, Germany, Japan,
and New Zealand. It is still a growing movement—but one that has proven
important. It presents a different way of rendering the quest for "normal."

---

[20]Pelka, *What We Have Done*, 328–9.
[21]Shapiro, *No Pity*, 197. Shapiro relies on Heath as one of his sources, though he skips over the
events of the first, Vancouver conference.
[22]Heath described how visible this was in his own work with a custodial institution: "I recognized the fact that people who lived in institutions felt very uncomfortable in making decisions
for themselves" (Pelka, *What We Have Done*, 326). This was a motivating force in Heath's later
advocacy work.

Now, Payton is not structured as a self-advocacy organization, since its primary mission is the provision of services (although advocacy has never been far from its task, either). Perhaps the most notable impact of the self-advocacy movement in Payton's history is its name change: from the Retarded Children's Committee to The Payton Center. The former CEO of Payton described the tensions around the decision:

> . . . the parents who founded Payton, many who were still involved, twenty and thirty year involvements, were proud of the name. In fact for them, they thought they showed pride in that name ["Retarded"] not to hide from it. That people were not talking about the mentally retarded, people were in the closet, even parents who were ashamed, or didn't have a place to go. And so, there's a context of people's pride in the name, not just that it was our first name, but that it was, for them at the time, "coming out" and saying it to the community. It's who we are, it's who we serve, and we're proud of it, not ashamed of it . . . so when the staff, the professional staff came to the board to change the name, there were real feelings, and hard feelings about it, from just a few people. The majority of the younger generation of parents, and newer board members understood, that a person at Payton Industries didn't want to get a check from the [Committee], and label them retarded.[23]

Changing the nonprofit's name may not seem like much. Still, it signaled a shift, a change from the old generation of parents to a new generation of parents and self-advocates alike. Note how the emotions connected to the original name are described in the terms of the parents' perspectives— it's their "coming out," not that of their children. The change, by contrast, echoes the desires of the clients, how they wished to be labeled. In fact, Payton would go on to be very active in "R-word" campaigns around Indiana.[24] Payton heard a demand, listened, and acted.

Self-Advocacy and Normalization in Disability Services

The agency made possible among self-advocates is deeply interwoven with the nondisabled. People First meetings are assisted and guided by the nondisabled, and chapter presidents (people with IDD) often have to

---

[23]Former CEO, Personal Interview, July 28, 2015.
[24]Best known in its current incarnation, "Spread the Word to End the Word," there has been a longstanding cultural campaign to remove the use of the word "retarded," both as diagnostic language but more specifically as a pejorative (akin to cultural pressure against terms like "gay" as casual insults in everyday slang). See: "Spread the Word to End the Word," www.r-word.org.

rely on the expertise and agendas set by the nondisabled social workers and community organizers that accompany them—although it should be emphasized that many social movements turn to experts in areas where they want to promote action. Self-advocacy presents a place in the disability rights movement where self-representation and interdependency meet, rather than treating them as a tradeoff. What emerged in People First has cross-pollinated with service providers, to the extent that in some places, such as the UK, self-advocacy is integrated into the rhetoric of disability services, if not actual practices.[25] The hazard of this setup, as Dan Goodley argues, is that it may fail to recognize or validate places where self-advocacy resists or rejects what service providers seek:

> "Person-centered planning," "service consultation" and "user empowerment" are all terms that reveal a non-conflict position in relation to services and empowerment. There appears to be an assumption that all is well with the status quo so long as people with learning difficulties are consulted about and participate in shifts in policy, provision and practice. But as we have seen above, self-advocacy's focus on the complicating qualities of resilience highlights a more critical view of society and its understandings of people with learning difficulties . . . self-advocacy is more in line with the criticality of the disabled people's movement than it is with the philosophies of policy-making and service provision.[26]

What Goodley points to here is an entanglement of power, self-advocacy, and service providers that originates with Nirje, Wolfensberger, and the early debates about normalization.

When Nirje, first proposed normalization in the 1960s, he also worked with Wolfensberger when the latter started his research on normalization at the University of Nebraska. Wolfensberger himself cuts a strange figure in the history of disability. A trained clinician, Wolfensberger also crossed disciplines into theology, influenced by a mashup of Michel Foucault and Henry Stringfellow. As a clinician, Wolfensberger was focused on supporting his theory with empirical data; he was also finely attuned to the role of language in stigma and perceptions of dehumanization. And yet, despite his sensitivity to language, Wolfensberger often clung to terms that he thought had empirical, clinical precision long after advocates had stopped using them: for example, he insisted on handicapped over disabled, Negroid over Black, and used "mental retardation" long after

---

[25]Dan Goodley, "Empowerment, Self-Advocacy and Resilience," *Journal of Intellectual Disabilities* 9, no. 4 (2016): 333–43.
[26]Goodley, "Empowerment, Self-Advocacy and Resilience," 341.

advocates had shifted to IDD.[27] As an amateur theologian, Wolfensberger held a strong suspicion of the idols of modernity—including technology, science, autonomy, and even "empowerment" (as commonly used by self-advocates).

Wolfensberger's now-classic text, *The Principle of Normalization in Human Services*, took normalization (defined as "making available to the mentally retarded patterns and conditions of everyday life which are as close as possible to the norms and patterns of the mainstream society") and proposed a two-part process of *interaction* and *interpretation*, on three levels: personal, primary and secondary social relationships, and the broader society.[28] *Interactive tasks* were direct actions that would develop "normal" behaviors in clients (then called "consumers") and provide spaces and services that were equal to and (preferably) integrated with services for the nondisabled. The *interpretive tasks* were related to de-stigmatization and re-defining "deviancy," which Wolfensberger believed had ultimately caused segregated practices. Wolfensberger's overall hope was for the de-segregation of people with IDD as a social group: in 1972, when the book was released, there were still large numbers of people with IDD in institutions, and the Willowbrook lawsuit had just been filed.

At the time, normalization was revolutionary, but by 1983 Wolfensberger had become frustrated with how the terminology was being received.[29] Wolfensberger had intended "normal" to be received as a statistical term, not a moral one.[30] Unfortunately, after over a decade of use, he had to come up with a new term, since

> relatively few people have found it possible to separate the different meanings attached to it by various users of the term. . . . Also, in part because of its name, people have failed to take the principle of normalization seriously as a tightly-built, intellectually demanding, and empirically well-anchored megatheory of human service and, to some degree, relationships.[31]

---

[27]Hank Bersani Jr., "Wolf Wolfensberger," *Journal of Religion, Disability & Health* 4, nos. 2–3 (2001): 1–9.

[28]Wolf Wolfensberger, *The Principle of Normalization in Human Services* (Toronto: National Institute on Mental Retardation, 1972), 26.

[29]Wolf Wolfensberger, "Social Role Valorization: A Proposed New Term for the Principle of Normalization," *Intellectual and Developmental Disabilities* 49, no. 6 (2011): 435–40, originally published in *Mental Retardation* 21 (1983): 234–9.

[30]Wolfensberger, *The Principle of Normalization in Human Services*, 28. Given Lennard Davis's assertion that "normal" developed with inherent value judgments (due to the relationship with eugenics), it may be that Wolfensberger's task of keeping "normalization" descriptive and not prescriptive was doomed from the start.

[31]Wolfensberger, "Social Role Valorization: A Proposed New Term for the Principle of Normalization," 435.

Instead, Wolfensberger now proposed "social role valorization" (SRV) for the terminology. The benefit of the terminology was that it was both more neutral than "normalization," and what connotations it did have were associated with "value," that is, increasing the human value of people with IDD. In this shift, he also adjusted the description of the theory: "Enhancement of Their Social Image" replaced "interpretive tasks," and "Enhancement of Their Personal Competencies" replaced "interactive tasks." The tripart levels ceded to categories such as physical settings; relationships, and groupings; activities, programs, and other uses of time; and language and other symbols.[32] The revisions to SRV may have actually rolled back the radical potential that Nirje's normalization once held (though Wolfensberger called this claim "revisionism").[33] The interpretive tasks of normalization involved a deconstructive element: they were meant to challenge social stigma. While *normalization* is still a live component of the vocabulary in social services, I do not recall ever hearing *social role valorization* among the staff and administrators at Payton. Now, the word du jour that captures the essence of Wolfensberger's theory is "community inclusion," sometimes "community integration," and "natural setting." These terms point toward the need for community, and therefore a certain kind of interdependence.

Yet, Wolfensberger's understandings of normal, value, and even inclusion ultimately reject the role of empowerment in favor of what he considers empirical practicality. Wolfensberger himself insisted that SRV included "*both* capitalizing upon cultural values, *and* the need to change at least some of them."[34] He describes SRV as a series of "if this, then that" statements: for example, if an agency with a derogatory term for IDD in its title wishes to improve the social value of the people it serves, then the title of the agency may need to change (as we saw demonstrated when Payton changed its name).[35] This change may come with a cost: the work of signage and rebranding could stretch the budget of a smaller nonprofit. *If* the organization chooses not to change, Wolfensberger argues "they should *then* honestly and overtly accept the image loss to clients or the loss of potential image improvement."[36]

---

[32]Wolfensberger, "Social Role Valorization: A Proposed New Term for the Principle of Normalization," 438.

[33]Wolf Wolfensberger, "Social Role Valorization and, or Versus, 'Empowerment,'" *Intellectual and Developmental Disabilities* 49, no. 6 (December 2011): 469.

[34]Wolf Wolfensberger, "Social Role Valorization Is Too Conservative. No, It Is Too Radical," *Disability & Society* 10, no. 3 (September 1995): 366, emphasis author's.

[35]Wolf Wolfensberger, "An 'If This, Then That' Formulation of Decisions Related to Social Role Valorization As a Better Way of Interpreting It to People," *Intellectual and Developmental Disabilities* 49, no. 6 (December 2011): 458–9.

[36]Wolfensberger, "An 'If This, Then That' Formulation of Decisions Related to Social Role Valorization As a Better Way of Interpreting It to People," 459, emphasis original.

On the one hand, he clearly disagrees with the latter decision, saying that it incurs a loss in value not only for the clients served but also for various stakeholders in the hypothetical organization. On the other hand, he allows for the possibility of such a decision because SRV can only hypothesize what can happen if you make the moral choice to improve the social value of a marginalized group. Wolfensberger makes the strange decision to remove value from the SRV methodology: "the values people draw on to select one option in preference to another must come from a higher level above that of social science."[37] Wolfensberger holds tightly to this fact-value distinction, even while arguing that objective social laws exist which are "(a) universal and (b) ascertainable."[38] This seems to imply that while SRV does not determine social values, there are immutable social (daresay moral) laws that SRV should be used to support.

Nonetheless, Wolfensberger's trust in universal social laws cannot avoid the inevitable conflicts of competing for moral values in a pluralistic society. By absconding from the issue of where values originate from, SRV cannot actually articulate why it is wrong, for example, to infantilize people with IDD. Take the example of ARC, which changed its name from "children" to "citizens"—Wolfensberger approves of the change because he thinks children are not given the same value as adults. Yet, another person could insist that actually children are *more* valued than adults, and that is why they need relatively higher levels of protection. In this case, infantilization is not a moral problem, but considered a sign of care.

The second example of an if-then statement from Wolfensberger's defense of SRV sheds more light on this tension. Wolfensberger writes of someone with a facial disfigurement that causes a lot of stigma and rejection by others: "If many more people are to be more accepting of that person, then the malformation will have to be addressed, perhaps by cosmetic means, grooming, attire, or even surgery."[39] Should this person not want to undergo surgery (it seems that Wolfensberger sees this as an issue of will, rather than resources, e.g. lack of coverage by health insurance), then they "must be prepared for the rejection that will almost certainly come . . . efforts to shame or browbeat people into being accepting instead of rejecting cannot be expected to be very successful . . .."[40] What is important in this example is that social rejection due to facial disfigurement is taken as one of the "universal and ascertainable" rules about social values—Wolfensberger cites

[37]Wolfensberger, "An 'If This, Then That' Formulation of Decisions Related to Social Role Valorization As a Better Way of Interpreting It to People," 459.

[38]Wolfensberger, "An 'If This, Then That' Formulation of Decisions Related to Social Role Valorization As a Better Way of Interpreting It to People," 461.

[39]Wolfensberger, "An 'If This, Then That' Formulation of Decisions Related to Social Role Valorization As a Better Way of Interpreting It to People," 459.

[40]Wolfensberger, "An 'If This, Then That' Formulation of Decisions Related to Social Role Valorization As a Better Way of Interpreting It to People," 459.

literature that makes the claim this is a genetic response seen even in young infants who reject disfigured faces.[41] One can question these assertions in a practical sense: what if someone cannot afford this surgery? What if there is no surgery or pattern of grooming that can really "fix" the disfigurement? Wolfensberger's response would likely be that this is an inherent limit in SRV: the if-then statements can only make probable hypotheses, not guarantee positive results. It is a probable outcome that without correcting the disfigurement, social rejection will continue.

Yet, there is an additional moral claim in this example that Wolfensberger is overlooking: by contextualizing the reaction to disfigurement as a part of human nature (one that even infants engage in), he is refusing to challenge the discrimination that results from the disfigurement. In fact, he is openly skeptical that such patterns of discrimination can be corrected, since this is a deeply ingrained social response. Despite Wolfensberger's insistence to the contrary, he does not create the space for successful challenges to prevailing social norms that cause stigma and social exclusion. Instead, he rests the burden of change on disabled persons and their support professionals. This is reflected even in his new vocabulary for SRV theory: "Enhancement of Their Social Image" replaces the deconstructive "interpretive" tasks of normalization and identifies the problem with the persons who lack value, not with the persons who withhold value—people with power.

In fact, Wolfensberger openly rejects consideration of "power" in his employment of SRV.[42] He asserts that even in its original formulation, normalization was "only partially concerned with rights," and rejects the idea that empowerment or self-determination are goals of SRV by offering three key differences between his theory and the supposed ideology of power.[43] Empowerment, he claims, relies on coercion, is ideologically driven, and presumes that choice and autonomy are necessary for achieving the "good things of life." By contrast, SRV relies on empirical data and persuasion as a change strategy, while also assuming that the pursuit of a good life does not require self-determination (at least when understood as an autonomous power of choice). Rather, SRV creates the conditions for the possibility of a good life through identifying "what is in the minds of those who do the treating and affording, and, most specifically, whether and to what degree they perceive the party in valued social roles." According to its founder, then,

---

[41]Wolfensberger, "An 'If This, Then That' Formulation of Decisions Related to Social Role Valorization As a Better Way of Interpreting It to People," 459.

[42]Wolf Wolfensberger, "Social Role Valorization and, or Versus, 'Empowerment,'" *Intellectual and Developmental Disabilities* 49, no. 6 (December 2011): 469–76.

[43]It seems to me that this is the point where Nirje diverges from Wolfensberger—the former's formulation of normalization was concerned with rights, and his frameworks developed along those lines to highlight rights more strongly. Hence, Nirje's conceptual framework appears more in discussions of self-advocacy, while Wolfensberger appears more in service providers. Wolfensberger, "Social Role Valorization and, or Versus, 'Empowerment'" 469.

it would seem that SRV cares more about how other people treat disabled persons than about what the disabled person wants.[44]

This may seem like a strange position for someone who has spent his career improving the living conditions for people with intellectual and developmental disabilities to take (it is). Wolfensberger's concern here is connected to the second aspect of SRV—"Enhancements of Their Personal Competencies." That is, Wolfensberger is concerned about the impact of empowerment on people with limited mental competency, as he argues that the greater the limitations, "the higher becomes the risk that attempts at such exercise will cause harm—possibly of major extent—to self, and usually also others."[45] He does not define or really offer any sense of threshold at which "empowerment" might create risk, so it is not clear if he sees someone like Danny (from the opening of this chapter) engendering the same level of risk as someone like Kelly (the micro-encephalic young woman that Reinders writes about)—if asked, his answer would likely be that SRV serves both Danny and Kelly, so a philosophy of disability services that leaves one (or both) out will ultimately fail. In this belief Wolfensberger has theological company. While the work of Reinders and Swinton attempts more nuance around power than Wolfensberger, they also see only a limited role for justice in their conceptualization of inclusion.

The Claim of Insufficiency for Disability Rights

Alisdair MacIntyre's notorious comparison of human rights to unicorns and witches has cast a long shadow over theology. Unfortunately, his pithy take (that was really a criticism of "natural rights" when divorced from communal politics) seems to generate a postliberal hermeneutic of suspicion whenever rights language is deployed. Postliberals, in rightly wanting to emphasize how inclusion is a communal responsibility, fail to recognize the lived, deeply interdependent expressions of rights embedded in disability justice.

The cornerstone of postliberal criticisms of disability rights is their disagreement with the social model of disability.[46] Reinders first articulated this criticism, arguing that the many forms of the social model presume self-representation, which includes claiming a disabled identity, engaging in political activism, and constructing a sense of self over and against structures

---

[44]Wolfensberger goes on to identity those others as: "the majority of society; sometimes, 'they' may be only its ruling minority, or the members of a societal subculture of close relevance to the party at issue." "Social Role Valorization and, or Versus, 'Empowerment'" 471.

[45]Wolfensberger, "Social Role Valorization and, or Versus, 'Empowerment'" 472.

[46]Reinders, *Receiving the Gift of Friendship*, 59–87. For how Reinders relates this specifically to Eiesland's text, see 167–9.

of oppression. When someone with a profound intellectual disability like Kelly cannot display a "sense of self" or participate in political resistance, it seems as if she is left behind: "Within its [the social model's] imagery of empowered people there is nothing to be gained for human beings like Kelly," argues Reinders.[47] Instead, Reinders offers an "ecological" approach to inclusion: this actually shares some principles in common with the social model, insofar as it seeks an *environment* in which someone with IDD can flourish. While Reinders acknowledges that rights can be helpful, he also warns that "rights and choice are about you making other people comply with what you want because you want it, without being dependent upon their approval."[48] Like Wolfensberger, he is skeptical of both the concepts and rhetoric around choice and independence, in that they rely on coercion rather than appreciation of human dependence. Although insisting that his ecological approach is "distinct from—*not opposed to*—a political approach," Reinders does not appear to place much moral value in the political approach, finding it at best weak and at worse antagonistic to the kind of sacrificial love he sees as proper to Christians relationships with the IDD community.[49]

Swinton is more moderate in his critiques than Reinders: he agrees that inclusion makes useful political rhetoric, to help "allocate resources and provide benefits and protection to people who need them," but he also warns that the political use of the term "disability" is a "double-edged" sword.[50] Precisely because "disability" has an expansive application (in order to inclusively mark a variety of conditions and impairments that need greater resources and protection), Swinton argues that it generates only a "thin" concept of disability, and therefore a "thin" concept of what serves the good of the disabled community. The result—at least in a liberal democracy that lacks the "moral torque" to create genuine acceptance—is that people may be included, but they do not "belong."[51] To illustrate this point, Swinton employs his own qualitative research with the example of Kevin. Kevin is a man with IDD who is regularly brought to a church by his direct support professionals, but has no real relationships with the members of the church: in the course of three months of attendance, Swinton testifies that "not one person spoke to him. One person patted him on the head in passing but

---

[47]Reinders, *Receiving the Gift of Friendship*, 86.
[48]Hans Reinders, "The Power of Inclusion and Friendship," *Journal of Religion, Disability & Health* 15, no. 4 (October 1, 2011): 433.
[49]Reinders, "The Power of Inclusion and Friendship," 434.
[50]Swinton, "From Inclusion to Belonging," 174. It also worth noting that such moves are also present in social science literature, not just theology. See: E. Hall, "Spaces of Social Inclusion and Belonging for People with Intellectual Disabilities," *Journal of Intellectual Disability Research* 54 (2010): 48–57; Alyson L. Mahar, Virginie Cobigo, and Heather Stuart, "Conceptualizing Belonging," *Disability & Rehabilitation* 35, no. 12 (2013): 1026–32.
[51]Swinton, "From Inclusion to Belonging," 174.

that was it!"[52] Although Kevin may have been physically present in the services, he did not have a real place in the community.[53] Kevin had access to space, but no relationships. Inclusion as a political concept relies on law, but imperatives of the law are empty without relationships.

A key theological problem here is the presumed difference between justice and love that has a longstanding history in Christian ethics, though perhaps most influentially established in Reinhold Niebuhr's views of justice. Swinton echoes this when he argues that "We can develop protective legislation, but unless people's hearts are warmed nothing will really change."[54] In a Niebuhrian framework, justice is a tool of restraint among self-interested individuals, while Christian love transcends self-interest.[55] Hence, Wolfensberger and Reinders view empowerment and rights as coercive, and Swinton's critique that you cannot legislate relationships—a statement I actually agree with. Nonetheless, Sandra Sullivan-Dunbar's examination of Niebuhr (drawing from longstanding feminist criticisms), identifies how his framework suffers from a narrow conception of justice, one that neglects material scarcity and human finitude. Indeed, Niebuhr presumes scarcity is a result of self-interest, "that if human persons could perfect their wills and become perfectly other-regarding, natural scarcity and conflicting embodied needs would cease to be a challenge."[56] As pessimistic as Niebuhr tended to be, this claim is surprisingly optimistic, even naïve, about the availability of both material and human resources.

Even assuming that most material scarcity is the result of unjust distribution, this neglects the hard limits of time and labor: if you spend an hour doing task A, that is an hour you cannot spend doing task B. An hour that a single mother has to spend earning a wage at her job is an hour she cannot spend caring for her child. She may hire someone else to care for the child during that hour instead but said person is therefore not caring for members of his or her (but more commonly her) own family. In this sense, scarcity of time and labor may be passed along, but it never disappears. Both Reinders and Swinton overlook the problem of scarcity and therefore underappreciate how rights have been rhetorically and strategically vital to addressing the particular vulnerability of the disability community to scarcity. As we saw in the previous chapter, every advancement in inclusion has suffered when scarcity increased. At the very moment that social welfare structures were needed most, they became harder to access. Social vulnerabilities also magnify scarcity: poor communities experience greater

---

[52]Swinton, "From Inclusion to Belonging," 180–1.
[53]Swinton, "From Inclusion to Belonging," 180–1.
[54]Swinton, "From Inclusion to Belonging," 175.
[55]Sandra Sullivan-Dunbar, *Human Dependency and Christian Ethics* (Cambridge: Cambridge University Press, 2017), 86–9.
[56]Sullivan-Dunbar, *Human Dependency and Christian Ethics*, 95.

losses in recessions than wealthy ones, communities of color are more at risk than white ones, and disabled communities risk losing the very labor and material resources they need to simply survive. Swinton and Reinders (in the vein of Niebuhr) may argue that this is precisely why we might need a *sacrificial* love, rather than justice. However, while we certainly cannot legislate relationships, we can (and should) legislate distributive justice. The kinds of ecological inclusion and belonging that Reinders describes requires a baseline material well-being; social value certainly cannot be improved when basic needs are unmet.

Still, this discussion of rights may seem to support the initial criticism that they are insufficient—that they create merely the bottom levels of Maslow's hierarchy, and love renders meaning to life through community, relationships, and belonging. Wolfensberger raises some applicable questions here. He seems aware of scarcity, declaring that "humanity is beginning to be beset by environmental catastrophe and the return of an age of plagues, and as both Western societies and the world order—such as it was—are collapsing" but believes these are made worse by the insistence on choice and empowerment.[57] It is his belief that power and autonomy are being viewed as the ends, rather than instruments to a good life. I agree with Wolfensberger on this point: a model of disability services that imprudently relies on autonomy could certainly fail to promote a good life for people with profound intellectual disabilities.

I would contend, however, that the depiction Wolfensberger, Reinders, and Swinton offer of how choice and self-determination operate in disability services and self-advocacy is a flattened caricature. Wolfensberger questions whether self-determination requires autonomy, yet a better question is whether the autonomy that postliberals embed in their criticisms of rights language actually exists in practice. Autonomy and interdependence may not be the opposites that these men assume. Choice, for disabled and nondisabled persons alike, can only exist within a set of given restrictions, is only enabled through existing material structures and relationships. I cannot choose to flap my arms and fly to a desired location; I can choose to purchase a ticket for a plane built, maintained, and flown by other people. Limitations, necessary and unnecessary, tend to be amplified in the context of disability services. In fact, we saw Goodley argue that in many cases choice plays the quite opposite role of what Wolfensberger fears: choice may only be rhetorically deployed, fails to challenge aspects of disability services that may be too limiting, and fails to contribute to flourishing. To better understand the way that interdependence is actually a feature of independence and autonomy, we can turn to the concept of "disability justice," which renders a thicker understanding rights and justice than postliberals recognize.

---

[57]Wolfensberger, "Social Role Valorization and, or Versus, 'Empowerment'" 474.

Disability Justice as Necessary
for Disability Rights

Disability justice is not a systemic, theorized approach to justice. Rather, it is grounded in living practices, imprecise but also asserting that distributive justice and relational justice are interconnected, but not reducible to one another. Sins Invalid, a disabled-led performance collective, offers one of the many explorations of justice in relationship to disability. They assert the need for distributive justice of material goods (especially with respect to environmental access, healthcare, and employment), while also acknowledging that interpersonal barriers (such as stigma, prejudice, and practices of exclusion) indelibly shape how a disabled person may be able to pursue her own human flourishing. This definition of justice is capable of including both Danny and Kelly: not only do both need distributive justice with respect to material needs like food, water, and medicine, but they also need relationships with others (including, but not limited to long-term care workers) for flourishing, as well.

When we look at how current rights activists use disability justice, we also see that solidarity is deeply embedded in the concept. Sins Invalid's manifesto offers ten principles for disability justice: "(1) intersectionality, (2) leadership by those most impacted, (3) anti-capitalist politic, (4) commitment to cross-movement organizing, (5) recognizing wholeness, (6) sustainability, (7) commitment to cross-disability solidarity, (8) interdependence, (9) collective access, and (10) collective liberation."[58] All of these principles speak to a deep relational sensibility, but I want to highlight two of these. First, *recognizing wholeness*: "People have inherent worth outside of commodity relations and capitalist notions of productivity. Each person is full of history and life experience."[59] A principle like this acknowledges Kelly's life, dependent as it is, is nonetheless valuable, that her body holds her own history and story even if we cannot understand how she communicates it. Second, Sins Invalid ends on *collective liberation*: "No body or mind can be left behind—only mobbing together can we accomplish the revolution we require."[60] This shows the depth of the principle of solidarity in the disability rights movement. These principles should resonate strongly with postliberals, while also showing how disability rights challenge the very presumptions of independence and autonomy so closely associated with rights language.

---

[58]The work of Sins Invalid is influential for Leah Lakshmi Piepzna-Samarasinha's work on disability justice. See: Sins Invalid, "10 Principles of Disability Justice," September 17, 2015, available online: https://www.sinsinvalid.org/blog/10-principles-of-disability-justice (accessed July 9, 2020); Leah Lakshmi Piepzna-Samarasinha, *Care Work: Dreaming Disability Justice* (Vancouver: Arsenal Pulp Press, 2018).
[59]Sins Invalid, "10 Principles of Disability Justice."
[60]Sins Invalid, "10 Principles of Disability Justice."

When we look at disability justice as the framework in which the ADA and self-advocacy function, we see a persistent interweaving of autonomy and interdependency that refuses to be flattened or simplified. Disabled persons seek their own good with the help of personal assistants and direct support professionals, as seen in the CILs and People First. In the process of creating access—whether it was a man in an iron lung attending college or people with IDD gathering for a conference on normalization—the social imagination was shifted. That which may have seemed impossible becomes possible when disability advocates push at the edges of "normal." And some impossible things, like community housing in the Olmstead decision, slide from merely possible to something which belongs to the disability community, a material and social right. The further these boundaries are pushed, the further they can go. This is what ultimately leads to the social role valorization, daresay the *belonging* that postliberals advocate for: a change in the social imagination around possibilities.

Empowerment, rights, and self-determination all circle around the issue of agency, and of granting a presumption of agency (not the same as autonomy) to all persons, including the most profoundly intellectually disabled persons. Kelly's body, history, and person has a complex agency that must be recognized, just as Danny does. This agency relies on extensive structures—but in that regard, I would argue the difference between Kelly and Danny, or even Kelly and Danny and a nondisabled person, is a difference of degree, not kind.

When Inclusion Reaches Belonging: Current Practices and Debates

One thing that postliberal theologians and disability rights advocates agree on is the importance of community inclusion: disabled persons have a rightful place and presence in our communities, and exclusion (on the basis of either physical or social obstacles) is unjust. For people with IDD, research into practices of inclusion does include both a spatial sense of inclusion, and a relational sense—the "sense of belonging" that Swinton and Reinders seek.[61] These categories interact with one another: for example, the size of

---

[61]Mahar et al., "Conceptualizing Belonging," 1026–32; Attracta Lafferty, Roy McConkey, and Laurence Taggart, "Beyond Friendship: The Nature and Meaning of Close Personal Relationships as Perceived by People with Learning Disabilities," *Disability & Society* 28, no. 8 (2013): 1074–88; Paula Sheridan, "How Friendship Is Understood in Adults with Intellectual Disabilities across Three Life Stages" (Master's thesis, University of Limerick, 2013), available online: https://ulir.ul.ie/handle/10344/3243 (accessed May 20, 2017); Katharine White and Lynette Mackenzie, "Strategies Used by Older Women with Intellectual Disability to Create and Maintain Their Social Networks: An Exploratory Qualitative Study," *British Journal of Occupational Therapy* (2015), doi:10.1177/0308022615586419; A. Kamstra, A. A. J. van der Putten,

social networks for people with IDD is often correlated with their living situations, whether they live at home, in assisted living, in group homes, or in the few remaining larger custodial institutions.[62] That being said, the literature still holds a strong focus on spatial access, in large part because geography shapes the possibilities for new relationships, though there are important challenges against *purely* spatial conceptions of inclusion.[63] For example, one New Zealand study warns that where the community is defined as "the opposite of segregation or isolation in 'special' facilities or services which only include disabled people and those who are paid to support them," we must be careful to acknowledge biases that would see "relationships and friendships between adults with an intellectual disability . . . as somehow less desirable or less valuable than relationships with non-disabled people."[64] Most of the studies mention that their subjects' networks are limited to some variation on "family, staff members, and other people with disabilities."[65] While it is certainly important to note the limits of social networks, we must resist the ableism of discounting the value of relationships among people with IDD.

This problem infiltrates Reinders's turn to the language of friendship rather than rights. He describes his friendship with a man named Ronald, which occurred almost by happenstance. Meeting Ronald on a visit to his group home, their friendship grows through regular visits, where Reinders

---

and C. Vlaskamp, "The Structure of Informal Social Networks of Persons with Profound Intellectual and Multiple Disabilities," *Journal of Applied Research in Intellectual Disabilities* 28, no. 3 (2015): 249–56. These studies all use qualitative research to investigate the extent, nature, and benefits of social networks. Sheridan (2013) and White and MacKenzie (2015) do this with interviews of people with IDD; Kamstra et al. (2015) interview caretakers and partook in some observation, though this is in large part because their work focuses on people with profound disabilities, and therefore extremely limited verbal skills.

[62]Kamstra, van der Putten, and Vlaskamp, "The Structure of Informal Social Networks of Persons with Profound Intellectual and Multiple Disabilities," 254–5.

[63]Robert A. Cummins, and Anna L. D. Lau, "Community Integration or Community Exposure? A Review and Discussion in Relation to People with an Intellectual Disability," *Journal of Applied Research in Intellectual Disabilities* 16, no. 2 (2003): 145–57; Pamela Cushing, "What Counts as a Community? Alternative Approaches to Inclusion and Developmental Disability," *International Journal of Developmental Disabilities* 61, no. 2 (2015): 83–92; Paul Milner and Berni Kelly, "Community Participation and Inclusion: People with Disabilities Defining Their Place," *Disability and Society* 24, no. 1 (2009): 47–62.

[64]Anne Bray and Sue Gates, "Community Participation for Adults with an Intellectual Disability: Review of the Literature Prepared for the National Advisory Committee on Health and Disability to Inform Its Project on Services for Adults with an Intellectual Disability," *National Advisory Committee on Health and Disability* (2003): 2–4.

[65]Kamstra et al., "The Structure of Informal Social Networks of Persons with Profound Intellectual and Multiple Disabilities"; Lafferty et al., "Beyond Friendship: The Nature and Meaning of Close Personal Relationships as Perceived by People with Learning Disabilities"; Sheridan, "How Friendship Is Understood in Adults with Intellectual Disabilities across Three Life Stages"; White and Mackenzie, "Strategies Used by Older Women with Intellectual Disability to Create and Maintain Their Social Networks: An Exploratory Qualitative Study."

takes Ronald outside his home to go out to eat or shop in music stores. Reinders comments that he doesn't think Ronald has any other friends— though Ronald lives with other people with IDD, Reinders reports that Ronald does not see these relationships as friendships: "He is stuck with them, which he takes as another fact of life. It is an asset to have a friend in this kind of social environment. Having a friend from 'outside' is a cause of envy: such a friendship enhances your status"[66] If Reinders is accurate about Ronald's feelings, it would seem that because he had no choice in his living arrangement, these roommates cannot be friends (since friendship, per Reinders, is a relationship of choice).

Ronald faces a common dilemma: many people with IDD do not have any choice in where they live. While this doesn't eliminate the possibility of becoming friends with a roommate or two, it can also lead to struggle and resentment. A social worker in Payton's Protective Services talked about a client having a near breakdown when a third roommate was brought into his living situation.

> I have a client who [is] in a waiver site. And umm, did fairly well with another roommate. And then we added a third roommate, and the dynamics changed completely when there was a third roommate. Because you're not only adding another person, you're also adding more staff, and . . . he is struggling with this so much. Because as much as you train staff not to treat individuals with IDD like children, as much as you tell them don't treat them like your own children— remember don't always tell them what to do—it happens. I think we underestimate how difficult it must be for an adult to live in their home and not be in control of all they're doing, twenty-four hours a day, and having somebody else tell them what to do, when to do, how to do it. And my client today refused to go into the psychiatrist. And he was clearly upset, and he said "I've had it, I've had it, I'm not going to let any doctor put me on any medication, I'm done, I'm done with it, I've just had it,—, I just can't do it anymore."
>
> We knew this was coming. And you want to change things but your options are limited. Because if you only have two consumers and only one staff, they always have to do things together. My client is a free spirit and he likes to be able to go to Dollar Tree when he wants to go to Dollar Tree, not when the other, when staff can take him, when it's convenient. And it's so challenging for him . . . we have consumers that are always having behaviors in this kind of a model because it's so demoralizing.[67]

---

[66]Reinders, *Receiving the Gift of Friendship*, 356.
[67]Protective Services Caseworker, Personal Interview, July 17, 2015.

These arrangements are understandably frustrating, and so it is not surprising that this might hinder the development of genuine relationships not only with other roommates, but also with staff, or even other members of the community: if everything has to be done with another person, then family is hard to see, and friendships or romantic relationships are difficult to cultivate. Although these clients have a community-based living arrangement (of the kind sought by Olmstead, deinstitutionalization, and self-advocates), scarcity intervenes yet again through limits on staff and even the need for more roommates to make the housing more affordable. Relationships alone will not solve this problem.

In Ronald's case, it does seem like Reinders's friendship grants him opportunities for community engagement that might not otherwise be available. This affirms Reinders's point about friendship: Reinders has money, time, and transportation that he is able to share with Ronald. Yet I have my doubts that such a friendship would solve the frustrations of Payton's free-spirited client, above. Having friends that would go to Dollar Tree with him would still put him in the position of relying on other people to meet his desires, and in this respect, having more available, paid staff might actually be a greater benefit—they could respond more immediately to the client's desires. Furthermore, there is unacknowledged ableism in Reinders's perception that the only relationships which count are those with the nondisabled.

Still, for the moment, we can accept the presumption that inclusion, and eventually belonging, ought to entail relationships with nondisabled community members beyond paid staff and assistants. Another point of agreement between Reinders and Swinton and the social literature is the distinction between active involvement and passive presence. To reach the goal of inclusion, people with IDD should have an active role in a community. In describing his ecological model of inclusion, Reinders offers another story, that of "Larry."

> Larry is a man with all sorts of limitations and problems, not the least of which is that he tends to scream with his high-pitched voice in such a way that you rather would not have to be around him. Because of his screaming, people avoid his company. Larry, however, likes company. So the more people avoid him, the louder he screams. . . . In the actual case, Larry went to support a senior men's volleyball team. They took him in, screaming and all, as their number one fan, which made him a lot of friends. And, of course, after a while Larry virtually stopped screaming at home.[68]

There is much to commend in the idea Reinders is advocating: he calls on us to ask, "What is it that makes Larry's screaming into a gift?"[69] This is

---

[68]Hans S. Reinders, "The Power of Inclusion and Friendship," *Journal of Religion, Disability & Health* 15, no. 4 (2011): 435.
[69]Reinders, "Power of Inclusion and Friendship," 435.

a compelling view, one that has the potential to respond to each person's particularity when making decisions about where to live, who to live with, or where to work. Yet, in order to make the case for such an integral, ecological approach, Reinders has to shape Larry's narrative into a story of successful reform: he made friends with people without disabilities, and therefore he stopped screaming. He became more "normal." What if Larry had continued to scream at home as well as at the volleyball matches—would that have undermined the importance of his place in the stands or his relationship with the team? The important, daresay salvific relationships in this story are with the ostensibly nondisabled team members. This renders the labor of others invisible, such as the direct support professionals who would have driven Larry to games.

This raises a second important point about inclusion: institutions, families and guardians, and staff are critical to facilitating active involvement in a community.[70] It is not enough to work on the competencies of people with IDD or bring them into shared spaces, the community must also be prepared (and possibly challenged) as an inclusive space. Payton recognizes this obligation, especially in its vocational rehabilitation programs. Supervisors and coworkers need to be trained to work with clients, just as clients need to be trained for the demands of competitive employment.[71] This is both a moral and pragmatic obligation: the success of placement depends on how well employers are prepared for clients. The bi-directionality of inclusion must also be recognized in other areas of the clients' lives that lack the same financial incentives as employment. While laws like the ADA have limits, and relationships with people with disabilities cannot be legislated, it is nonetheless a mistake to underestimate how geographical and spatial inclusion creates the conditions for the possibility of relationships: it is the foundation on which friendship or belonging is built. Stigma continues to be a major hurdle for building relationships with people with IDD, but improvement in reducing stigma comes from the increased visibility that spatial inclusion makes possible.[72]

Structured Independence: Payton Industries

If community inclusion represents an ideal goal of disability rights and self-advocates, then segregated facilities like Payton Industries seem sorely

---

[70]Angela Novak Amado, Roger J. Stancliffe, "Social Inclusion and Community Participation of Individuals with Intellectual/Developmental Disabilities," *Intellectual and Developmental Disabilities* 51, no. 5 (2013): 363.

[71]Personal Interview, Job Coach, September 22, 2015.

[72]D. Morin, et al., "Public Attitudes towards Intellectual Disability: A Multidimensional Perspective," *Journal of Intellectual Disability Research* 57, no. 3 (March 2013): 279–92. doi:10.1111/jir.12008.

out of date. In the previous chapter, we saw how the project of inclusion slowly rejected separate instruction for students with disabilities: although special education classrooms still persist, mainstreaming is the dominant preference. The HCBS waiver is also starting to push organizations like Payton away from segregated services, especially in housing. There are strong moral reasons for this trajectory, and yet a site like Payton Industries does provide a certain sense of social inclusion, a sense of *belonging* that should not be underestimated. Payton Center relies on a complex network of people, including both paid staff and volunteers that allow clients agency and (relative) autonomy. This provides a sense of "normal" if not "normalization." The question is whether this network, geographically segregated as it may be, nonetheless promotes agency and flourishing.

When you walk into Payton Industries for the first time, the first thing that hits you is the noise. Not in a surprising way (it is an active workshop, machines and all). It is more the overlap of noise of machines, music, and announcements over the loudspeaker. The thump of a big machine at work is easily mistaken for the bass of a pop song. The second thing you notice is the movement. The workshop has a lot of moving parts: machines, people, walkers, and wheelchairs. There are large conveyor belts that move boxes of organic cat treats through a thin sheet of plastic, a heated blade to seal the plastic, and then an oven to shrink the wrapping tight. There are people at these machines, stacking the newly sealed packages, lifting and closing the sealing blades, and moving pallets piled with neat cubes of packages via hand-cranked forklifts. There are people filling the bottles with the cat food treats and screwing the lids on tight; or cutting lengths of string for window blind repair kits; or pulling apart toy derby car kits to sort the damaged and undamaged parts. Supervisors sit at desks working on productivity counts, doing quality checks on stuffed boxes of wooden boats, or running bottles through a labeling machine before they are filled with cat food. Program assistants push someone in a wheelchair to the restroom because they need assistance with toileting; or a fellow client guides a blind friend to the cafeteria for their fifteen-minute morning break.

All of this movement helps us understand more than the day-to-day tasks of the client-workers of Payton Industries. Like most factory work, a product passes through many hands, each one specializing in just a small part of the process of completion; someone like Danny is at Payton both as a worker and as someone being worked on (i.e., Payton Industries is meant to be training him for community employment). He, too, relies on a large network of workers, each one offering support in a specialized way. Let's see it in action.

A Day in the Life

Most mornings, Danny arrives at the workshop just around 9:00 am. I see him walking each morning, driven to work, and dropped off by staff, with an insulated lunchbox in hand that swings with his long stride. He lives in one of Payton's residential homes and has worked at Payton Industries for quite a long time. Though I meet Danny at 9:00 am, his day actually begins much earlier, in his residence. There are on-call staff members for all of Payton's community homes, and Danny's day begins with them working alongside him and his roommates. I only see these staff members at a glance, the profile of whoever is driving the large, silver van in which Danny and his roommates and some other residents arrive. Danny is dependent upon this form of transportation. Some clients take the bus, but they often have alternative living arrangements. Whether or not Danny can take the bus isn't the point—the members of his residence travel back and forth from work as a group, his schedule partially dictated by the roommates he may not have had much choice in gaining.

Danny's work group is assigned to the production of cat treats, among a cluster of big machines on the left side of the building. He places his belongings in a locker and then sits down for the morning at a tall metal table with a stool. He tends to stay in the same location for weeks at a time, then moves (this is possibly supervisor-prompted), stays for a while, moves, etc. Danny begins by filling a plastic bin with the small, fish-shaped cat treats from a large bag in a corner of the workshop. The bag is about 8 feet high, made of a thick-coated canvas, and provides for all of the dozen clients or so that fill bottles. I've seen the forklift used to replace it, lifting the old bag out of a wooden container with sides about 3 feet high, and carefully putting in the new one, straining at the seams of the handles and the bag itself. Generally, it lasts for a few weeks at a time, but when other groups lack work, they will be assigned to fill cat treat bottles, as well. More than a few times, this has resulted in depleting the supply early and leaving clients with a lot of downtime for several days, sometimes even a couple of weeks.

On a regular day Danny carries the bin; or, if he's in an especially helpful mood, he will fill a couple of bins and wheel them back to his working area on a small cart. Then he gets a bin of empty bottles, and a bin of lids and goes to work. Wearing latex gloves (most clients who work on the cat treats wear these, though some who are allergic to latex do the task barehanded—one or two clients keep a pair of cotton gardening gloves they use regularly), Danny proceeds to systematically fill as many bottles as possible. His coworkers all seem to have their own idiosyncratic way of doing this. His is to use the bottle itself to scoop up a large amount and then top it off with several curled fistfuls of treats. He often dumps two to three fistfuls over the bottle long after it's been filled to the top. Then he screws on the cap. The bottle stays on the table until they are collected for another bin, sometimes by his Training Supervisor, Natalie, and sometimes by another client. Sometimes Danny himself collects bottles from others. Danny keeps track of the number of bottles he filled with a small silver counter, pressing the button on it each time he finishes one. His supervisor takes the count a few times a day. Tracking their counts, reassigning people to new tasks, and even sometimes doing the grunt work of labeling bottles or filling them if the group is behind, the training supervisors bear the burden of daily oversight for the clients. Danny rarely has conflicts with other clients; but when he does, Natalie is one of the first persons to respond.

The bottles then end up arranged on a table next to the heated oven. Some of them are neatly placed sideways into a long, ramped wooden shelf, where they can roll into a bin, picked up by coworkers whose sole job is to slip the plastic seal over the cap before putting it on the belt through the oven that shrinks the plastic cap into a safety seal. Out of the oven, they fall into another large bin, where someone else arranges them in cardboard display packaging, three rows of four bottles for each package. These packages are neatly stacked into a tall plastic bin. All of these steps are contained within the narrow, left-side area of the workshop, and each one is done by a different set of clients. I have seen up to a dozen clients working on filling the bottles; some work on re-filling bottles that weren't done properly the first time. Two clients work on placing the seals; a few more work on placing the bottles in their packaging and into the bin before being moved.

When the bin is filled with packages, a client can take it, using a hand-cranked lift, over to the machines on the far side of the workshop. There, the boxes are placed on another conveyor belt, where it goes through a pocket of plastic sheeting, which is sealed by a heated frame around the box. This is lifted and closed by a client. Then, the box goes through an oven again, emerging with the plastic newly shrunk, and rolls around a curve to come back to its bin. When that is filled again, it is taken to the back of the warehouse, where it's made ready to ship. A single bottle that Danny fills will change hands at least half a dozen times, and cross the entire workshop before it is set to be shipped. Since each client, like Danny, does only a small piece of the process, their work is deeply interwoven and reliant on each other. The cat treats are one of the more consistent, flexible jobs, but even so, they rely on an essential network of coworkers to be completed. Other jobs are easily held up when one link of the chain is slowed down, or stumbles.

Danny's first break is a snack break, in the cafeteria. Most days, it's the same: a set of cheese and cracker sandwiches, a snack package of Oreos, and a pop. While it is possible that Danny packs his own lunch, the material in his lunchbox is another sign of the unseen (to me) staff members that work in his residence, who assist in grocery shopping and meal planning. He grabs a paper towel from a dispenser in the cafeteria and lays out each type of food in precise piles of two. Most days, he decides he doesn't want all of it, and gives away the last half of the crackers to nearby friends. Betty, a friend of his, pointedly asks why he packs food that he doesn't seem to want to eat. The answer that Danny could give (but hasn't yet) is that he does not pack his own food. Instead, he ignores her inquiry and keeps asking if someone else wants the crackers. He doesn't chat much during the morning break (it is only fifteen minutes after all) and returns to work promptly when done.

Some days, Danny leaves after his morning break to go out and do his volunteer work, or "community hab." Danny goes to a nursing home where he helps set places for meals—at least, that's what I think he told me. Community hab for other clients may involve volunteer work at the Humane Society or delivering with Meals on Wheels. Other times, Danny has been taken out by a "friend"—as he tells me—to get breakfast or go to a movie. I've seen him walking in or out with the same woman on several occasions, who volunteers at several Payton programs. I've been told that Danny is emancipated, but I suspect the woman is a kind of guardian or family member. But Danny doesn't say when I ask him, instead points me to his boss, Natalie.

When Danny is out on his community hab day, he gets lunch offsite. But most days, he has the third lunch, at 12:20 pm (following an 11:00 am and 11:40 am). At lunch, Danny has a more varied menu: leftovers, or a Lunchable, yogurt, and juice. One afternoon, he had a couple of leftover slices of pizza that he heated in the cafeteria microwave. He showed this meal to me with pride, telling me about how they cooked it themselves last night—from the kind of crust, I suspected it was a store-bought crust they may have cooked in an oven. Since lunch times are determined by working groups, Danny eats with the same people he works with and a couple of other groups, too: the two groups that work on cat treats, a group that works on the big pressing machines in the back corner, and another group that spends more time idle, but on occasion works on labeling or stuffing parts of toy wooden boats into boxes.

Lunch is a collaborative affair. They give away or swap food; some clients take the opportunity to grab a soda from the vending machine. They aren't supposed to give one another money; but I've seen economic exchanges done surreptitiously when a friend purchases the soda with their own money and gives the drink away. Most clients drink at least a can or bottle of soda during the day. Though Danny is not a regular soda drinker, I've seen him with Kool-aid or iced tea pretty frequently. The motor skills are varied among the clients, and they often pass off plastic containers of applesauce, Jello, or pudding to others for help in peeling back the foil and plastic lids. My own dexterity is in high demand at any table where I sit, and Danny frequently passes me cans of Chef Boyardee to pop open.

This is also a prime social time for the clients. When it's nice out, some clients will eat outside, though Danny shows a general preference for eating inside. The most notable difference between inside and outside—aside from fewer people at each table—is that outside a lot of clients and staff alike take the opportunity to smoke. Danny doesn't smoke, but a few of his coworkers do. Some afternoons, Danny plays verbal games with his friends and coworkers. For one game, they take turns saying "boo" to each other, testing reactions (mostly, dissolving into chuckles and giggles). Almost anyone sitting at their lunch table can be wrapped into the game—*boo* has been called out from one end to the other, though it's not always heard in the din of a crowded lunch. Another game seems to be one of imitation.

Danny verbalizes something, then suddenly and abruptly strikes a pose. Clients around him mimic the pose. I think they're probably mimicking a person, but I haven't heard them use a name for what—or who—they're doing.

At the end of lunch, clients often politely collect each other's trash—one client at the 12:20 pm lunch takes great pride in wheeling the trash bin around, through the aisle, and squeezing between chairs, to collect the trash. For a while, the trash can was locked in a closet until the last five minutes of the lunch in order to prevent a couple of clients from digging through and trying to drink the leftover soda in the discarded cans. The lack of access disturbed a lot of clients and perplexed Danny. Eventually, they compromised by keeping the trash in a corner, behind a table where the training supervisors sit.

Lunch wraps up at 12:50 pm, and Danny returns his lunch bag to his locker. He continues to work for the afternoon—because of how late his lunch is, he doesn't get an afternoon break. This was a change instituted just a few months before I started at the workshop. The structure used to be two breaks (one in the morning, one in the afternoon) and a lunch. Now, some groups have a morning break and later lunches, and others have an early lunch and an afternoon break. The schedule was changed in order to help clients focus on work, and more closely resemble what their experience in a community job would be. This was done along with several other adjustments—increased number of supervisors, smaller work groups, reassignments among the groups, and once-a-week classes on job skills training. I still hear grumblings about the changes, from clients who no longer get to have lunch with their friends, or who get very hungry without the extra snack time. The change disrupted their abilities to spend time with certain friends.

But I don't hear these complaints from Danny. Danny follows directions, and rarely expresses displeasure. There is a shape to his face that naturally seems to scowl, but that is actually his neutral setting. On the rare occasions that Danny has been upset, it's expressed physically—he slams down a bin of bottles or smacks a hand on the table. Very rarely does he shout, though if he's on edge, that can happen, too. But he's generally deferential to the authority of the program coordinators and training supervisors that intercede.

After lunch, Danny works steadily until 2:00 pm or 2:30 pm. Starting around 2:00 pm, there's a general, workshop-wide slowing down. Many clients who take the Access Bus have to be ready by 1:45 pm—the bus can arrive anytime between 1:45 pm and 2:30 pm, a forty-five-minute window. Danny's staff will pick him up, so he works until his name, and those of his roommates, are called over the loudspeaker. He collects his belongings from his locker and heads outside the re-opened entrance.

Some afternoons, they are brought to recreation events: I've already mentioned Danny's participation in the theater program, but Danny also likes to bowl, and on weekends he'll attend some of the events that Payton hosts. Payton programs have plenty to keep the clients busy on the weekend. I know Danny has family that he travels to see—for the long fourth of July weekend, he excitedly told me about packing a bag to visit his sister, though he couldn't quite tell me where she lived.

Over the years, I've described Danny's day to different audiences: ethicists, theologians, parishioners, and so on. As I talk about the seeming structure of Danny's day, I get a comment along the lines of: "well, that sounds terrible!" I understand the reaction: it may seem as if Danny is constrained or restricted. It is very true that Danny does not have a lot of options. Although Payton Industries is meant to be a vocational rehabilitation program, not many of the clients in the workshop make it to community placements. I don't know if Danny has ever had an "outside" job—meaning a community job—but they do not seem to be options for him now. Payton may be the only place he can work, not because of his competencies, but because of complications concerning hours, transportation, and other supports that are more readily available at the workshop. His relative independence exists only because he is dependent on so many of the things Payton offers.

Danny, though, does not seem unsatisfied with life. Some Payton clients are (more on that later). But Danny? He laughs with friends, trades his food, and in many ways has a life that is unremarkably ordinary, living the kind of working day that a lot of people in a manufacturing town would have. The direct support professionals, training supervisors, and others who enable his labor are sometimes as much coworkers as they are care workers. This dependency labor makes it possible for Danny to have a good life, one with meaning and friendship, and daresay flourishing. Care work, the subject of our next chapter, operates through complex, difficult relationships; relationships that demand justice in order to render justice.

3

Speaking to Each Other

Dependency, Care Work, and Grace

To locate grace within the life of someone like Danny, we must recognize how much of his flourishing is enabled by the relationships and support networks in which he is embedded. These relationships fall under the broad umbrella of "care work," and perhaps more specifically as "dependency relationships." Yet the term "dependency" troubles the disabled community: it seems to imply a lack of agency and denies the ways Danny does pursue his own goals and flourishing. We must also remember, as many feminist analyses of care work have named, that care *workers* are also subject to dependencies, both with respect to the client and to other relationships and community structures. Care work and dependency emerge as places where flourishing and agency are negotiated: between persons, within communities, and as enabled or restricted by social and institutional structures.

The present task is to examine that process of negotiation, from both clients' and care workers' perspectives. The core question is where and how grace is found among the care work and dependency relationships at Payton. Although dependency can be a fraught term, it does name a shared human trait, however much we might be tempted to distance ourselves from it. Given this, I ask: are dependencies experienced by the IDD community different in kind or in degree from "normal" dependence? In most morally relevant aspects, I argue that these are differences in degree, not kind—nonetheless, there are real worries about people with IDD being particularly vulnerable to *exploitative* dependency relationships. I contend that dependency relationships and care work can be sites of grace when they are shaped by justice on structural and interpersonal levels. To achieve that justice, we need to address the problem of scarcity within the context of care work, the obligations of a worker to a client (epistemic humility), and the obligations of clients to workers (the reception and uptake of care). In the previous chapters we have seen how the disability rights movement has tried to address justice, especially distributive justice; now, we see the kind of world that has shaped for the present.

Defining Care Work in the Context of Disability

Paid care work has always played a central role in disability advocacy: from the live-in nondisabled assistants that served in the first Centers for Independent Living in the 1970s, to supervisors and program assistants in sheltered workshops and vocational rehabilitation programs today. Such labor is vital for the project of inclusion. On the one hand, care workers of every stripe are instruments through which disabled people claim their own agency, and on the other, we must remember the workers are agents themselves. The intersection of client and worker agency provides a particularly salient site for recognizing dependency and interdependency in the pursuit of human flourishing.

Care work is an expansive category not limited to disability services, and also includes healthcare and education (though these do intersect with disability services). In the most general sense, care work does the following: (1) supports the physical, mental, and social well-being of the person, (2) relies on significant "human infrastructure" to offer these supports, in particular direct, face-to-face contact, and (3) is done for persons who cannot meet such needs on their own power (whether permanently or temporarily).[1] Though face-to-face contact is common for this kind of work, there are divisions between what's called "nurturant" and "non-nurturant" forms of care work. Nurturant care work relies on interpersonal contact (e.g., the direct support professionals (DSPs) who do everything from driving clients to budgeting, grooming, and toileting).[2] Such roles enable clients to work, play, and exert a relative amount of independence in their lives. It is important to recognize non-nurturant forms, as well—since they act as the human infrastructure that allows the nurturant roles to function (e.g., administrative workers or physical maintenance, or Payton's nondisabled factory workers who organize shipping and receiving on the back end).

---

[1]Amy Armenia, Mignon Duffy, and Clare L. Stacey, "On the Clock, Off the Radar: Paid Care Work in the United States," in *Caring on the Clock: The Complexities and Contradictions of Paid Care Work*, ed. Clare L. Stacey, Amy Armenia, and Mignon Duffy (New Brunswick: Rutgers University Press, 2015), 4–5.
[2]Armenia, Duffy, and Stacey, "On the Clock, Off the Radar: Paid Care Work in the United States," 5.

Yet, whether in a nurturant or non-nurturant role, these care workers are structurally and economically undervalued, which creates ongoing challenges for the provision of care. Nationally, the turnover rate for DSPs is "astronomical"—a problem that the AAIDD has named a "crisis" for disability services.[3] The estimated rate of turnover in any given year is between 25 percent and 27 percent.[4] Such scarcity of care work labor points to a deeper issue: the problem of moderate scarcity, or the sense that there just may not be enough resources to fully meet all needs, everywhere. The problem of moderate scarcity undergirds a great deal of modern political theory and is particularly relevant to care work and dependency.[5] We saw in the disability rights movement that the burden of "economic hardship" allows many organizations to be exempt from accessibility regulations precisely because disability invokes fear of scarcity: if you force a business to spend money to put in an elevator, they might have cut other budget lines that affect nondisabled employees. If too much is given to this small minority, then there won't be enough left for the rest of the majority. Of course, scarcity inevitably affects disabled persons more profoundly: scarcity makes those who are already vulnerable even more so in material, social, and psychological ways.

Payton runs on multiple forms of care work and labor, from DSPs in residential communities to training supervisors and program assistants in the workshop itself. Since my research was restricted to the workshop, I had limited interactions with the residential DSPs, but I did interview ten of the fourteen training supervisors, who do much as their name suggests: they supervise groups of about ten clients doing assembly work within the workshop. Their form of care work is perhaps more readily described as "front line supervisors," defined as workers that: "(1) are in occupations with a low threshold to entry (typically a high school degree with little additional training), (2) provide direct care or support services, and (3) typically make under $40,000 per year."[6] Though the title "training supervisor" seems to indicate a more authoritative role than the DSPs, in day-to-day practices these individuals were responsible for similar tasks to the DSPs were: physical well-being of clients, management of client time, and emotional

[3]Carli Friedman, "Direct Support Professionals and Quality of Life of People with Intellectual and Developmental Disabilities," *Intellectual and Developmental Disabilities* 56, no. 4 (August 2018): 235.

[4]Matthew D. Bogenschutz, Amy Hewitt, Derek Nord, and Renee Hepperlen, "Direct Support Workforce Supporting Individuals With IDD: Current Wages, Benefits, and Stability," *Intellectual and Developmental Disabilities* 52, no. 5 (September 23, 2014): 322.

[5]Sullivan-Dunbar, *Human Dependency and Christian Ethics*, 47–51.

[6]Janette S. Dill, "Are Frontline Healthcare Jobs 'Good Jobs'? Examining Job Quality across Occupation and Healthcare Settings," in *Caring on the Clock: The Complexities and Contradictions of Paid Care Work*, ed. Clare L. Stacey, Amy Armenia, and Mignon Duffy (New Brunswick: Rutgers University Press, 2015), 54.

labor of dealing with client conflicts (both with one another and with staff). There also seemed to be a pipeline between other care work positions and the training supervisor position: four of the fourteen supervisors had previously been either DSPs for Payton's residential system, or program assistants (people who help with food and toileting) in the workshop. About four more had been CNAs or worked as aides in the local public schools. At the time of my interviews, only three of the training supervisors had been in that particular position for more than a year; the rest had been there anywhere from ten months to a few weeks. In the six months that I was present, I saw three more training supervisor positions change over, and a recently hired program assistant was promoted to an open position.

The cost of turnover in care work is high, both personally and economically: replacing a dependency worker costs $2,500–4,000 per position (a hefty expense for nonprofits running razor-thin margins), and the unstable workforce of DSPs makes access to HCBS services difficult, resulting in waiting lists that in some states are more than a decade long.[7] The reasons for such instability in dependency labor are manifold but can be roughly grouped into three categories: training and personal support, organizational culture, and low economic support.[8] As a result, many of the dependency workers that Payton relies on experience their own "secondary dependencies" (more on that later). In this initial portrait of care work within disability services, I want to stress that inclusion will succeed or fail based on its ability to address justice for workers and clients alike, which means it needs to recognize how categories like dependence and independence are not opposed to one another, but rather exist together within the same set of relationships.

Care Work: Where Dependence and Independence Meet

I want to take a moment to note something about the language employed in this chapter—thus far, I've been using both "care work," and "dependency," which could be viewed as somewhat interchangeable. Yet "dependency" is often avoided in specifically disability-centric discussions of care work because it can reinforce negative stereotypes. At the same time, dependency plays an important role in some critiques of inclusion: we saw Reinders argue that the reliance on liberal presumptions of autonomy and independence

---

[7]Bogenschutz et al., "Direct Support Workforce Supporting Individuals With IDD: Current Wages, Benefits, and Stability," 320.
[8]Friedman, "Direct Support Professionals and Quality of Life of People with Intellectual and Developmental Disabilities," 236.

will inevitably create a hierarchy of disability that places IDD communities at the bottom.[9] For him, universal dependency on God and grace creates an equalizing foundation for theological anthropology. Others argue that dependency is valuable precisely because interrupts liberalism's false equality by highlighting inequities of power—such as Eva Feder Kittay (philosopher and mother to Sesha, a woman with profound intellectual disability).[10] Kittay suggests these inequities offer a shared starting point, therefore *difference* rather than sameness is the foundation on which justice must be built.[11]

Where Reinders uses his experiences of friendship as a model of inclusion, Kittay draws on her personal experiences of motherhood as a way to understand difference and dependency: we are all "some mother's child."[12] In choosing our shared origins not only within a womb, but also as a process of care and growth, Kittay turns equality from being an intrinsic trait *possessed* by a human person into a "connection-based equality," that relies on relationships of mothering (very broadly construed—not limited to biological inheritance or female-identified labor).[13] Rather than construing dependence as the great unifier, Kittay argues that our dependence only makes sense in light of difference: the person requiring care has needs that can only be served by someone who is less dependent, or dependent in different ways.

Which is also to say that dependence reveals the "construction of independence."[14] Using the example of the CILs and associated Independent Living Movement, Kittay displays how even among disability advocates, "independence" had multiple meanings. It was less about self-sufficiency than about a "measure of control over their circumstances comparable to those without physical disabilities."[15] For example, activist Irving Zola

---

[9]Reinders, *Receiving the Gift of Friendship*, 24–7.

[10]Kittay, *Love's Labor: Essays on Women, Equality, and Dependency* (New York: Routledge, 1999), 9–17. Kittay posits dependency as a critique of specifically Rawlsian views of equality, and one which intersects with other feminist critiques.

[11]Kittay, *Love's Labor*, 16.

[12]Kittay uses Sarah Ruddick's framework for mothering (preservative love, fostering growth, and training for social acceptance), with adjustments that I will address later in the chapter. Kittay, *Love's Labor*, 31–3. Kittay presents an "origin-based" definition of personhood; Reinders explores this possibility in his own work (looking specifically at Thomistic theological anthropology) but ultimately dismisses it. Reinders, *Receiving the Gift of Friendship*, 88–94. Sullivan-Dunbar also critiques this principle, on the grounds of people who did not experience positive "mothering"; though she does acknowledge that this goes against Kittay's obvious intentions with the phrase. For Sullivan-Dunbar, the main problem is that Kittay does not offer enough substance or content to what human flourishing may look like. Sullivan-Dunbar, *Human Dependency and Christian Ethics*, 225–7. I would suspect that Kittay leaves the content open-ended because she is hesitant to overly prescribe an understanding of flourishing that could potentially leave someone like her daughter, Sesha, out.

[13]Kittay, *Love's Labor*, 25.

[14]Eva Feder Kittay, *Learning from My Daughter: The Value and Care of Disabled Minds* (Oxford: Oxford University Press, 2019), 148–9.

[15]Kittay, *Learning from My Daughter*, 148.

admitted that his insistence on being "physically independent" often left him too exhausted to do the advocacy work he valued. So Zola turned to personal support assistants because it improved his flourishing by strengthening other areas of his life.[16] This provides an example of how dependence and independence are deeply intertwined.[17]

Kittay also offers two cautions for the rhetoric around independence, the first of which is pursuing independence (in all its complexities) for disabled people out of a mercenary desire to cut the cost of care, rather than because it supports flourishing. On the contrary: to provide the kind of support structures that disability advocates demand will be labor-intensive, which means it will also be expensive. Part of the structural problems that affect care work consists of an unwillingness to recognize how cost-intensive this kind of work is: in emotional energy, time, and money. So, justice for the clients requires support that meets "genuine needs and legitimate wants"— that is, those goods that are required for human flourishing.[18] At the most basic level, this means that care has an objective end, if not always a clear one: promoting the cared-for person's well-being. The objective ends of care can range from the very small (providing nourishment) to the much larger and harder to quantify (developing a sense of belonging).[19] But those ends are there, nonetheless: the good intentions of a worker—or an entire system—that do not meet those ends also fail to contribute to flourishing.

Given this, the discernment of those needs and wants is a necessary skill for care work; one that may be less intuitive than we want to believe, especially with respect to people who have significant communicative barriers.[20] This brings us to Kittay's second caution, concerning agency in dependency relationships: "might not the supposition that the disabled person is 'independent' render the assistant invisible and effectively subordinate his (or more often her) status and interests to the disabled person she serves?"[21] We should seek out how both dependence and independence are created in care work, without losing the agency of either client or worker. Once genuine needs and legitimate wants have been discerned, they must also be met in such a manner that does not violate the dignity of the client.[22] Paternalism is at risk not only in the process of discerning needs and wants, but also in the material practices that seek to meet those needs.

---

[16]Kittay, *Learning from My Daughter*, 148.

[17]Kittay notes she values the emphasis on "inextricable human interdependence" that comes in some work on dependency, but maintains the need for "dependence" as its own category, given the reality that "there are some ways in which we are simply dependent and unable to respond to others' needs or to reciprocate another's care." Kittay, *Learning from My Daughter*, 146.

[18]Kittay, *Learning from My Daughter*, 135-9.

[19]Kittay, *Learning from My Daughter*, 217.

[20]Kittay *Learning from My Daughter*, 209.

[21]Kittay, *Learning from My Daughter*, 150.

[22]Kittay *Learning from My Daughter*, 197-200.

There is another way that vulnerability affects dependency relations: people doing dependency work need to be cared for, too.[23] Kittay refers to this as a secondary dependency, and it also calls our attention to what is just for the people serving in such roles.[24] Care and dependency work is heavily gendered and racialized, and this contributes to secondary dependencies. At Payton, twelve of the fourteen training supervisors were women; at least four were women of color, and both the male training supervisors were men of color. I almost exclusively saw women of color acting as DSPs, though I had far less contact with them. Many of the women I interviewed told me they were single mothers.

These kinds of layered dependencies illustrate how care work presents a unique case for considerations of justice and entangled human flourishing: as care work links together both dependence and independence, justice for the client and the worker is also bound together, but not indirectly correlated ways. Rapid turnover prevents the development of trust between client and worker; failure to support the cost of care damages worker and client alike. We do not need to see worker burnout as an inevitability: both external factors (such as a sense of supervisory and peer support) and internal factors (such as access to personal mental health care), can mitigate the effects of work stress, lowering levels of depression and increasing the quality of life of DSPs.[25]

Structural supports for care work are vital, but it is also important to remember that care work exists within a relationship: the client owes something to the worker that is not reducible to material or social support. This is what Kittay terms the "uptake of care." If the care offered by a worker must actively contribute to flourishing, the client is also an active participant in what the worker does:

> it is necessary (though not sufficient) for subjects to have the subjective sense of living a flourishing life . . . to say, however, that such endorsement must be a matter of autonomous choice is too strong . . . just because we cannot be certain of rational reflection, it is not to be assumed that endorsement need not be sought.[26]

---

[23]Kittay is also careful to distinguish between this kind of vulnerable dependency work and professionals—such as doctors or therapists—who may be charged with caring for the well-being of a person, but whose title and education render them in a different social position of power. Kittay, Love's Labor, 38–40.

[24]Kittay, Love's Labor, 42.

[25]J. A. Gray-Stanley, N. Muramatsu, T. Heller, S. Hughes, T. P. Johnson, and J. Ramirez-Vallesz, "Work Stress and Depression Among Direct Support Professionals: The Role of Work Support and Locus of Control," *Journal of Intellectual Disability Research* 54, no. 8 (2010): 749–61. This illustrates another one of Kittay's concepts, "diffused reciprocity,": rather than reciprocity moving back and forth between A(the worker) caring for B(the client), reciprocity spirals outward, that C cares for A, while A cares for B. Kittay, Love's Labor, 32.

[26]Kittay, Learning from My Daughter, 200.

By emphasizing the active reception of care as a part of the caring relationship, Kittay not only recognizes the role of agency on behalf of the client but also imposes a kind of moral obligation on the client toward the worker—something often overlooked among theologians who highlight care work and dependency.[27] A robust sense of the tangled nature of dependency is needed to understand how care work is or is not just, and therefore is or is not a source of grace and flourishing.

Grace for Clients within Care Work

One of the key themes of this chapter is that the presence of justice in dependency relationships helps point toward whether or not they contribute to human flourishing, and therefore are experiences of grace. This includes both an objective element (meeting "genuine needs" and "legitimate wants" of the clients) and a subjective element (the "taking up" of care). To clarify the objective elements: a need is genuine when "if not attended to, [it] will cause harm or impede the flourishing of the one in need"; and a want is legitimate when it can be satisfied "without harming others."[28] So now we consider how the clients experience care work and dependency: in the previous chapter, Danny had a positive relationship with the dependency structures of Payton, in that they seemed to meet his genuine needs and legitimate wants (albeit with some frustrations). Betty is another client who lives in a Payton residence with roommates and participates in frequent recreation events: dance, theater, art class, and weekend trips. But her relationship to care work is more ambiguous, both in terms of its reception, and where she performs care work, herself.

Betty is chattier than Danny (when she's in the mood), and high functioning in a diagnostic sense—she can read, and write in a messy print, and speaks clearly and rapidly, even if there are often long periods of silence while she thinks of her answer to your question. She often steps into a mothering role for her social group (she and Danny share several friends in common), but is also often ignored when she offers chastisement.

Danny's day is one of activity, but that is not true for all clients at Payton Industries. Of the different work groups, only four to five appear to have consistent enough work that their downtime is rare. Danny's group and the

---

[27]Kittay runs through a number of examples of how this might work, including the example of someone in a coma who cannot actively respond to the care given. In this case, Kittay emphasizes the material nature of care: the body itself performs the "uptake" of care. This is a particularly illuminating example for Reinders's case of Kelly: his insistence that agency cannot exist for her can be refuted if you take the activity of her human body itself as an expression of human agency. Kittay, *Learning from My Daughter*, 200–3.

[28]Kittay, *Learning from My Daughter*, 138.

others that work on the cat treats, are busy most of the time; as are the clients who work on stuffing repair kits for window blinds. Betty's group seems to be more ad hoc in their assignments, and of the groups, hers often appears the most idle, the most bored. I was not able to interview Betty's TS, so I never learned if there was a specific reason for this. One time, I saw a few of her peers working on the cat treats, but Betty wasn't. I asked her why, and she told me she was allergic, and they caused a rash on her hands. Occasionally I saw her group working on the small wooden boats, or rare projects like the assembly of boxes. But mostly, Betty simply sat, head resting on her hand, fingers curled against her lip, and elbow on the table, staring at nothing in particular. Some days, she flipped through a magazine. Sometimes, I heard her laugh at a conversation with other clients in her work group. But mostly, her area was quiet, except for pop music coming from the radio on the training supervisor's desk.

Despite this, Betty rarely expressed open frustration at her low workload. Still, I regularly saw her outside the workshop at recreation events, and I could see a difference in her energy levels. In art class she was chatty and amiable; in the workshop, she was a bit more sarcastic (though this might have been partially egged on by a peer). It seemed to me she wanted to work, but here we have the question of discernment and scarcity: the lack of supplies for projects Betty can do (like the wooden boats) leaves her group without regular work. But is work (especially in a sheltered workshop) a "genuine need" or "legitimate want?" Is Betty harmed when she *lacks* work? I admit there are no clear answers on this point, but I think asking the question does challenge how we construe the relationship between care work and other forms of labor.

The workshop isn't the only site of care work Betty receives. She lives in a Payton community home with a couple of roommates who work at Payton with her, and one roommate who is in the Seniors class (a Day program for clients who have "retired" or aged out of the vocational rehab programs). Her schedule requires ongoing negotiations with the schedules of her roommates, particularly the one who is in Seniors—Susan.

I knew Susan a bit from the theater program, an older woman with salt and pepper hair and a subtle stubborn streak (Susan had actually played the Auntie Em to Betty's Wicked Witch in the Payton production of the Wizard of Oz). Betty complained on more than one occasion that Susan "refused to get out of bed" and made the whole group late that morning. In fact, time is a pretty consistent concern for Betty—and yet it's something that she and most other clients have very limited control over. Care work done in the residences often seems to come down to balancing competing needs in a place where time is experienced through scarcity.

While some of the demands on a direct support worker can be alleviated by including clients in the labor, time is still ultimately a zero-sum resource.[29]

---

[29]Jack Levinson's ethnography of a group home illustrates this—although client involvement in housekeeping labor or even the care of other clients (doing hair and nails among women,

When there are limited drivers and transportation, bringing a client to one activity or appointment means another has to reschedule or miss out on something she might want to do. Betty frets about her schedule, wondering aloud whether she will be able to attend the events she finds meaningful, like a friend's birthday party. This is also to say the events she most values are places where her friends, boyfriend, and others she cares about are present: seeking the genuine need for a relationship with others. The DSPs provide conduits to the places where Betty's needs are met, and even where she may experience grace.

Betty's ability to foster fulfilling relationships is also impacted by the support structures that other clients do or do not have. She has had a boyfriend for several years now—they were a well-established couple when I first met Betty, five years ago. And yet, spending time with him outside of the workshop is difficult. Her boyfriend lives separately from his parents, but they still support him, despite their limited income. His presence at recreation activities has dwindled: "his parents haven't got money, so he can't come to art anymore," she tells me. She's not resentful of this, it's just a fact of life—a common one, I think, for the clients, though few are as self-aware of their income limits.

And yet, clients find small ways to reclaim their time and pursue their genuinely desired relationships, sometimes even by adopting practices of care labor themselves. Betty regularly helps a fellow worker, who is legally blind, get to the bathroom. This friend likes having an arm to guide her to the bathroom where she can otherwise tend to herself, which is different than the clients who need more direct assistance with toileting. Hence, Betty is able to step in instead of a program assistant. This gives Betty a modicum of control that other clients don't have: she can collect her friend and bring her to the cafeteria early, both offering a service and providing an opportunity for Betty to get to the microwave before the crowd. Then, in turn, Betty can reserve seats for her boyfriend and friends in other working groups (like Danny). In these microtransactions, Betty builds meaningful relationships, facilitated through her own caring conduct.

One of Betty's coworkers and good friends, Camilla, also makes use of these small exchanges in care and social capital. Once, a member of Camilla's work group lost track of a plastic bag of valued items (it was not clear to me what was in the bag, only that this client was upset enough about losing it to cry). Camilla spent her afternoon systematically tracking down the missing bag: first, checking with Danny (who had been in charge of it at lunch), then searching along the lockers in the cafeteria, which is where the

for example) is not framed as labor in the same sense that it is for direct support professionals. These actions become part of "behavior plans" designed to improve independence. Jack Levinson, *Making Life Work: Freedom and Disability in a Community Group Home* (Minneapolis: University of Minnesota Press, 2010), 5, 69–73.

bag was discovered (even if its provenance was never determined). I saw Camilla return the bag to her friend, walking with her as she slowly crossed the room.

"You found the bag? That's great!"

"She didn't find her bag, you know. She's real upset, you know." Camilla turned her head toward me, but her eyes never quite focus on my face. They always seem to be looking just down and to the right.

"I know, she's been upset all afternoon."

"I just went into the lunchroom, and it was there. Just right there, in the lunchroom." Her alto voice chuckled softly—*so many tears*, it seemed to say, *and it was where she left it all along*. This mix of sincere care and bewilderment marked a lot of Camilla's interactions, with me and others.

To take a step back and reflect on these examples as illustrative of genuine needs and legitimate wants, we see the importance of the subjective element in the results of care. Relationships are genuine needs, and the clients at Payton desire them. Care work becomes a barrier when it pits clients' needs and wants against one another: for example, such as one client's doctor's appointment against another client's recreational activity. On the one hand, these tradeoffs are not unique to the IDD community: I've certainly had to cancel plans in order to attend to more pressing needs, like illness. Perhaps in an ideal world, this tradeoff wouldn't have to happen, but with existing limits on time and sheer human vulnerability, they are inevitable. The difference is that I am able to take ownership over the ability to forgo one want for another, to meet one need, and delay something else. For the IDD community, especially people who live within institutional or group home settings, that is less likely to be the case. They will unwillingly be late to work, miss out on birthday parties, and have to drop out of art class. This is where the subjective element is important for care: discerning genuine needs and legitimate wants means preserving human dignity, means creating space where, whenever possible, needs and wants are both/and, not either/or.[30] And, in the times when it must be an either/or, ensuring that clients have the ability to participate in that process and name their own priorities is a part of preserving that dignity.

Camilla gives further insight into how the care work relationship can be a site of grace when it protects the subjective elements of flourishing. Camilla's kindness is often tinged with anxiety. She tells me she worries about working hard enough, about her problem ankle, about her loud upstairs neighbors. As best I can tell, though Camilla has aides through Payton, her actual residence qualifies as assisted living, not a group home (though she does have at least two roommates who also work at Payton). She has a guardian with Payton's Protective Services Board, and they have a close relationship— Camilla frequently brings up her guardian in conversation.

---

[30]Kittay, *Learning from My Daughter*, 200–13.

Over the summer I was at the workshop, Camilla was faced with a significant health decision: whether or not to have surgery on the bone spurs that were causing pain in her ankle. Although medicated for the pain, her ability to walk had slowly gotten worse. For a few weeks, Camilla was low on work (she was a part of the cat treats group with Danny) while they waited on a new shipment, and this only made her more agitated and anxious. She liked working, she told me, she liked having something to do: "I don't like just coloring all day. I want to work, can't earn money if I'm not working." In the absence of materials, her days looked more like Betty's: coloring books and puzzles spread over the large metal table, half complete, none of them as interesting to Camilla and her table partner as filling bottles. With all this downtime, Camilla often brought up her leg. It was clearly weighing on her mind, especially without regular work to distract her.

She seemed to have a fairly clear understanding of what surgery entailed: she expressed anxiousness about being put "asleep" for the surgery, for an hour or more, and that there would be a long recovery time. She didn't like the thought of missing at least a week and a half of work and staying in a wheelchair for longer. She also told me that she was worried the spurs could come back after the surgery, making it seemingly pointless. Other alternatives to surgery included a new walker, one with a seat that Camilla could use to rest on when standing or walking for a long time (as she does working with the cat treats at Payton). As the summer went on, this seemed to be the choice she was leaning toward, and she would tell me about the type of walker she wanted: lightweight, with a basket to hold her stuff.

Camilla felt a strong connection with her guardian, who was making an effort to give Camilla a sense of agency in this decision: she told me repeatedly that her guardian had said the decision was up to her. I don't know exactly how realistic the option of foregoing surgery altogether may have been, but subjectively Camilla expressed a sense of control over the process. It was something she was thinking over, not something she was being told to do. As autumn arrived, I saw Camilla with her new walker, with a soft leather seat and a nice basket for her purse, just as she had described.

Agency and Epistemic Justice in Care Work

The way Camilla and her guardian worked through her health questions displays a notable virtue: testimonial justice. While Kittay rightly insists that moral judgments are integral to doing care work, the deliberation behind these judgments often seems spontaneous in the immediacy of offering care.[31] In this respect, the kind of moral judgment engendered by care work

---

[31]Kittay, *Learning from My Daughter*, 174–6.

most closely resembles virtue ethics: dependency workers need to develop habits of attention and epistemic humility that help identify the clients' genuine needs and legitimate wants. Care work also relies on the role of the affective in care labor: in order to be grounded in "the concern for the well-being (or flourishing) of a person *for their own sake*," care work necessitates some sense of attachment between worker and client.[32] Yet the desire to do the best for another means that care has also gone hand-in-hand with paternalism. Disability history is a testament to the fact that paternalistic "care" is very often euphemized for violence (see: institutions, eugenics, and forced sterilizations). While Kittay relies on critical reflexivity for the carer to unpack and deconstruct paternalism, there are also structural issues around epistemic justice that need to be addressed. These can be illuminated through Miranda Fricker's work on testimonial and hermeneutical justice.

Although dependency workers are intended to be at the service of a client, in many settings like Payton there is still a differential in power experienced between carer and client. Overarching principles like normalization and professionalization may incentivize care workers to be more loyal to "behavior plans" than to client desires in the belief that they are doing what is best for long-term care.[33] It can also be the case (as with nondisabled persons) that clients' expressed wants and needs do not promote their physical or psychosocial well-being: perhaps they are in harmful romantic relationships, or perhaps they have self-harming behavioral patterns. Essentially, this presents a problem of *phronesis*, practical reasoning. On the most local level, this is why care work demands reflexivity and self-examination on behalf of the worker, including "whether or not she has used her power qua carer to dominate and impose her own will, whether or not she has the requisite competence to assist in the situation, whether or not she should seek help or advice from another and so on."[34] It asks care workers not to presume that their assessment of client needs is right without first taking seriously the client's standpoint: What is the client's understanding of his or her own flourishing, genuine needs, and legitimate wants? Clients may not be right about their genuine needs and legitimate wants in all cases, but workers are nonetheless required to respect the epistemic vantage of clients.

---

[32]Kittay, *Learning from My Daughter*, 177, emphasis in original.
[33]Levinson describes group homes as "technology of governments," by which he means patterns of inducing control among free agents. Behavior plans are an important element in this structure of the group home, and a sign of the primarily "clinical orientation" that staff in the group home—the care workers—take on. I think he is generally right about the role of behavior plans and their connection to patterns of control (by which I don't mean a Foucauldian panopticon, but a more a clinical view of reduction of risk and increase of competencies), but there may a dissonance between my fieldsite and his, since the "clinical orientation" of staff that he observed all had greater professional training (all had a bachelor's degree, many were working toward a masters) than the staff I encountered. Levinson, *Making Life Work*, 44–8, 96–9.
[34]Kittay, *Learning from My Daughter*, 209.

Care without such a foundation of respect will veer into paternalism; it will cease to be real care.[35]

Fricker develops the constructive virtue of testimonial justice in this work of practical reasoning and building epistemic respect. The problem of epistemic *injustice* begins with the assertion that when a "speaker" communicates information to a "hearer," the receiver of the information makes an almost immediate, generally unreflective judgment about credibility.[36] Such judgments are inevitably colored by beliefs and values that cannot always be articulated by the receiver. Rather, they happen implicitly, shaped by the social imagination of the culture(s) in which both the communicator and receiver exist. When these credibility judgments are negatively impacted by derogatory stereotypes, the result is testimonial injustice.[37] It is not hard to imagine how these implicit judgments harm the credibility of intellectually disabled persons: the paternalism so common in disability services operates on the presumption that the guardians and professionals who surround a client with IDD know better than the client herself what contributes to her human flourishing. Any testimony that someone with IDD might give which contradicts professional opinion is undermined by their diagnosis, even in asserting the most mundane desires for certain life choices (e.g., what to eat), let alone larger decisions like where to work or live.

Introducing testimonial justice into interpersonal exchanges within care work can build the kind of reflexivity that Kittay calls for among dependency workers, but it is not entirely sufficient without also attending to structures of knowledge production—the shift from testimonial justice to hermeneutical justice. Hermeneutical injustice occurs when a marginalized group (from a lack of what Fricker calls "identity power") struggles to articulate their own experience because the heuristic lenses they have for reflecting on those experiences belong to the groups that hold power.[38] For hermeneutic

---

[35]Kittay, *Learning from My Daughter*, 210.

[36]The initial language Fricker uses potentially re-inscribes ableism, but for the sake of clarity I include them here at the outset—"giver/receiver" of testimony can also work within the conceptual framework that Fricker employs. Miranda Fricker, *Epistemic Injustice: Power and the Ethics of Knowing* (Oxford: Oxford University Press, 2007).

[37]An example that Fricker uses is Tom Robinson's trial in Harper Lee's *To Kill a Mockingbird*: as a Black man existing in a world where "all negroes lie," the white jurors at his trial refuse to grant him any credibility, even to the point of ignoring the physical evidence that supports Robinson's account of what occurred with Mayella Ewell. The example speaks to a number of identities and kinds of power: race, gender, and class are all wrapped together in Robinson's trial. And so is disability—Tom Robinson has a lame arm from a childhood accident with a cotton gin, a point of evidence that is central to Finch's defense. Fricker does not foreground Robinson's disability in the discussion of how he is subjected to epistemic injustice, instead looking at the triad of gender, race, and class. It is an interesting gap—and one that magnifies the injustice. The jury, so focused on race, overlooked an empirically challenging element of Robinson's embodiment to render their guilty verdict.

[38]For further discussion of hermeneutical marginalization and injustice, see Fricker, *Epistemic Injustice*, 152–61. An illustration is found in early feminist organizing around sexual harass-

justice to take root, those in positions of power and privilege not only must include the testimony of those without identity power, but they must also trust those without privilege to name and interpret their own experiences. Yet, for the clients at Payton, this raises another potential obstacle, one that affects the subjective element of care: learned helplessness.[39] That is to say, testimonial injustice affects the construction of a person's sense of self: if a person spends their entire life being told "you can't," eventually that person comes to believe "I can't," that he or she is incapable of learning new things, or taking on Perske's now-famous phrase, "the dignity of risk."[40] Deference to professionals, limited spaces for sharing and reflecting among others with IDD (without authority figures, such as counselors and doctors, present), and persistent tendencies toward infantilizing people with IDD all work against giving credence to their own accounts of meaning-making and flourishing.

Gemma's Decision

In some places, some structural changes are being made in disability services to account for this gap, primarily by invoking "client-led services." Client-led services attempt to grant more agency to someone with IDD in determining their goals and plans. Yet, questions still remain about whether client-led services give genuine interpretive power over to clients with IDD,

---

ment in the workplace. Though many women shared similar experiences of intrusive verbal and physical exchanges in the workplace, they initially lacked a language for describing the experiences, let alone advocating for social and legal protections against them. Through sharing experiences and consciousness-raising activities, the term "sexual harassment" emerged as a way of categorizing the shared experiences, and that's what advocacy groups mobilized behind. But it took time and space for sharing and reflection for women to be able to generate this kind of heuristic lens. Fricker, *Epistemic Injustice*, 149–52.

[39]Learned helplessness is a behavioral theory arguing that men and women who are consistently treated as "helpless" eventually internalize the perception of their capabilities, despite whatever actually strengths and capacities they might have. This is only one behavioral model among many, but it is particularly popular in examinations of mental illness and cognitive disabilities. For a brief historical overview and lengthy list of studies, see: Bruce Overmier, "On Learned Helplessness," *Integrative Physiological and Behavioral Science: The Official Journal of the Pavlovian Society* 37, no. 1 (March 1, 2002): 4–8.

[40]Fricker, *Epistemic Injustice*, 53–4. A point should be made here about a site of dissonance between Fricker and the theologians such as Reinders and Haslam. Fricker asserts the fundamental nature of being a "knower" to personhood, a claim that Reinders and Haslam would disagree with. They would likely argue that to assert knowing as a foundational component of our anthropology is a mistake that excludes people with IDD from the conversation at the very start. They would likely question if this testimonial injustice can exist in the case of a person who cannot actually give testimony, who cannot communicate sufficiently to convey information about wants and needs. I think this does locate a weak spot in some of the broader metaphysical claims that Fricker is drawing on; nonetheless, I would again assert that many people with disability are knowers, and deserving of testimonial justice. Minimally, I can assert that the clients I work with at Payton all show a capacity for testimony, and it would be an injustice for me to presume their stories are false or erroneous.

or adequately account for the spaces shaped by learned helplessness, where clients became accustomed to ceding to authority figures.

Over the summer, my conversations with a client named Gemma had indicated increasing frustration with her family, and the restrictions they placed on her. Gemma lives with her family, but is able to walk to most of her favorite places in her neighborhood. She dates regularly, is adept at navigating social media such as Facebook, and seems to do a lot of entertaining by hosting parties for friends. Yet, she often tells me about arguments with her mother, mostly concerning money. I am under the impression that although Gemma is a high earner for the workshop, she doesn't get to control her money. She seems to receive a limited allowance that allows her to go shopping at places like the Dollar Store and Five Below, but she needs her mother's approval for significant purchases (one example Gemma vented to me about was a new pair of pink sneakers—her mother refused to buy them because she had "too many pairs" already).

Gemma's sister and nephew had been living in her parents' home while they struggled to sell their former house and purchase a new one. This was a source of the growing conflict. She complained that her nephew didn't respect the privacy of her room, and that he used her things.

"I think I need to move out," she told me one afternoon.

"Yeah? Where to?"

"I could get an apartment with my friends," she said. Some of them had openings in their assisted living situations.

"Would your parents allow that?" Gemma was able to sign her own consent forms, so I knew she had some level of autonomy. Even if Gemma was legally independent, though, her parents' financial control would be a significant obstacle.

"I'm going to bring it up with my annual meeting." The annual meeting was something done with all the clients involved with Payton services. From what the clients told me, it was a meeting with guardians (whether family, Protective services, or other), the client, sometimes a supervisor (if in employment services, like Gemma), and someone who seemed to be either a case manager or counselor. The meeting updated behavior plans and set goals for the upcoming year.

"I think you should, if you feel strongly about it." I was trying to be neutral with my response, but internally I hoped that Gemma was serious. A goal like independent living (even if assisted through Payton) would likely be a multi-step process that had to start there. If her parents did have a lot of control over Gemma, articulating her desire to move out in the annual meeting could be a good place to get support if needed. I was cautiously optimistic—I had known Gemma for a couple of years in both the Rec programs and the workshop, and sometimes wondered if Gemma had been holding herself back.

The annual meeting date came and went, so I checked back and asked Gemma how it had worked out.

"Hey, so I wanted to ask, how did the annual meeting go?"

"Oh, it was good. They said I'm doing good."

"Did you ask about moving out and into an apartment?"

"Yeah. I don't think I'm going to. I don't need to." Her tone was nonchalant—you would never know the frustration she had been expressing just weeks prior. It was almost as if I was the one bringing the idea up for the first time.

"Oh. So, are things better at home?"

"Oh yeah, they're good. Much better."

These moments remain opaque to me as an observer: what did or didn't happen in that conversation? Did things improve at home, first? Or did Gemma ask to move out first, and instead they decided to have a conversation about what she needs in her current home, to mediate the current situation? And I must ask for my own epistemic humility: to what degree was I allowing my own prejudices about preferred living situations to color the hopes I held for Gemma? Did I connect with her parental and sibling frustrations because that's how I felt as a young adult? Gemma is not known for caving to the pressure of authorities—she finds loopholes and small sites of resistance to rules and regulations. It is entirely possible, even likely, that she changed her mind of her own volition: perhaps the enormity of moving out started to worry her, or perhaps she gained some new degree of control that brought her living situation back from the brink of intolerable.

As it turned out, things started to get better for Gemma—at least for a while. Her sister and brother-in-law finally purchased a house, moving out of their parents' home. And then her parents announced that they were going to sell their own house and get a larger place, one "big enough for a dog," Gemma excitedly told me. But other things stayed the same: just a week after the annual meeting, Gemma complained about her parents being hard on her, again. She repeated that she wanted her own place, but told me that her parents wouldn't let her move out.

Epistemic Justice and Profound Intellectual Disability

Gemma presents an example of how structurally enabling clients to express their needs and desires can create ambiguous outcomes for testimonial justice, hermeneutic justice, and the pursuit of the goods of care. It is also worth noting that such examples of client-led services are employed among people like Gemma, who are able to communicate with relative ease. This does not account for people with much more limited communication. It would seem that in those cases, the epistemic exchange that Fricker proposes may not be possible. Yet, even here Kittay insists that we need to resist paternalism. While Kittay acknowledges that a "lack of epistemic access here means we are also lacking moral access, that is, access to the moral possibilities of interaction with this person,"[41] nonetheless she insists that every subject has some form of agency to exert, that we must respect that agency to the degree that we *do* have epistemic access. This means that Sesha (Kittay's daughter) expresses her agency not in language but in bodily movements, in resistance to medications that taste poorly, and in subtle facial expressions that Kittay has learned, patiently over time. When Sesha resists taking seizure medication, it doesn't mean that Kittay stops giving something necessary to Sesha's well-being (i.e., ceasing care); but it does mean that she tries to find alternative ways to administer it that avoid the elements Sesha dislikes.[42]

Molly Haslam also illustrates this in her experiences with physical therapy for clients with profound intellectual disabilities. Haslam's clients have less communicative resources than Sesha; they are more like Kelly, perhaps, but they still respond to stimuli, and still reflect a form of engagement with the world. Haslam is less assertive about agency than Kittay; nonetheless, she presents a case for subjectivity (and therefore a kind of agency) grounded in responsiveness, rather than intentionality or "conceptualization."[43] She describes Chan, a client with his "perlocutionary" communicative development (a stage that typically lasts from birth to about nine months old), which is typically "preintentional," but still relational insofar as "his or her behavior affects the caregiver, and thus serves a communicative function."[44] Yet, Haslam troubles the assumption that a perlocutionary stage is intrinsically preintentional, since some people with profound IDD do learn to use behaviors and gestures in a way that communicates intention (e.g., humming and looking back and forth between a meal and caregiver).[45] Determining such intentionality takes a great deal of time and attentiveness to the client—it also means that the caregiver needs to presume subjectivity on behalf of the client, to be willing to find patterns of intentionality even in nonverbal behavior. Caregivers also cannot write off "problem" behaviors as irrational resistance: there may well be a reason that the client cannot articulate, much as Kittay figured out the problem of taste for Sesha's resistance to her medication.

Chan magnifies these challenges: his behavior does not seem to have enough of a pattern to indicate even this kind of subtle intentionality in his perlocutionary communication.[46] He also cannot roll over, hold his head up, or sit up unsupported: he requires physical support even when sitting in his wheelchair. Such physical limitations create barriers to even the subtle

---

[41]Kittay, *Learning from My Daughter*, 212.
[42]Kittay, *Learning from My Daughter*, 204–5.
[43]Molly Claire Haslam, *A Constructive Theology of Intellectual Disability: Human Being as Mutuality and Response* (New York: Fordham University Press, 2012), 53.
[44]Haslam, *A Constructive Theology of Intellectual Disability*, 55.
[45]Haslam, *A Constructive Theology of Intellectual Disability*, 55.
[46]Haslam, *A Constructive Theology of Intellectual Disability*, 57.

kinds of communication just discussed. Does Chan represent the "problem" of Kelly that Reinders finds unavoidable? Still, even here Haslam (through Chan's caregivers) finds patterns of embodied responses that illustrate how Chan exerts an almost imperceptible agency, one that Kelly may also exert. In the presence of a familiar caregiver (Philip), Chan "exhibits more 'awake behavior' . . . [t]he motor activity of his arms and legs increases, his eyes remain open, he smiles, and he begins to vocalize at the sound of Philip's voice."[47] Chan does not respond similarly to other, less-known caregivers. This interaction with the world is a particular product of Chan's relationship with Philip, a relationship of obvious dependency but one which nonetheless prompts and facilitates Chan's subjective expression. Indeed, Chan's physical therapist, Sara, uses Philip to engage Chan:

> Knowing that Chan is especially responsive to Philip's presence, Sara positions Philip in front of Chan. . . . Sara notices the increased activity in the muscles along the back of Chan's neck as his head slightly elevates and the gaze of his eyes moves upward in the direction of Philip's face. After several seconds in which Chan attempts to elevate the position of his head in an upright position, Sara intervenes and assists Chan in the completion of this task.[48]

In this slow, careful anecdote, Haslam illustrates precisely the principles of respect and dignity that Kittay argues are structurally necessary for care. It is true that eventually, Chan's physical therapist had to complete the task of lifting his head, but this was not an act of paternalism. Sincere efforts were made to understand what would help and motivate Chan, and he was given the opportunity to complete the task on his own terms, before Sara intervened.

Despite the limits of language, despite the limits of Chan's body, a sense of reciprocity emerges, paternalism is resisted, and respect is brought forward. These elements can be overlooked in the name of efficiency—especially when structural pressures force care workers into pursuing efficiency over the preservation of dignity. As we move to the next section, it is important to keep in mind that justice owed to care workers (both in terms of the clients and the organizational structures that surround care work) goes hand-in-hand with the preservation of agency, dignity, and flourishing for the clients they serve.

Care Workers, Justice, and Grace

As indicated earlier, though my interactions with residential and direct support staff have been limited, several of the Training Supervisors

---

[47]Haslam, *A Constructive Theology of Intellectual Disability*, 58.
[48]Haslam, *A Constructive Theology of Intellectual Disability*, 60–1.

I interviewed had started in residential services at Payton or elsewhere before moving into their positions at Payton Industries. They provide valuable insight into the nature of care work in that environment—which also helps to understand the peculiar nature of the care work done within the workshop space. I'll take "Sarah" as my example here: she had been an in-home support professional at Payton for over six years.[49] She was one of the few supervisors with a Payton employment history of over a year, and she spoke somewhat fondly of her time in residential. She had gotten her job through the encouragement of a family member: Sarah had an autistic cousin (who was a client with Payton), her aunt noted that Sarah was "good" with her cousin, and told her to apply for a position at Payton during a job fair. Sarah did, and was hired that day, actually to work with said cousin.[50]

"Residential's a lot different than out here," she told me, more plainspoken and blunt than other supervisors. She made the shift to Payton Industries because she had a baby, and the lengthy shifts (sometimes sixteen hours straight) would no longer work with her new mothering duties—and she was not the only supervisor who indicated they had taken the Payton Industries position to gain hours more amenable to childcare. She noted several differences between her old position and her new one:

> . . . [in] residential you get to know the clients in their environment, their home, they are completely laid back. You're, uhh responsibilities there: you have to give medication, make sure house chores and the house is kept neat and clean. And food, make sure that they're fed and uh, make sure all of their doctor's appointments—if they're on your shift, you need to take them to all doctor's appointments. If they have any activities, you have to drive them to their activities and stay with them at their activities. Just basic needs that we don't think about you needing help with, like showering, bathing, hygiene. Just—and a lot of them just need a reminder. "Hey, you need to go brush your teeth." Because if they didn't have that they wouldn't do it. It was completely laid back, home environment. Here, they are not, they are not the same. Like, I have clients here that I worked in their home. And I get to see the difference. Like, they might be not shy at home, but they are completely shy here, they don't talk as much. At home you can't get them to be quiet, and here they won't even converse with you. Or, just the opposite. They are completely different here. At home they're more laid back, here they are just edgy.[51]

---

[49]Training Supervisor, Personal Interview, August 31, 2015.
[50]In the course of the interview, Sarah indicated that her cousin had left Payton because they weren't equipped to adequately meet his needs. Personal Interview, August 31, 2015.
[51]Training Supervisor, Personal Interview, August 31, 2015.

One of the biggest challenges for Sarah in her relatively new position was the new negotiation of boundaries. She spoke with a clear sense of former intimacy with the clients she had worked with in residential services:

> The first house that they stuck me in, in residential, I had a lady who was bi—dual diagnosis. Severe schizophrenia, and severe bipolar. And then you add on the, uh, MR to that, and she was basically a hot mess type. They actually had to re-locate her just recently, because they, we are not equipped to handle how severe she was. Her schizophrenia was so severe she might scream out "someone's raping me" and "someone's outside my window, they want to get me." Then she'd go into man—her manics, and she would refuse to take her medicine. She would refuse to get out of bed and this means that she would soil herself, and all over her bed, and she would lay in that for days. And you, we uh, depending on the caregiver we're supposed to—uh, in supported living they're supposed to be independent. So, certain one of the caregivers would just let her stay. Me personally, I had an attachment to her, I couldn't—we had a certain relationship. She would call me her daughter. And, I wouldn't, I wouldn't allow her. I would say, "okay, miss, you're gonna scream at me or hit me, but I—I love you too much to have you lay here and get sores because you refuse to get up and be changed." So I would basically—and some people might've thought that as kind of abuse, because they want them to be independent. But to me, like, I'm helping her. And if she can't help herself, I'm going to help her. That was . . . it changed me as a person, just having to deal with that.[52]

Sarah names a potent tension here in dependency labor and care work: the will of the worker vis-a-vis the will of the client. Sarah acted against the explicit will of the client not only for the client's health but also for Sarah's own emotional needs. This is hard territory to navigate: when carers assume the goods they themselves would seek are the same goods their clients ought to want, we enter the realm of paternalism. At the same time, we've also seen the need for an objective effect of care, and Kittay herself would warn against a distorted view of independence that allows clients to interfere with their own objective flourishing. This can prevent what Kittay calls the "completion of care." In the previous case of Sesha and medication, the completion of care required that Kittay not forgo medicine, but find an alternative way for Sesha to take it.[53] Do such examples perhaps *ask* for paternalism?

To a certain extent, these cases highlight the indeterminacy of care work, in that the completion of care is not always the result of the worker's

---

[52]Training Supervisor, Personal Interview, August 31, 2015.
[53]Kittay, *Learning from My Daughter*, 206–7.

efforts. Sometimes, care cannot be completed because the person being cared for does not accept it (what Kittay refers to as the "uptake of care"). This heightens the moral stakes for the worker, especially when there is an emotional investment.[54] Sarah made a very reasonable decision to conduct her care on the basis that preventing hunger and bed sores contributed to this client's flourishing, but she also made this decision in light of her own personal feelings regarding the client: "*I had an attachment to her.*" The difference between this decision being a function of paternalism or a function of care is the degree to which Sarah tried to understand the client's own subjective viewpoint. We see that Sarah reports explaining her rationale to the client, making an emotional appeal by naming it as an act of love. It is also not unreasonable to assume that Sarah knew the client well enough to know that when she was not experiencing this kind of mental health crisis, she would want to be taken out of bed and appropriately cared for.[55]

As an outsider to the situation, there are limits to my ability to judge the morality of this specific incident; still, this capacity for discernment, even if occurring in the immediacy of a crisis, is an important virtue to cultivate among care workers. It is not difficult to imagine that a care worker in charge of material necessities like budget and cleanliness may more often operate in an authoritative register than a subservient one: *yes, you have to brush your teeth, no you can't buy that snack*, and so on. It is also not difficult to imagine someone taking actions similar to Sarah's, but without the emotional processing she describes—perhaps ensuring the client gets out of bed is merely prescribed as a part of a behavior plan, or because the worker is worried about job sanctions if they fail to act. In such cases, these ostensibly caring actions become functions of paternalism, and lack the respect for subjectivity that is so important to caring done well.

Secondary Dependencies and Care Workers

Such is the fine ethical line that DSPs must walk—not just with one client, but often with 3–4 clients living together and a second DSP on-site. Yet,

---

[54]Kittay articulates this tension in a recent article: "Caregiver A is free to offer care. Care recipient B is equally free to refuse it. But care is more complex than the coordinated action of two actors. The care that A (that is, the caregiver) offers must be for the sake of B (the care recipient) and must be guided by B's needs, as best as A can discern them. To act on behalf of B for B's sake, A must set aside her own view of needs or desires, and understand the matter from the position of B." Eva Feder Kittay, "Caring for the Long Haul: Long-Term Care Needs and the (Moral) Failure to Acknowledge Them," *International Journal of Feminist Approaches to Bioethics* 6, no. 2 (Fall 2013): 82.
[55]Kittay, *Learning from My Daughter*, 205.

they are rarely offered the formation or education that helps to do this work well. Some literature on care work indicates that is at least partly because the gender disparity in care work can lead supervisors and other leadership to see this work as "natural" or instinctive—likening it to the work of parenthood.[56] Sullivan-Dunbar indicates a similar historical narrative, where care work became marginalized in political and economic discourse precisely because as "women's work" it was placed in the "private" sphere of the family.[57] But even if the skill set between parents and DSPs is similar (and I had one training supervisor specifically use that comparison to describe her work) I would argue that says more about the necessity of resources needed to parent well, rather than the ease of care work itself.[58] Whether referring to parents or paid workers, the work of care is *skilled* work: "If A lacks the requisite skills and competencies to correctly assess B's needs as B sees them, or is inept in meeting those needs, A lacks the wherewithal to succeed in caregiving."[59] It would seem then, that at bare minimum, the justice we owe care workers must include supports that enable them to discern and meet the needs of their clients.

Several elements immediately come to mind, and these echo what Kittay calls "secondary dependencies."[60] The kinds of vulnerabilities that care workers are subject to often result from the clear economic devaluation of care work, resulting in insufficiencies in struggles to meet their own personal needs. To achieve distributive justice with respect to dependency labor, we have to assess not only pay and wages, but also time, energy, and the ways that care workers themselves often need other kinds of care (and human labor) to support them.[61]

While all of these elements will be addressed in turn, let me start with the most obvious one: material resources. Across all the interviews I did with training supervisors, the refrain rang clear when I asked what Payton could improve:

"More overtime," says Sarah—by which she meant not the number of hours she worked, but the ability to earn higher pay by working those sixteen-hour, overnight, or holiday shifts.

---

[56]This gendered view of the work is also, unsurprisingly, connected to the low wages that persist in care work. Paula England, Michelle Budig, and Nancy Folbre, "Wages of Virtue: The Relative Pay of Care Work," *Social Problems* 49, no. 2 (2002): 455–73. It is interesting, however, that this gendered view of care work can also enable certain forms of microresistance, though that topic will be taken up in more detail in the following chapter. Jillian Crocker, "'We Will Handle It Ourselves': The Micropolitics of Resistance in Low-Wage Care Work," *Sociological Perspectives* 62, no. 1 (2019): 42–58.

[57]Sullivan-Dunbar, *Human Dependency and Christian Ethics*, 27–35.

[58]Training Supervisor, Personal Interview, July 16, 2015.

[59]Kittay, "Caring for the Long Haul," 82.

[60]Kittay, *Love's Labor*, 46–8.

[61]Sullivan-Dunbar, *Human Dependency and Christian Ethics*, 188.

"Except for money, this would be the perfect job," says another training supervisor.[62] And a third: "There's a lot of bullshit you have to put up with, and you don't get paid much. But the clients bring us back every day."[63]

At the time of writing, the federal mean wage for DSPs is $11.26/hour—a wage that, at a full forty hours/week, places a family of four a few hundred dollars below the federal poverty line.[64] There is a structural reason why wages are so low: since this type of dependency work falls under Medicaid's HCBS waiver, each state sets a reimbursement rate for DSP services. Service providers then set their wages by budgeting their reimbursement against need, with nonprofit service providers often making up differences between wages and the reimbursement through their own budgetary lines, endowments (if they are lucky enough to have one), and fundraising. When I was at Payton, the average salary in Indiana for a DSP was $10.20/hour, which is where Payton's wages were hovering (depending on the length of time and experience)—and then, a year and a half after I finished my fieldwork, Indiana passed a bill (one that Payton lobbied heavily for) to increase DSP services reimbursement by 5 percent, or a total of an extra $10 million (something that several other states have recently done or are pursuing). This was a positive gain—but, perhaps not enough, since the economic data suggests that until wages reach $15/hour (i.e., a living wage) they will continue to experience high turnover and labor instability.[65]

Wages constitute only one part of the picture for economic security, though: fringe benefits and other aspects of the social welfare net are infrequently accessible. Less than half of all DSPs have employer-provided insurance, and about 18 percent use public insurance programs.[66] When I interviewed Sarah, she had to pause the interview to take a phone call—her son was getting tubes in his ears to solve a recurring ear infection problem, and the call was her waited-for approval for coverage of the pre-surgery antibiotics he needed to take. There is no small irony in the fact that mothers like Sarah, being paid through Medicaid waivers, had a high likelihood of being on Medicaid themselves. Other resources, such as paid time off, retirement accounts, and more are not readily available to DSPs.

Of course, this is not a problem limited to DSPs: this is a problem for all hourly workers that aren't being paid a living wage. Nonetheless, it says something peculiar about our social values that the work of caring for the vulnerable among us, a form of work with apparently sky-high demand and

---

[62]Training supervisor, Personal Interview, July 16, 2015.
[63]Training supervisor, Personal Interview, September 15, 2015.
[64]Friedman, "Direct Support Professionals and Quality of Life of People With Intellectual and Developmental Disabilities," 324.
[65]Bogenschutz et al., "Direct Support Workforce Supporting Individuals With IDD: Current Wages, Benefits, and Stability," 318.
[66]Bogenschutz et al., "Direct Support Workforce Supporting Individuals With IDD: Current Wages, Benefits, and Stability," 319.

low supply, is still so drastically, deeply undervalued.[67] It seems to defy free-market beliefs in how supply and demand ought to work concerning wages. On the one hand, this could be an argument about what role the state ought to have concerning distributive justice, given the impact that Medicaid has on shaping wages. Funding structures like Medicaid heighten the political problem of moderate scarcity: ongoing debates about how much to fund Medicaid or how expansive its program should be are often cast in terms of taking from some (via taxes, or cuts to other social welfare programs) in order to give to others.[68] On the other hand, I think this is primarily an argument about the social capital such work entails: given the history of excluding care work from the economic sphere, given that such work is primarily done by poor women of color, perhaps the low wages associated with care work is less about the labor market than it is about a refusal to see this work as valuable, performed by valuable people and done for valuable people (in this case, the IDD community).

Payton's leaders recognize this issue, though it was not articulated as distorted social capital, but as a frustration for the type of candidate they end up seeing for work that is intellectually, emotionally, and physically exhausting. One vice president spoke about the difference in client satisfaction rates between adult programing (typically very low) and Payton's expanding Autism centers (typically much higher). She attributed a large part of that discrepancy to the fact that most of the people Payton hires in Autism services require Master's degrees, which engages a different kind of worker.[69] A former CEO more bluntly commented:

> When you're paying people $9.50 an hour you're not going to get the cream of the crop staff. . . . I mean, that's reality. And uh, we have to take that into account. . . . People that we are counting on every day to provide 24-hour, 7-day a week care at entry level positions that we start at $9.50 an hour. And we're—I'm going to try to say this nicely—but

---

[67]For a history of care work and its devaluation, see Emily K. Abel, "A Historical Perspective on Care," in *Care Work: Gender, Labor, and the Welfare State*, ed. Madonna Harrington Meyer (New York: Routledge, 2000), 8–14; Mignon Duffy, "Beyond Outsourcing: Paid Care Work in Historical Perspective," in *Caring on the Clock: The Complexities and Contradictions of Paid Care Work*, ed. Clare L. Stacey, Amy Armenia, and Mignon Duffy (New Brunswick: Rutgers University Press, 2015), 14–26.

[68]Sullivan-Dunbar discusses this element of justice as "sacrifice." Social welfare programs, like SNAP, are "widely seen not as part of the communal relations of giving and receiving . . . but as impositions" (191). Continuing with the thread of hunger, Sullivan-Dunbar asserts (correctly, I believe) that "feeding the hungry elsewhere in the world will claim our resources, perhaps to a significant degree," and therefore "we cannot rely on the sporadic and heroic sacrifice of individuals for this purpose" (192). To meet the vast needs of dependency care requires the willingness of a total community to sacrifice, and potentially requires the coercive power of the state to enforce that.

[69]Vice President, Personal Interview, July 8, 2015.

we're asking them to take care of adults and put them in a position, and to, to help them to buy groceries, help them to plan meals, help them to manage money. And let's face it, if we really did a test on a hundred percent of our employees, how well would they do on just managing their own money?[70]

Although unfortunately framed as an individual limitation on the worker, I think these comments really indicate other areas of distributive justice that need addressing, namely, interpersonal and organizational support. When care workers don't have the resources they need—whether in terms of material resources, interpersonal support, or professional development—they are left unable to complete the task of care they have been given.

Take, for example, the category of time: there are certain ratios of DSPs-to-clients that Payton must abide by for regulations of their residences. Generally, a home with two clients can function with one staff present at all times, three to four needs at least two staff at all times, and so on (the scale increases as the size of the home increases, but for Payton, their group homes are no larger than eight residents, with three to four staff around at all hours). Ostensibly, these ratios are meant to grant direct support workers enough time in their shifts to adequately attend to the needs of their residents, and more residents require more time, ergo, labor. Yet, as the ratios increase, a zero-sum game is created: even just one staff serving two clients might find the clients have needs that directly compete for time, and the staff is left deciding which need takes priority. And this drain on time doesn't only impact the workplace: it also creates drains on staff's energy and time for their personal lives, too. Working overtime (for material gain) drains care workers of hours they might spend caring for families, or attending to other relationships and social support. A solution to this might be to add staff above and beyond what the regulatory ratios might be, but this is hard to do when there's not enough consistent labor to meet the regular demand, let alone hire extra. And so time and labor in residential systems continue to fall short of what distributive justice ought to look like.

Organizational support forms another branch of distributive justice for care workers. Indeed, organizational culture is one of the top reasons given for the labor shortage in DSPs, something I saw even among the training supervisors at Payton. I do not think it is a coincidence that those who had the longest job history with Payton were people who had been through some kind of formation process which gave them the intellectual and emotional skills to navigate the tricky boundary of being both a boss and care worker.

One corner of the workshop was run by a paired set of training supervisors, Mary and Jane—both of whom came to Payton first as program assistants

---

[70]Former CEO, Personal Interview, July 29, 2015.

before getting promoted to training supervisor. Prior to Payton, they had both worked as teaching assistants for students with IEPs in the local public school system. The experience seemed to offer them a stronger intuition for what they should be providing the clients, but they also admitted to feeling a lack of institutional clarity concerning their roles as training supervisors:

> Mary: Well I think one of the biggest challenges is, in the school setting you know you have set disciplinary codes, set actions that take place for behaviors or you know, to assist you in shaping your client, your student. Here, there really, I don't think there really are any set boundaries or rules, if you will. Uhm, and if there is a violation of anything you would consider to be somewhat of a rule, there's really no consequence here. I mean I guess that for me has been the biggest adjustment, because . . . if I have, if I have a client speak rudely to me, there's really nothing I can do about it other than tell a supervisor.
> Jane: [echoing] Tell a supervisor. And they know that, the clients know that. Yeah.
> Mary: They do, they know that.
> Jane: You know there's no like, you know in a high school, if you're gonna fight somebody, you're suspended. They don't have that here. I think that's been a challenge because then it's, it's putting more strain on your role as a supervisor.
> Mary: Right. And too sometimes they think if you show them a little respect, they kind of appreciate that, and then their behavior will turn around. Whereas in a school it was always kind of a threat, we had to hold something over their head, you know, like, suspension or, or extra homework, or whatever. But here, here if you treat them like the adults that they are, sometimes that helps. Not always.
> Jane: Right.
> Mary: Just depends on who, who you're talking to.
> Jane: That's been a challenge because, you know, they are adults. So, you know, giving them certain boundaries and freedoms that, you know, I don't expect them to tell me every time they go to the bathroom, or I don't expect them to ask me to use the restroom. Uhm, I just like the mutual respect that, they tell me where they're going kind of a thing.[71]

In the comparisons with their time in the school system, Mary and Jane indicate that they miss a clear set of procedures and rules, but also, perhaps, a sense of authority. This register of authority, embedded within care work is precisely what makes the work difficult. Mary and Jane were used to having

---

[71]Personal Interview, Two Training Supervisors, September 15, 2015.

structured rules and repercussions, and without that they were unsure of what to do.

Lack of clarity or support for the supervisors in their care work prevents the completion of care. Part of what supervisors are told to do is socialize clients into standard workplace expectations (per Wolfensberger's normalization): Mary and Jane cited things like professionalism, hygiene, etiquette, and even personal space as a part of their task. Kittay's analysis of care work acknowledges that this is a major element of dependency labor, but she also describes this as a two-way process: not only do carers prepare their clients for socialization, but they also need to prepare their communities to accept their clients.[72] This is further supported by the social science literature, which consistently notes the role that institutions and supporting staff play in facilitating inclusion and deconstructing stereotypes.[73] So in this respect, we come back to the way material resources (e.g., paying workers well) enable interpersonal support (e.g., more "soft skills" building vocational preparation) and organizational capacities (e.g., creating more community access for people with IDD). It is vital the voices of care workers *and their clients* are involved, so as to avoid the problem of paternalism that Kittay identifies: one of the biggest obstacles for justice in disability services is that so many policies are made about the disabled community without any of their input.[74] The obstacles to distributive justice may appear overwhelming, but this is a task central to constructing just relationships between care workers and those cared for, allowing those relationships to become sites of grace.

The "Need to Understand, Respect, and Serve Everyone"

Although my central claim for this chapter is that we need to create just relationships for care work to be sites of grace, I did observe one strategy among supervisors to find grace within work that is still very much distorted by the social and economic problems just detailed. This often came in the form of invoking relationships with clients, even expressing a sense of vocation in the work.

---

[72]Kittay, *Love's Labor*, 161.

[73]Amado and Stancliffe, "Social Inclusion and Community Participation of Individuals with Intellectual/Developmental Disabilities," 363.

[74]Sullivan-Dunbar emphasizes "the moral knowledge of marginalized persons giving care in oppressive or exploitative circumstances," rather than the persons receiving care (*Human Dependency and Christian Ethics*, 193). Client contributions would likely come in generating her "epistemologically humble account of the good" (*Human Dependency and Christian Ethics*, 192), but in the case of this policy both the goods identified and the structures that enable them are hard to untangle.

I will confess that when I interviewed training supervisors and heard this invoked, I was often skeptical: *You don't get paid much, but the clients bring us back.* The conditions under which the supervisors worked were hard, and, as with any client-facing position in an organization, some of the clients were *very* antagonistic and resistant (more on that in the next section). On the one hand, this might indicate that the employees need something "irrational"—in the economic sense—to keep bringing them back to work, so relationships were indeed a part of their motivation. At the same time, jobs were not easy to find in this corner of the country: unemployment was hovering between 7.5 percent and 5 percent at the time I was doing these interviews, rapidly declining but still making its way down from the double-digit peak of the Great Recession. I wondered: *was having a job more important than what the job was? Might these supervisors think that expressing attachment to the clients was simply what I wanted to hear, and what would make them look good as employees?*

When I could put my cynicism aside, I could see that many of the supervisors did go above and beyond, and their actions lent depth to a sentiment that could otherwise feel trite. For Faith, this was particularly apparent, and I give her that pseudonym because she was one of the only supervisors I interviewed who directly referenced her faith life. A woman of color in her early sixties, Faith had worked at Payton for two years and initially taken an early retirement just four months prior to our interview. But, she told me, she "quit in March and was back by April," not because she needed the money, but because she missed the Payton community.[75]

Faith had a wide range of experience in care work, having first felt a vocation (admittedly my language, not hers) to nursing, a story she recited to me with the musical lilt of a Baptist preacher:

And for me, I remember, I was like nine, ten years of age, and I thought the little ladies, the ladies with the white uniforms and the little nurses cap you know, they were like God's angels to me. And I said at that age, you know, I want to be a nurse when I grow up. And I was a little girl, you know, I was—I was at work one day and I was sitting down and just thinking to myself, you know [Faith], why did you really want to be a nurse? And you know, we take words, and we break down those letters and we do a lot with them. And, I realize that I have the need to understand, respect, and serve everyone, and that's why I'm a nurse. And that's what it spells: the need to understand, the [N]eed to [U]nderstand, [R]espect and [S]erve [E]veryone. If you take those first letters that's what it spells, it spells "nurse."[76]

[75]Training Supervisor, Personal Interview, August 27, 2015.
[76]Training Supervisor, Personal Interview, August 27, 2015.

(In fact, Faith had a lot of acronyms like that—including one for Payton's real name, though it was strictly shared "off the record"—Faith feared that the acronym could get her in trouble.) Through nursing, Faith had a lot of experiences in the disability community, including working in a group home in Chicago and for a VA hospital. At some point, her nursing work dropped to part-time, and she was working the third shift in the same industrial complex where Payton Industries was located when she applied for and got the position of training supervisor.

With both a nursing background and a manufacturing background, I would venture to say Faith was uniquely prepared for the kind of hybrid care work of being a training supervisor: she both understood the nature of manufacturing work and had a necessary level of comfort with some of the caring needs entailed by working with the IDD community. She explicitly expressed a sense that Payton was "different" than her other experiences with the disability community—again, placing my own gloss on this, I would speculate that Faith's previous experiences were primarily in clinical environments, ruled by a medical model. Here at Payton, the medical model (though not entirely gone) could be sidelined.

> . . . [W]hen I worked at the VA hospital and when I worked at the small group home in Chicago, my position wasn't the same. I didn't actually have to train them to do anything other than your normal activities that they remember. But here, it's different because we're actually trying to help prepare them for jobs out in the community. Which is different from what they are accustomed to in here. . . . Because here, not only is this a place where we're trying to learn them and prepare them for work on the outside, but this is a place where this is a social gathering for them as well.[77]

But most importantly, perhaps, Faith's sense of vocation—that mission to "understand, respect, and serve," seemed to help her articulate client needs as a matter of their subjective development, not their capacities for productive output. While some supervisors spoke of the relationships between clients as potential distractions and obstacles to their vocational rehabilitation, Faith articulates this as a part of the value of Payton's work: she sees the value of the workshop from the clients' perspectives. Where other supervisors noted the piecework pay but accepted it as a part of the limitations of client capacities, Faith told me about the empowering experience clients have in actually receiving a paycheck: she told me a story about one client's excited tears when she received her first paycheck, in own her name, for just a dollar.

---

[77]Training Supervisor, Personal Interview, August 27, 2015.

This is part of the tangled, uncertain nature of grace. Christian views on labor and justice would decry the low wages entailed in piecework (which I strongly agree with). At the same time, even amid these structures that range from unjust to imperfectly seeking justice, there are these small moments of grace, small moments of effect, and relationships that help resist potentially overwhelming obstacles to flourishing. While Faith told me she was once again contemplating retirement, she also expressed a sense of transformation from the experience: "You know, whenever my last day comes, I'm sure, without a doubt, I'll miss them so much. I'm thankful, every day I'm thankful for the opportunity I've had to be employed here, I really am, because, ah, it's an awesome experience and like I said, I'm a 'N.U.R.S.E.'"[78]

What Clients Owe Care Workers

The labor of dependency care work, contrary to popular perception, does run in both directions: this means that for care work to be both just and effective, the clients have certain responsibilities to their care workers. Kittay calls this the "uptake of care," and it's a critical element to the completion of care. One of the reasons why theologians of disability tend to reject discussions of agency as unhelpful is precisely because they view dependency relationships as entirely passive on behalf of the dependent. Yet, as Kittay argues, good care depends just as much on the person receiving care as the person giving it.[79]

While Gemma's home life had initially started to improve after the late-summer annual meeting, her health suffered in the fall. Gemma was heavyset, and one of the consistent conflicts with her mother (that she told me about) concerned her weight: her mother was insisting that Gemma had to exercise more, and had to lose weight. Concern for weight is a complicated thing, especially in the context of care. Many healthcare and medical professionals see weight as a clear indicator of health and well-being, and losing weight is a common recommendation for a number of problems (such as chronic joint pain, which Gemma struggled with in her knee and ankle). On the other hand, health and weight are not always directly correlated, and disability theory frequently points out that "fatness," like all forms of abnormality, is subject to the same social construction as a disability. Gemma's bad ankle, for example, is something that Gemma attributes to a fall, not her weight. So Gemma's mother, in attempting to care for her daughter, maybe using a rubric (weight loss) that does not necessarily address the real cause of

---

[78]Training Supervisor, Personal Interview, August 27, 2015.
[79]Kittay, *Learning from My Daughter*, 185–97.

her troubles, and therefore may not make an objective contribution to her overall flourishing. That being said, the kinds of things that Gemma was being encouraged to do can be considered goods in and of themselves: moderate exercise does contribute to health, even if it doesn't result in weight changes. And Gemma did do some forms of exercise regularly, such as a Zumba-like class called "Move and Groove" once a week, and she liked taking walks around her neighborhood. So she was active, but her mother seemed to want greater activity, or more precisely a specific set of results from that activity. In fact, when Gemma's ankle started acting up, she claimed that her mother wouldn't take her to the doctor, because "he'll just say that you're overweight."

In October, I was away for a week while traveling, and when I came back I learned that Gemma had been hospitalized overnight for a bad bladder infection. Shortly after, she came down with what she told me was a "bad cold." Since a number of clients were immunosuppressed, either as a result of their conditions or a result of medications taken for their conditions, these kinds of infections could present real dangers. Though Gemma insisted she was feeling much better, I started to worry. I had known her almost the longest out of the clients I was working with, and though I tried to keep the nature of our relationship at a professional distance, I cared for her.

The following week, Gemma was at the emergency room, again—this time leaving the workshop sick while her mother picked her up. On Monday, Gemma was back, and told me the problem was her foot, "bad circulation." This was a warning sign for diabetes (which runs in her family), and so she was waiting on the results from several tests to see what was wrong. Her voice dipped down as she told me the story, and I saw her eyes get red around the edges. I'd never seen her so upset—not even when a good friend of hers had died from a sudden infection about a year prior. I didn't know what to say to her as the story poured out, imaging that she was still in a lot of pain. So I said the only thing I could think of: "I'm so sorry—that sounds so scary."

She responded: "I'm worried that if the tests come back positive I'll have to give up pop." Gemma loved soda; buying her own soda was one way she took control of her own spending, her own desires. It was a love language her boyfriends used, buying her sodas from the workshop's vending machine. A small thing made so significant, that it was the only fear she could articulate at the moment. In the face of a health issue like diabetes, Gemma's legitimate want of soda potentially becomes illegitimate, especially in the eyes of her carers: wants and needs end up pitted against one another, again.

First, Gemma had good news: the test for diabetes came back negative. And then, the bad news crashed down. The last week I spent on-site, I saw Gemma sitting quietly at her workstation, crying instead of working. I walked over, and as soon as she saw me, she started trying to speak—but her voice was muted, hard to hear among the noise of the machines. I asked her to repeat herself as I come around the edge of the table.

"I'm not feeling well."

"Oh, no. Are you sick again?"

"I found out last Tuesday that I have stage three kidney disease."

I was shocked still for a moment. The previous weekend was Thanksgiving. She was told two days before Thanksgiving that she had kidney disease—stage *three* kidney disease. Of course, she had been so unwell for the last couple of months. And of course, she'll have to give up a lot of stuff. I hurt for her, silently shedding tears of fear and discomfort. "I'm so sorry. That's so hard to hear before the holiday."

She went on to tell me that her family was sick for the holidays, and that she thinks she has the flu they had. She wasn't feeling well Sunday but was fine yesterday. Today, not really. So her mother was on the way to pick her up, any minute now—that's why Gemma wasn't working. Then Gemma paused, and then seemed to rally. The tears cleared up, and she asked after my own holiday. I said it was good, but was noncommittal in my details (I didn't really want the conversation to become about me). Gemma's boyfriend walked by, and she told me that he didn't know, yet. Not many people did. In fact, as an act of sympathy, one friend had given her a bottle of Mountain Dew. She took it out of her bag to show me, musing that she could just give it to her boyfriend when he passed by again.

"That's a good idea. I guess you're probably not allowed to drink that anymore?"

Gemma disagreed. "I can probably have a little bit." She held onto a small string of hope and control. She began to put on her coat and wait for her boyfriend to double back.

I was not on-site long enough after Gemma's diagnosis to find out if she did give up soda. To give some context: stage three kidney disease is prior to the stage where dialysis is necessary. Typically, it is managed by diet, and in particular, sodium and phosphates need to be watched (which can impact a wealth of foods that we enjoy: cheese, peanut butter, chocolate, and "cola beverages").[80] Sugar isn't the problem, as it would be for diabetes, so drinking diet sodas don't solve the problem. Altering Gemma's diet means more than soda, it means a significant lifestyle change. If she progresses, stages 4 and 5 might require dialysis. Without dialysis, someone with advanced or end-stage renal failure may survive some months to years; with dialysis, that can be extended. However, dialysis itself bears significant risks, and ongoing dialysis without a transplant still has high mortality rates. A patient who has been on hemodialysis (the most common type, at 90 percent

---

[80]National Institute of Diabetes and Digestive Kidney Disease, "Eating Right for Chronic Kidney Disease," *NIH.gov*, available online: https://www.niddk.nih.gov/health-information/kidney-disease/chronic-kidney-disease-ckd/eating-nutrition (accessed October 15, 2019).

of dialysis patients) has a 35 percent survival rate after five years.[81] So, if we are thinking about the objective outcomes of care, evidence tells us that Gemma needs to make these dietary changes (including giving up soda) for the basic preservation of life and to prevent the worsening of symptoms that impact the things she does value—for example, hemodialysis entails long hours tethered to a machine in a clinic, which would impact Gemma's work and social life.

So what happens if Gemma refuses? What happens if she continues to sneak sodas, chocolate, and cheese? If she does so, it means the work of care cannot be completed, and its objective goals cannot be met. Care fails because Gemma did not take up the care offered. On the one hand, I want to be clear that Gemma is not obliged to receive all forms of care offered. Gemma would not have an obligation to take up incompetent care, care that does not actually address real needs, or exploitative care.[82] However, assuming this care is done with the right intentions and out of respect for her subjectivity, it seems that Gemma ought to "graciously" receive this care, per Kittay, because it could further some of the goals she values. As a result, the refusal to adjust her diet and cease drinking soda is not only bad for Gemma but also "does an injury to the caregiver and the relationship between them."[83] Her refusal can make it impossible for those caregivers to fulfill their duties to the clients.

This is where the inclination to paternalism is the strongest: some might say it does not matter if Gemma subjectively agrees to the parameters of care, it must be done regardless. Earlier, in Sarah's story of the client she removed from the bed, I proposed that her actions could be just under the assumption of a counterfactual, that "if this client were not having a depressive episode, then she would want to be taken from bed." But the stakes in Gemma's case are even less clear than in Sarah's (which was already fairly complex). Gemma does seem to understand the problems that soda presents, and she's keenly experiencing the limitations that her health problems have been causing. But the issue of soda, and her diet in general, seems to be meaningful for her in a way beyond the care for her body. Soda represents freedom, or perhaps a connection with others, given its place in the gift economy at Payton that she shares with friends. We cannot simply ascribe Gemma's resistance to a "failure to understand" (and frankly, even if we could, that still does not justify paternalism). There is an aspect of Gemma's views of her own human flourishing that seems to run counter to medical views of her flourishing.

---

[81]University of California San Francisco, "The Kidney Project," *UCSF.edu*, available online: https://pharm.ucsf.edu/kidney/need/statistics (accessed October 15, 2019).
[82]Kittay, *Learning from My Daughter*, 216–17.
[83]Kittay, *Learning from My Daughter*, 218.

On the one hand, this could reveal a weakness in Kittay's theorizing of care work. Sullivan-Dunbar identifies this when she comments that Kittay fails to offer enough substantive content to flourishing and her concept of the good.[84] Kittay identifies a different issue—because Kittay insists on the subjective element of care, rather than accepting paternalism or even violence as necessary, a situation like Gemma's represents a problem of "moral luck." Those in the position of providing care will, through no moral fault of their own, find themselves with clients who refuse the uptake of care, and who frustrate the objective completion of care. Kittay rightfully notes that it is "difficult to accept that someone who prima facie does what we expect of a carer can be deprived of her laurels because the individual for whom she cares fails to take up her acting as caring."[85] Yet, laurels for the provision of care are not the goal of care. Recognizing both the uptake of care and the role that moral luck play keeps the carer's values and desires from overdetermining what care looks like. Moral luck also highlights parts of care that are structural, rather than interpersonal:

> ...the failure to have our care taken up occurs because certain background conditions required for successful care are not present: the parent lacks the resources to adequately feed her child because of poverty, and there is no third party to take up the responsibilities inherent in the dependency relationship; the caregiver of a disabled person gets no relief and so fails to be able to carry on successfully; the caregiver of a disabled person cannot obtain the needed equipment or other support to adequately care; the mother is the caregiver for a disabled man who is at times violent and aggressive, and she is left alone to try to care for someone who endangers himself and her, but whom she loves . . . all these cases display what care ethicists have so often emphasized: namely, that rather than being a simply dyadic relationship, the relationship between a carer and a cared-for sits in a set of nested dependencies.[86]

It is important to remember that moral luck does not mean these structures are the result of powers beyond all control, only that they are the result of factors beyond any *single* person's control. These structural obstacles are

---

[84]Sullivan-Dunbar, *Human Dependency and Christian Ethics*, 225–7. In fact, there are places where Kittay seems to openly resist an overdetermination of what constitutes flourishing—for example, she cites Martha Nussbaum's list of conditions needed to flourish, but implies that viewing the list as "what *all* people require" is limiting itself (Kittay, *Learning from My Daughter*, 198, emphasis original). The problem is largely because there are clearer objective criteria for when someone is not flourishing, than for proving that someone is flourishing (Kittay, *Learning from My Daughter*, 198).
[85]Kittay, *Learning from My Daughter*, 214.
[86]Kittay, *Learning from My Daughter*, 215.

also a result of capitulations to normalcy, and the long history of devaluing intellectually disabled persons.

This is why "caregiving is morally hazardous," why seeking justice for both clients and their workers is so important.[87] Their agencies are bound and entangled together, and what is good for one helps improve the flourishing of the other. More time, more skill, more relationship-building, and more resources might help a caretaker convince someone like Gemma of the value of her care, leading Gemma to the uptake, and then completion of care. Or, more time, more relationships, and more resources for Gemma herself might make the sacrifice of something like soda much less significant, as she finds meaning and a sense of control in other spaces—again, leading to and supporting the completion of care. Even in the scenarios where the uptake of care is attempted but is not possible (perhaps Gemma does give up soda and change her diet, and still her kidney disease progresses to dialysis) it does no moral harm to have respected Gemma's dignity and subjectivity along the way. Rather it affirms the dynamic, active (and not passive) nature of care relationships, and the obligations those create.

Care: Differences of Degree, Not Kind

When we examine the nature of care work, we can see that both care workers and clients experience dependency. Both clients and workers have structures they need in order to meet their needs, and both have to respect one another in order for care to be successful. So, although dependency is often connected to intellectual disability as if that is a problem unique to IDD, in reality, I would argue that what we see in Camilla, Betty, and Gemma is merely a difference of degree, not kind from other dependencies. I would even argue that what Haslam identified with Chan is a difference of degree—an extreme degree, but nonetheless requiring similar kinds of care and dependency that Gemma needs, or even that Sarah needs in her position as both a mother and a care worker.

This becomes even more apparent when we think about the structural obstacles and injustices that prevent just care. Sociologist Christine Kelly has theorized that in its current iteration, violence is actually an integral part of care.[88] In her interviews with personal care workers, they express awareness of the ever-present risk of their labor of care becoming violence, while "paradoxically, [care] includes the abuse and coercion of marginalised workers who, at times, actively enjoy their work."[89] Violence occurs because

---

[87]Kittay, *Learning from My Daughter*, 214.
[88]Christine Kelly, "Care and Violence Through the Lens of Personal Support Workers," *International Journal of Care and Caring* 1, no. 1 (2017): 97–8.
[89]Kelly, "Care and Violence Through the Lens of Personal Support Workers," 109.

of paternalism, and it also occurs in the policies, structures, and cultural institutions that devalue the work of care, even though it is something that every person needs. Thus far in this chapter, I have avoided the language of sin, but as we move into the next chapter—which takes that topic directly on—we must start to see these injustices as expressions of structural sin. In order to pursue justice for clients and workers, we must also pursue practices that resist sin and its influence on our social imagination.

4

Difficult Conversations[1]

On one of the many afternoons when work was slow, I was spending time with Gemma's work group, which usually assembled boxed "regatta" kits: balsam wood, cloth, and string for making small toy boats. They were out of the materials for the moment, so instead, Gemma had been coloring, with some stray puzzles in various stages of completion scattered around.

Gemma was eager to have a listening ear. This was prior to her annual meeting when she was agitated with her home life and started to talk about wanting to move out. From Gemma's telling, her mother nagged her with a laundry list of complaints, including Gemma's poor diet, her lack of exercise, and saying that Gemma had been stealing money.

The last one startled me—a far more serious complaint than the others. So I asked about it: "Why do your parents think you're stealing money?" I was expecting some complicated issue with her Payton Workshop wages and the SSA office.

Instead, a completely unabashed Gemma simply stated: "Because I did. I took money from my Dad's wallet."

This incident is curious for a few reasons—but I want to start with intention, even though Gemma's intent is rather opaque. The temptation, because of Gemma's disability, would be to excuse her actions, to assume that she doesn't know any better. Or, if we are to hold her responsible for stealing, it is *despite* her disability. Diagnostically, Gemma would be called "high functioning." She reads somewhat, writes in a messy print, and speaks without any speech impediment. In some environments, she can "pass" as nondisabled. So she may be deemed "rational" enough to be held

---

[1]A much shorter version of this chapter has been previously published as an article. See: Lorraine Cuddeback-Gedeon, "Sin, Sins, and Intellectual Disability: An Ethnographic Examination of Moral Agency and Structural Sin," *Journal for the Society of Christian Ethics* 41, no. 1 (2021): 55–71.

accountable for wrongdoing—for sin. Both of these positions assume that Gemma's agency is causally connected to her ability to reason.

I want to complicate these positions on Gemma's culpability by troubling the role that intent plays in our understanding of sin. In this regard, I am not only examining personal sins in the light of intellectual disability but also taking a new view on the debates we have encountered so far on the agency and IDD, which have generally avoided the question of culpability and sin among disabled persons themselves. This was not always the case: eugenics understood "idiocy" and "feeblemindedness" as *moral* failings. However, the Parent Movement flipped the eugenics narrative: now, people with IDD are rendered inherently saintly instead of sinful. To acknowledge the capacity for sin among people who defy modern understandings of both reason and agency is to raise a difficult conversation, indeed.

Yet, as Nancy Eiesland warned: "the person with disabilities is either divinely blessed or damned: the defiled evildoer or the spiritual superhero. As is often the case with such starkly contrasting characterizations, neither adequately represents the ordinary lives and lived realities of most people with disabilities."[2] So, in tackling the thorny issue of sins and intellectual disability, I also hope to raise questions about agency in the face of structural sin that even we nondisabled can learn from.

If the previous pages sought to illustrate how the flourishing of clients at Payton relies on structures of dependency and care, this chapter will illustrate the various ways that clients act as agents, resisting (and at times, ceding) to the structures that surround them. The primary form of sin which theologies of disability engage is the structural *sin* of ableism, but this often leaves out a discussion of personal complicity in *sins*—a distinction parsed with help from Darlene Fozard Weaver's work on sin in Catholic moral theology. With Weaver's work, we can understand ableism—or more precisely, normalcy—as the primary form of *sin* that shapes the *sins* of clients and staff alike at Payton Center. Social theorists such as James Scott and Michel de Certeau offer alternative accounts of agency that resist postliberal criticisms which see agency only as a construction of liberalism.

Sin, Intent, and Agency

Physical disabilities have often been conflated with sin: either as analogies for sin or the results thereof.[3] The connection between intellectual disability

---

[2]Eiesland, *The Disabled God*, 69–70.
[3]The most common complaints about this conflation have to do with the use of scriptural metaphors like blindness as references for human sin, and historical accounts of disability as either punishment for sin, or redemptive suffering. For just a few examples: Leviticus 21:8 forbids men with "blemishes" (blindness, lameness) from approaching the altar; Psalm 69 invokes

and sins is more difficult to analyze, given the anachronism of a very contemporary term, yet a look at the eugenics movement shows how morality and agency have had a longstanding relationship in approaches to intellectual impairments. In fact, eugenicists made moral failing an integral part of their diagnosis of mental impairment: moral deviancy was one of the essential components that defined "feeblemindedness."[4] Eugenicists did not appeal to the term "sin," per se, but nonetheless presumed the criminality of the feebleminded, including a distinct category for "moral imbeciles." By some accounts, these were the most dangerous kind of feebleminded persons, because they could "pass for normal."[5] In making this a function of genetics, criminality—and in that capacity, an analogy for sinfulness—ceased to be a function of a person's own agency: moral turpitude was an inevitability, rather than a result of free will and choice.

Then, the Parent Movement rejected the moral deviancy argument in favor of their "special child" narrative (recall the title of Dale Evan Rogers's book, *Angel Unaware*—certainly, angels are not agents of sin). Given the long history of infantilization of people with IDD, it is not hard to see how the angelic special child remains as such, even in a grown-up, adult body.[6] This instrumentalization also marks a great deal of theological reflection on people with IDD: they are consistently cast as people that teach the nondisabled something about diversity, vulnerability, and dependency on God and others. As Eiesland warned, having a disability is given a theological weight that the nondisabled do not have, even if we have moved from inherent sinfulness to innocence. Authentic theological anthropology cannot hold people with IDD on either end of those extremes.

Here an objection can be raised, especially from within the Catholic moral tradition: since IDD is a heterogeneous category with a wide range of capacities, can we really hold people like Kelly or Chan accountable for sins? This objection results from the emphasis that Catholics tend to place on intent in the definition of sin. Culpability for sin typically exists when: (1) you know that the object of your action is not a moral good; (2) you fully intend to reach the object that is not a moral good, and (3) you fully consent to and will the actions you take to achieve the object. Exceptions to

---

blindness as retribution for persecutors while in Psalm 30 the speaker chastises him- or herself for being "deaf" to the Lord; in the opening chapter of Zephaniah, the Lord promises blindness as a part of his forthcoming punishment on Judah; Isaiah 6:10 calls deafness and blindness on the people to prompt their repentance; and the list could go on.

[4] Carey, *On the Margins of Citizenship*, 45, 70.

[5] Carlson, *The Faces of Intellectual Disability*, 58.

[6] And that is to say nothing, of course, about the contemporary bioethical issues around "pillow angels" or "the Ashley treatment," quite specifically designed to keep the body of people with profound IDD in a child-like state. For a more in-depth, theologically informed discussion of the moral implications of the Ashley Treatment, see Greig, *Reconsidering Intellectual Disability*.

culpability arise when dealing with intent: take, for example, the principle of double effect. If there are two outcomes to an action (a moral good, and a sinful object), then you have to be intending the morally good object to avoid culpability for the sinful object. Ignorance is another factor that can negate culpability: if you are unaware of the moral status of your actions, then you may not be culpable. This latter example does raise a counterpoint, in that the Catholic moral tradition also speaks of "culpable ignorance"—meaning, we have a responsibility to learn, as best we can, the impact of our actions on ourselves, others, and our relationship with God. Nonetheless, these factors in determining culpability still prioritize an individual state of mind or awareness; but in examinations of "social sin" or "structural sin," traditional understandings start to run aground. Superstructures like racism seem to defy the emphasis on knowledge and intention. Even if I, a white woman, am doing all I can to advocate for anti-racism and structural change, I will still very much benefit from my white privilege in a way that may reinscribe the power dynamics of racism and render me complicit—and I would argue *culpable*—in that structural sin.

This understanding of complicity is a tough sell to Catholic moral thinking. In 1984, John Paul II released an apostolic exhortation, *Reconciliatio et paenitentia*, in which he attempted to clarify the term "social sin." He does acknowledge some of these tensions: "now it has to be admitted that realities and situations . . . when they become generalized and reach vast proportions as social phenomena, almost always become anonymous, just as their causes are complex and not always identifiable. Hence if one speaks of social sin here, the expression *obviously has an analogical meaning*."[7] This sense of sin is merely "analogical" because when the causes of social phenomena become anonymous, they lose the tripartite structure of object-intent-action. Despite calling this only an analogous sin, it should be said that John Paul II does not mean to excuse human responsibility, asserting that "each may shoulder his or her responsibility seriously and courageously in order to change those disastrous conditions."[8] Nonetheless, he continues with an additional warning that targets the sense of "social sin" specifically developed by liberation theologies, which operates much more like racism, ableism, and other structures of power and privilege. John Paul II finds it problematic that in this final sense of social sin (which I refer to as structural sin) "blame for [sin] is to be placed not so much on the moral conscience of an individual, but rather on some vague entity or anonymous collectivity such as the situation, the system, society, structures or institutions."[9] Instead, John Paul II insists that "collective behaviors" always boil down to personal sins, therefore "real responsibility, then, lies with individuals."[10] Despite

[7]John Paul II, "Reconciliatio et paenitentia," 1984, par 16, emphasis mine.
[8]John Paul II, "Reconciliatio et paenitentia," 1984, par 16.
[9]John Paul II, "Reconciliatio et paenitentia," 1984, par 16.
[10]John Paul II, "Reconciliatio et paenitentia," 1984, par 16.

John Paul II's insistence that we are obliged to work against social sins, his final assertion fails to account for the moral opacity that we face with most of our everyday decisions, nor does it account for the restriction of options we might face. It may be that all the options available have a social impact that contributes to unjust structures beyond what the individual in question might intend, or consent to. Does that negate culpability for those effects? An affirmative answer places the role of social change in the hands of a few hypothetical individuals who do bear direct culpability, rather than on communities of persons who must challenge one another to, for example, unlearn implicit bias.

A few strategies have emerged to deal with this tension. Weaver's work documents a twentieth-century turn in Catholic moral theology from "act-centered" morality toward "person-centered" morality.[11] Where *act-centered morality* (i.e., the casuistry tradition) focused on sins as an individual, culpable actions, *person-centered morality* (i.e., primarily the fundamental option debates) displays "appreciation for the historical, socially situated, and dynamic character of human life."[12] The benefit to this growing theological emphasis on sin, singular (i.e., sin in its most general existence, writ large over time and place) is that it better accounts for how "sin preconditions choice" in particular actions, and recognizes the complexity of human connectivity and interdependence.[13] Yet Weaver is not willing to give up on acts: she also argues that this turn somewhat struggles to hold sin with sins, *plural*, which refers to specific actions and inclinations that structure a person's relationship to God, self, and others.[14] Instead, Weaver emphasizes the reflexivity of actions (sins) within that which limns our freedom to act (sin). In doing so, she describes our entanglement with sins as formative for our subjectivity and sense of agency. The moral nature of the actions we take, the good we seek, and how we relate to those, undeniably shape who we are.

I agree with Weaver on these points, and I think these offer a new entry point into the problem of how to relate social or structural sin to personal sins.[15] Weaver is also aware of this tension, acknowledging that structural

---

[11]Darlene Fozard Weaver, *The Acting Person and the Christian Moral Life* (Washington: Georgetown University Press, 2011), 9. Weaver admits that this may be "oversimplification," but nonetheless provides a helpful "orientation" to the development of moral theology.

[12]Weaver, *The Acting Person and the Christian Moral Life*, 13.

[13]Weaver, *The Acting Person and the Christian Moral Life*, 122.

[14]Weaver, *The Acting Person and the Christian Moral Life*, 52–3. Her precise definition of sin, singular is "the disruption of proper relation with God issuing in and resulting from the disruption of proper relationship to ourselves, others, and the world, and disruption that does not, and cannot, fit neatly into determinations of moral culpability" (52).

[15]Weaver uses the term "structural violence," and then the term social sin to give the problem of structural violence a theological framework. I'm choosing the use the term structural sin over social sin because there is some ambiguity about the definition of social sin in the Catholic tradition—sometimes it refers to interpersonal sins, sometimes to sins of one community against another (e.g., nation-states). I find that "structural sin" gets at the "impersonal" nature of the phenomena more accurately than social sin.

violence changes the shape of our agency, both causing it to affect more people further distanced from us, and mask the effects of the sins we engage in.[16] This means it affects analyses of both person-centered morality (insofar as it obscures how sin and sins connect us to one another) and act-centered morality (insofar as it prevents us from knowing the full impact of our actions on the goods we seek). When coupled with views of freedom and responsibility that hinge on autonomy, the result is that any discussion of our responsibility for sin or sins seems to stop at culpability—creating a shallow theological assessment of something that is integral to human experience and limiting the ability to determine how persons may actually combat structural sin.[17]

I find that the primary challenge Weaver and others encounter in this task is the role of intention: for Gemma, her responsibility (or culpability) for theft seems to rest on having some access to her interior intention that we may never have. The reflexive formation of the self that Weaver ascribes to moral acts does downplay intentionality, but cannot wholly escape it.[18] It may be comforting to know these challenges are not unique to the discipline of theology: anthropology has also wrestled with personal agency and structures, which is why I now turn to the discipline's practice theories of resistance.[19] These theories offer heuristic tools that recognize agency outside of intentional, voluntary actions.

Practice Theory and Intention

Practice theory arose as a way of carving out a dialectic space between the structuralism of Lévi-Strauss and the micro-sociology of Goffman.[20] Sherry Ortner uses practice theory to address the complicated role of agency when embedded in relationships of power and inequality, and intentionality is central to this issue.[21] She identifies a spectrum of agencies within practice theory, and placement on the spectrum is dictated by the role that intentionality plays. On the one hand, there are "hard definitions" of agency that make intentionality central, as represented by a forward or future-oriented capacity for desiring and acting. On the other hand are "soft definitions" which avoid intentionality, instead seeking agency in the

---

[16]Weaver, *The Acting Person and the Christian Moral Life*, 113.

[17]Weaver, *The Acting Person and the Christian Moral Life*, 116–18.

[18]Weaver, *The Acting Person and the Christian Moral Life*, 118.

[19]Indeed, part of Weaver's argument for recapturing the role of acts and sins is that it prompts theology to take the insights of other disciplines seriously, while also offering its own distinct contribution. Weaver, *The Acting Person and the Christian Moral Life*, 58.

[20]Sherry B. Ortner, *Anthropology and Social Theory: Culture, Power, and the Acting Subject* (Durham: Duke University Press, 2006), 1–2.

[21]Ortner, *Anthropology and Social Theory*, 132.

processes of acting, regardless of how "consciously" end goals are held in the acting agents' minds.[22] Emphasizing that the spectrum is permeable, but retaining the distinctions as useful, Ortner argues for a construction of agency that retains (in contrast to soft definitions) some difference between routine and intentionalized action, but (in contrast to hard definitions) does not need to be fully "conscious," or intentional, because agency is almost always unreflexively socialized into the shapes it takes.[23] She suggests thinking about agency in terms of projects: what are the ends that a subject is seeking? This might seem to lean on the hard end of the aforementioned spectrum, but this is set in the context of what Ortner calls "serious games": like games, the goals one can intend or desire are constituted not only through known rules but also through the opaque actions and projects of other players.[24] Thus one's own intentionality is always constrained by power, culture, and other acting agents in ways that one may not be able to know or recognize. So although intentionality plays a role in agency, it does not over-determine the effects we can attribute to a given agent.

Traditional Catholic views of sin would likely agree that there is often a disconnect between intent and outcome: hence how the principle of double effect works. But these are generally seen as exceptions to the rule, not the rule itself. Ortner suggests, instead, that agency has never been a thing restricted to intentional actors, but always operates in the relationship of actors to structures. In this sense, practice theory's affinity with Weaver's complex balance of sin and sins reveals how clients at Payton play their own serious games, sometimes perpetuating sins against a backdrop of sin. Understanding what sins means—per Weaver—means understanding the cultural context in which they are embedded.[25]

So what do sin and sins look like in disabled communities? Sin is a topic of some discussion among existing theologies of disability, first because of the aforementioned risk of conflating sin with a disability, and second, because of how the presumptions of normalcy—or structural sin—create distortions in theology. Conceptually, *normalcy* resembles ableism: a structure of social power that disadvantages people who don't meet the expectations of "normal." I choose to employ normalcy in this chapter rather than ableism because it also captures how intersectionality shapes disability: normalcy punishes not just impaired bodies, but also bodies whose race, gender, and class fall outside what is deemed "normal." This manifests at Payton through the phenomenon known as "passing," meaning that clients at Payton who can, under the right circumstances, pass as nondisabled enjoy implicit privilege and advantages that those whose disability is more obvious do not.

---

[22]Ortner, *Anthropology and Social Theory*, 134–6.
[23]Ortner, *Anthropology and Social Theory*, 135–6.
[24]Ortner, *Anthropology and Social Theory*, 144.
[25]Weaver, *The Acting Person and the Christian Moral Life*, 47–8.

Normalcy is the primary structural sin against which people with IDD are struggling for liberation and grace.

The Sin of Normalcy

"It's like a high school," the director of the workshop told me when I first toured the workshop, a sentiment echoed among staff. The parallels were not hard to see: a relatively small population with regular contact, a place of gossip, friendships, romantic relationships, and occasional fights. Still, I wanted to resist the label: these are adults, not teenagers. The "perpetual child" stereotype of people with IDD runs deep.

And yet, I also had to acknowledge a certain kind of appropriateness to the label: the more time I spent at Payton, the more I came to see the social hierarchies that influenced client and staff interactions. There were popular cliques, "good kids" and "bad kids," loners, smokers, cool teachers (in this case, training supervisors), and loathed ones. They held holiday celebrations, attended classes, and had assigned lunch periods. There were bullies, and people who stood up to bullies. There were friendships marked by deep loyalty, and there were deep betrayals, too. In some sense, high school itself is not unlike any other community that comes together consistently over an extended period of time. Payton's natural level of attrition is perhaps somewhat lower than a high school, which loses and regains a full quarter of its student population from year to year; but if anything, the consistency and longevity of Payton Workshop allowed the stakes in these relationships to rise.

More specifically, I see a benefit to the high school analogy that I am not sure the director of the workshop intended: high school is often invoked as a time of discovery, a time when young men and women start to eke out their own identities. Though often associated with rebellion, it can also mean embracing values that have been passed on through the network of relationships (dependent and otherwise) that have formed them so far. While the director playfully referenced clients' colorful dating lives and "drama," I reflected on my own recollections of high school: I was bounded on all sides by authority figures, operating within structures of power and merit, and yet also seeing myself as an independent actor. I celebrated and relished my own moments of resistance even as I regulated my behavior according to grades and social expectations of teachers and peers, alike. Payton provides a space that is both private (away from families and/or full-time staff) and clearly public (clients are all too aware of training supervisors' observing eyes). It is a place where, by both resisting and complying, clients reflexively strengthen their sense of self.

To think about Payton as a "high school" is helpful insofar as it demarcates a space and community in which clients are intentionally and programmatically educated into a set of cultural expectations regarding labor and workplace behavior. Much of the curriculum is influenced by normalcy, but not all—Payton's own relationship with normalcy is ambivalent. But we cannot let the analogy over-determine our perception of the clients as "kids"—because, really, who wants to stay in high school forever?

The Curriculum of Normalcy

In late July Sandra, the Pre-Vocational Specialist, saw me as I signed in at the front desk for the day.

"I've been looking for you!" She commented, friendly.

"I've stopped by your office a few times, but it always seemed dark."

She nodded at this. "I've been offsite a lot lately. Stop by later, I want to run something by you."

Later that afternoon, I saw the light on in her office—possibly for the first time since I had started in June. I knocked and entered the room, painted in a soothing, pale blue. Sandra wasn't in her office, but in the big meeting space in the middle, standing in front of a bunch of papers, all spread out on a large, heavy-looking wooden table.

"Ah, great! I was just going over the workstations." She gestured for me to come over, and started giving me a rundown of the new class curriculum. Last winter, Payton had run a set of pilot classes for vocational training, classes that would build up basic "soft" and "hard" skills for community job sites. Soft skills were building blocks like time management, teamwork, timeliness, and grooming. Hard skills were generally job-specific: alphabetizing files, data entry on a computer, wiping down a table, and assembling a sandwich.

The last skill was the one that Sandra was puzzling over when I came into the room. Sandra's plan was to divide up the classroom into five workstations, each representing a type of job that clients might be able to get: file clerk, grocery stocker, retail assistant, restaurant buser, and fast-food worker. At the moment, Sandra was trying to figure out how to construct the fast-food stations, modeled after popular chains for sub sandwiches. The setup would be called the "Payton Cafe," and Sandra had printed out a series of menus. At least one of the class sessions would be dedicated to letting clients play both customer and worker—someone orders, and the server has to assemble the sandwich. The food would be real (Sandra always tried to approximate, as close as possible, what the actual tasks would be on the job site), and they would get to eat the sandwiches after as a reward. "They're very food-driven," Sandra remarked in a side comment.

The problem was fitting in something like a sandwich bar in a room already crowded by three circular tables, two big wooden meeting tables, several filing cabinets, and a set of wooden shelves for stocking. Along with the menus, Sandra had printed out a list of fast-food skills and tasks taken from the Equal Employment Opportunity Commission's website, meant to help people in vocational discernment determine if they had the education, skills, and attitude for the job.

Eager to help, I walked through the setup with Sandra. I had worked in a sandwich shop during high school and was able to help Sandra visualize what pieces she would need: bins with lids and ingredients, a sneeze guard of some sort, and paper to wrap the sandwich in. With new clarity, Sarah headed toward an old kitchen to gather utensils and supplies. The room, painted bright salmon, was hidden just beyond the cafeteria, behind a locked door that always had a trash can in front of it (which I had honestly assumed was a closet). As I followed along with Sandra, I was amazed to see a fully functional, expansive kitchen space, with stainless steel counters and an industrial-sized stove.

As we searched the kitchen for supplies, Sandra became nostalgic—pointing me to photos on the wall and a recipe book near the door. She told me stories about "life skills" classes she used to offer. They would hold cooking classes (which generated the recipe book), or they would set up a movie screen in the cafeteria, pop popcorn, and have some of the clients play ushers while others were movie patrons. For a moment, Sandra wondered if the fast-food training should be held there, but quickly decided against it. "I don't want people to think I'm starting up cooking class again. They ask me about it all the time."

"Why did you stop?" I asked.

"They weren't billable hours." She shrugged.

That was a common phrase, and Sandra explained it to me in a later interview.[26] Billable hours were what could be billed to state funding sources for reimbursement, a critical source of income for Payton. Payton could certainly offer other programs, but most of them would be running at a deficit, a loss—not uncommon for nonprofits. Eventually, maybe in some budget tightening, things like cooking classes and movie nights had to go. Yet again, money determines the services that are "useful." In fact, the class that Sandra was preparing was only recently something that counted as billable hours. As Sandra explained to me, the old structure for vocational rehabilitation involved a flat fee: X dollars when you get a placement, Y dollars at sixty days there, and Z dollars at a certain number of months. The problem with this model was that the financial incentive was for quick placement, not necessarily a sustainable one. So Payton's vocational services had been focused on easily placed clients and neglected the clients with less experience, who would be more difficult to train.

Shortly before I started at Payton, Indiana changed its billing structure significantly. Now, people like Sandra could bill for her training classes, and other employment specialists could spend more time on-site, seeing the client

---

[26]Pre-Vocational Specialist, Personal Interview, July 7, 2015.

through the transition for an extended period of time. The change allowed greater individual attention and hopefully greater sustainability in employee placements. The transition, however, was still in process—even things that seem minor, like record-keeping and paperwork, were taking double the time as they changed systems and translated the old billing categories into new ones. There were still some strict regulations in place, too. One morning, when a large number of absences had reduced a vocational rehab class to just three participants, Sandra was unsure she could go forward with the class. She had to call one of the directors to make sure that she didn't need at least four people present to meet the proper billing regulations.

For clients, these changes meant that about fifty of them returned to class once a week, some at a beginner level and some at an intermediate level. The curriculum for the lower-level class and the upper-level class traced out the same topics, with the primary difference being time given to soft skills versus hard skills. The more advanced students—some of who were already working with job specialists outside of Payton—spent more time on hard skills, learning by practice how to fold shirts for a retail display or how to check the facing for cans on a shelf. The beginning students spent slightly more time on soft skills, like expectations about communication and attitude. Often, hard skills were taught to these less advanced classes by observing Sandra's example rather than a hands-on approach, though sometimes they got a chance to practice. For both classes one of the primary goals (explicitly named by Sandra) was socialization, to get them used to what the requirements of a community job would be. "You can't come late when you have an hourly job," Sandra warned them. Or, "how do you think a boss would react to that kind of language?" The task at this level was preparing the clients to behave in such a way that they could be seen as valued employees.

These classes represented Payton's own ambivalence toward normalcy. On the one hand, everything about the structure of the vocational rehabilitation program was about forming clients as good laborers; that is, so they fit into the capitalist expectations of workers. Even other "normal" life skills (like cooking) took a backseat to these expectations in terms of billing priorities. Clients needed to learn to be compliant, efficient, and obedient. On the other hand, these were all *relative* expectations. Sandra herself professed a "person-first" philosophy: she wanted to recognize the individual gifts and possibilities of each client, even if she was eventually trying to mold those possibilities into something economically useful. I heard this expressed in interviews with the Job Coaches, too—they understood vocational rehab to be a two-sided process. Job coaches talked about the need to train potential supervisors in community job placements just as much as the clients themselves.[27] In this sense, the vocational rehab program at Payton could

---

[27]Pre-Vocational Specialist, Personal Interview, July 7, 2015; Job Coach, Personal Interview, September 15, 2015; Job Coach, Personal Interview, October 30, 2015.

potentially disrupt some expectations of normalcy, even as they complied with it.

As students, the clients at Payton have their own ambivalence to normalcy. Most of their resistance operates on the level of relatively quiet, quotidian practices. Open client dissatisfaction with the powers and principalities of Payton Workshop tended to focus on local iterations: supervisors, dress codes, or the dullness of the work. Payton operates like something of a leaky umbrella, shielding the clients from some of the effects of normalcy, while other parts drip through. Some clients resent the leaks; others shrug, grateful for some coverage; and still, more find the leaks are beneficial.

Hard Agencies: Public Performances and Hidden Transcripts

To identify expressions of hard agencies that resist normalcy, I turn to James Scott's theories of resistance, derived from his anthropology of Malaysian rice farmers. Scott observed that the resistance of poor farmers to the widespread economic oppression of the state showed minimal strategic thinking for long-term improvement of social structures, but rather focused on immediate gains: thefts from the wealthy, shaming gossip, and even dragging their feet while working in the rice paddies.[28] Despite how ineffective (per Ortner) these practices seem against overwhelming economic injustices, Scott maintains that these "weapons" are signs that even the most rigid hegemonies have cracks in their control: no superstructure is absolute, not even normalcy.

Scott invokes two "transcripts" that shape resistance: the public transcript, written by the powerful to structure the performance of the weak, and a hidden transcript, used by the weak to maintain their own sense of identity in the face of structural oppression.[29] While "onstage," social performances "produce a public transcript in close conformity with how the dominant group would wish to have things appear."[30] However, offstage both dominant and subordinate classes have their own hidden script.[31] Recognizing a hidden transcript means a kind of "reading between the lines": for subordinate groups, the hidden transcript responds to the slights and denigrations of human dignity within the public transcript, sometimes by rejecting the values of the public transcript, and sometimes by reclaiming elements of the

---

[28]James Scott, *Weapons of the Weak* (New Haven: Yale University Press, 1985).
[29]Scott, James C. *Domination and the Arts of Resistance: Hidden Transcripts* (New Haven: Yale University Press, 1990).
[30]Scott, *Domination and the Arts of Resistance*, 4.
[31]Scott, *Domination and the Arts of Resistance*, 4.

public performance that can resist the claims of power.[32] When the hidden transcript starts to make its presence felt in the public performance, it often takes the form of subordinate classes asking the dominant classes to live up to their own purported ideals in the public transcript.[33] The disability rights movement arguably resembled this strategy: it was a successful bid for increased access and visible human dignity using the rights language of the American "public transcript."

This all implies a sense of intentionality to the private transcript: if not the intention of individuals, certainly a level of shared resistance and recognition among the weak that they are, indeed, oppressed.[34] The phenomenon of "learned helplessness" among people with IDD could compete with Scott's assertion that even "false consciousness" among the oppressed is still performative. Is it clear that clients at Payton view their situation as one of oppression? Even if they do not use terms like normalcy and ableism, clients definitely hold clear dreams about improving their lot, and many of these do circle around the idea of an "outside" job, or community placements. A related weakness to Scott's theory is in situations where members of the subordinate class are kept "atomized," or where the powerful class can enact total "abolishment of discursive freedom." In these cases, there would be no offstage space for the private transcript to develop. This is a real risk for people with disabilities, especially those who have twenty-four-hour attendants and the like: they never have a real sense of privacy. Nonetheless, for many clients, Payton Workshop itself operates as an offstage space. Some clients come to view staff (and volunteers like myself) as one of their own, people to whom it is safe to expose at least part of their private scripts. While there are times that clients at Payton do seem to cede to the public script, there is still a hidden one present, not hidden behind a curtain, but like magic tricks, navigated in open space while the audience is distracted.

Public Scripts: Euphemizing Normalcy

Payton's public transcript is shaped by normalcy primarily through an implicit emphasis on "passing": that is, the clients who are closest to passing as nondisabled, particularly in their speech and appearance, receive more leeway and implicit privileges in their on-site behavior. One process by which this is enforced is euphemization, which permeates all disability services. For Scott, euphemization is a ritual that disguises the

---

[32]Scott, *Domination and the Arts of Resistance*, 7.
[33]Scott, *Weapons of the Weak*, 186–92.
[34]Scott generally insists that what could be read as "false consciousness" is still performative ("laying it on thick"), he makes the valuable point that even if false consciousness is genuine, that does not prevent the existence of conflict between dominant and subordinate classes. Scott, *Domination and the Arts of Resistance*, 79–80.

effort of domination.[35] Phrases like "special needs" or "differently abled" are pervasive, soft euphemisms preferred over the hard reality of the word "disabled" (the term actually preferred by self-advocates). Threatening—or even just inconvenient—actions from clients are "behaviors." The people that Payton serves are "clients" or "consumers." Despite performing labor (at absurdly low wages), those who are disabled at Payton are clients, not workers. They are being served, not serving. Ostensibly diagnostic, these terms develop a life of their own, setting the clients against normalcy. Their skills, their behavior, and their persons are not deemed normal enough to deserve the rights of a worker.

"Clients" and "consumers" are of particular interest. Those with the longest history at Payton slip back and forth between client and consumer; those who have been recently hired stick exclusively to the client. On one level, it does preserve a technicality to the relationship that clients have with Payton: clients make use of Payton for residences, support staff, respite care, and even recreation. But this relationship is embedded in a triangle: there is the client, the service provider (Payton), and then there is the purchaser, that is, the state of Indiana. State money, under the Medicaid Home and Community Based Services waiver, goes directly to Payton for services without passing through the client's hands or bank accounts: Sandra's "billable hours." As a result, Payton's lines of accountability run in at least equal parts to Indiana's government as it does to the clients.

This triangle creates tensions. A long-term board member expressed concern about the shift that this change represents: "when you accept government funds that comes with conditions, that comes with bureaucracy that you have to deal with. The agency used to be much more family driven, where you're responding to the consumer as opposed to, in my mind the purchaser, the government."[36] Moreover, the state can be experienced as restrictive, according to one former CEO: "services have always had this strain of trying to be progressive, but also how far can we go? . . . Will the state be there, or will they pull the rug?"[37] This suggests that although both terms are meant to bestow a kind of dignity on the people served, with echoes of agency and choice, the ever-present threat of a tightened budgetary belt offers another sign of the overall framework of normalcy: disability services suffer chronic underfunding on both state and federal levels, precisely because they are for people who may not feed back into the economy. Whether called clients or consumers, the people who rely on Payton for services do not have the same level of choice or control over the use of their dollars that the nondisabled do. If the state of Indiana reduces

---

[35]Scott, *Domination and the Arts of Resistance*, 45–55.
[36]Parent and Protective Services Board Member, Personal Interview, October 2, 2015.
[37]Former CEO, Personal Interview, July 28, 2015.

funding to Payton, they have probably done the same for other service providers like Payton. It would leave the clients without anywhere else to go.

Clients euphemize, too. Some refer to staff and guardians as "friends," as in "I'm going on a solo trip with my friend," or "my friend who brings me to the hospital." This illustrates Scott's insight about how the public script can be used by the powerless against the powerful—as seen with Marie, a master at switching the script. Marie has a high, squealing laugh, and boisterous sarcasm. Ask her to get on stage for her scene in a play, and she objects: "I'm not ready," she tells you with a grin, "my throat hurts." Or, to staff: "You're gonna be nice to me, right?" And regardless of the answer, she responds with a high-pitched eruption of laughter. The laugh, I suspect, means the joke is on us. Marie knows we will be nice to her, that's our role in the script.

Euphemization is only one way the clients cooperate with the public script for their own ends—another way seemed to be the surprising (to me) habit of self-policing one another's behaviors. One client, Tim, was subject to an unusual amount of this policing by other clients. At forty-something, Tim was filled with the energy of a much younger man: sometimes, when you looked at him he seemed to quiver with it. When he was sitting, it appeared practiced, as if he would rather be standing and moving and waving his hands, but he just *doesn't*. Instead he sits, tense with the effort of repressed energy, trying to approximate normalcy. Tim is one of the few Black clients at Payton, wears thick glasses, uses an unusual cadence to the words he emphasizes while speaking, and has a killer high five—his go-to gesture for celebration. I started to avoid them, since they invariably hurt my hand, leaving the palm sore for a long while afterward. I simply figured that Tim didn't really have a sense of his own strength.

Tim also had a reputation for misbehaving which first seemed somewhat unfair. For example, Tim was known for repeating the last phrases of sentences that he hears, and whenever this happened there was a resounding chorus from the other clients: "Tim, no repeating!" His words had hardly interrupted their work, and the mass call to stop repeating seemed to take up more client attention than the initial incident. Tim, among others, had been tagged as a troublemaker, and staff and peers alike seemed to tread extra-carefully around him. For clients perceived this way, even minor behaviors (like sounds or intense expressions of emotion) were reacted to—perhaps overreacted to—with an immediacy that startled me.

Tim's appearance, especially his thick glasses and speaking patterns, impaired his ability to pass: a cursory glance or hearing a single sentence would quickly place Tim outside the bounds of "normal." Few other client behaviors were policed as adamantly as Tim's repeating, so I wondered why it mattered so much. Was this, like sitting still, a part of the project to conform the client to normalcy? Meanwhile Gemma, much more capable of passing, could judiciously bend the rules of the workshop: such as taking the long way to the bathroom to interact with friends or her boyfriend, even though the policy stated that clients should not interact with people in other work groups while on the factory floor. By contrast, Tim was viewed suspiciously even when he went to help someone clean up their trash at lunch (which several other clients did quite regularly and generously).

Hidden Transcripts: Gossiping

> *Lorax 2: We are the Lorax (put arm around [Danny] as you say the line)*
> *Lorax 1: We speak for the trees.*
> *Lorax 2: And We would like to say a few words, if you please. (Pause) Regarding the story that you're about to see, it actually happened,*
> *Lorax 1: Just take it from me! (after talking, stomp your foot)*
> *Lorax 2: But there's more to this story than what's on the page, (put arm around [Danny] again) So please pay attention while we set the stage.*

The excerpt given earlier, from the "Prolog" in Act I of *The Lorax* (as performed by Payton's theater class), indicates a key component in Scott's work on resistance: *there's more to this story than what's on the page,* and that makes up the hidden transcript.[38] Gossip and grumbling mark the hidden transcript, and they are common at the workshop. I heard stories of Payton Workshop long before I ever stepped foot inside. Gemma was a key conduit for this: memorable stories include gossip about a client with a pocketknife at work, and the firing of a beloved supervisor at Payton Workshop. The latter piece of gossip struck me because it came early on in fieldwork, and was one of the few times I heard grumblings about the power structure of Payton from clients. Those complaints came more regularly when I actually started observing at Payton Workshop. Just a few months before I began my fieldwork at Payton Workshop, they overhauled the personnel structure, but I was never able to get a full picture of the circumstances. I have only pieces of information: the "State" (as in the state government of Indiana) did something and subsequently, Payton let go of almost all of the training supervisors and hired several new ones. When I was doing my interviews only two of the supervisors who agreed to speak with me had been supervisors in the workshop prior to "State's" intervention—one had been temporarily retired during the incident, and the other simply declined to speak of it. Leadership at Payton that would have been informed about this were too busy to sit for an interview. Honestly, it is unclear whether this was even something that was specific to Payton—the changes could have just as easily been prompted by a policy change and enforcement (akin to the change in vocational rehab funding) as a targeted investigation.

---

[38]Prologue was actually misspelled on the copy of the script I had from volunteering.

Subsequent to the intervention, whatever it may have been (though this may be not have been caused by the intervention) clients were regrouped and their lunch times were changed. Client complaints about the switch up continued for at least a year afterward, when I started my research. Staff described these changes as a part of the effort to promote more professionalization (re: normalization), and create a schedule that looked more like a regular working day. That reasoning was unconvincing to Gemma. She had been separated from her friends in her new lunch placement, so she tried a few tactics to resist the change—for a while, she "helped" a friend by keeping her company when the friend had to eat early for dietary reasons. When she was told not to accompany the friend anymore, she settled for eating with her preferred lunch group just once a week, when she returned from service she did at the local ASPCA. Gemma would talk to me about these attempts without pretension: it was almost as if the rules she was bending did not exist. Or at least, she thought they didn't really apply to her.

The specter of State would resurface periodically. One week, the training supervisors had warned everyone to be much more careful about the dress code later that week. The dress code was pretty standard for factory work: closed-toed shoes, covered shoulders, etc. Not all clients abided by this code with great consistency, and while verbal chastisements would be given, I never saw a client sent home for a violation. Though the new workshop director was pushing for more stringent expectations of professionalization (like the lunch changes), it seemed to be a bit of an uphill battle. Appropriate clothing was also a touchstone of Sandra's work in the vocational rehabilitation classes, but although she told clients to leave class for behaviors or tardiness, I never saw her remove a client for dress code. It is possible that happened on a day I was not there, but it had to have occurred at a much less frequent rate than tardiness. Frankly, not every client had control over how they were dressed, and the relative laxity around the dress code was probably in light of that reality. But when State was on the way, that called more attention to aberrations from normal.

I was not there on the date they visited (by then I was in part-time fieldwork), but a client, Karen, updated me afterward: "Yeah, they were here. Bunch of guys in suits, walking around with [the director]. They didn't talk to no one, though." Karen was unimpressed. I was struck by the effort to present a public appearance: though clients, staff, and institutions alike were ambivalent about the dress code on a regular day, the external threat of authority nonetheless prompted reconstruction of the public transcript, of a public face. That one day of ceding to the public transcript of normalcy could preserve the hidden one resisting it.

Resisting the Script: Risk and Realism

Despite being labeled a troublemaker, Tim was a pretty good worker—in the sense that he was productive and reliable. Sandra had coached him through a few previous job placements, and so she included him in the new classes.

I had the impression she was kind of rooting for him. In late autumn, Tim entered his vocational class with big news: he had been on a job interview.

At first, Sandra tried to limit Tim's discussion of the interview and focus on the lesson plan (later, she told me she was worried other clients would feel left out), but he was not the only one who had been interviewed and his peers were riled up. Finally, she gave in and asked them to explain what was going on. The story was that Payton was partnering with a nearby steel factory, which had gotten a large job and needed more workers. Interested in investing in the community, the company had approached Payton about getting some part-time workers from their pool, to be paid at an hourly rate ($15/hour) rather than a piece rate. About half a dozen clients had been identified and interviewed the previous two mornings, Tim among them.

Tim talked about the job incessantly for a few days. Then, eventually, he stopped—not unusual, since he tended to fixate on events for a bit, and then move on. Still, when a couple of weeks passed without hearing anything more, I inquired with Sandra about what she knew: not much, it seemed. She knew the collaboration was happening, but she was not directly involved with it. Frankly, she had been afraid to bring it up with the clients who had been interviewed. Sandra worried that Payton had rushed the process, and prematurely set up clients' hopes—essentially, that they had taken too much of a risk by jumping into the apparently unrealistic collaboration.

Risk and realism were themes echoed among training supervisors, as well: while most supported community placements, in theory, there was also an undercurrent of skepticism and concern that it was not a "realistic" expectation for many clients: again, the risk of setting up hopes without follow through. Reducing risk is certainly not a bad thing—for example, the shift in vocational rehab funding described earlier is a result of reducing the risk of failed placements. Yet, when risk and "false hope" are used to deny opportunities to the Tims of the world, then we are talking about normalcy. Normalcy wants security and predictability. And it socializes the clients into that: routines to stick to, repetitive jobs, and good, "stable" behaviors over the unpredictability of emotions and expressions.

That risk is frequently denied to people with IDD is a longstanding problem, best identified in the 1970s by Robert Perske's famous phrase, the "dignity of risk."[39] Perske writes:

> The world in which we live is not always safe, secure, and predictable. It does not always say "please" or "excuse me." Everyday there is a possibility of being thrown up against a situation where we may have to risk everything, even our lives. This is the *real* world. . . . To deny any retarded person his fair share of risk experiences is to further cripple him

---

[39]Robert Perske, "The Dignity of Risk and the MR," *Mental Retardation* 10, no. 1 (1972): 24–7.

for healthy living. Mentally retarded persons may, can, will, and should respond to risk with full human dignity and courage.[40]

Clients like Tim express this desire for the dignity of risk in the private transcript when they hope and dream about their community placements and "outside jobs." In this respect, they offer a forward-thinking version of intentional, hard agency that resists normalcy precisely by rejecting normalcy's "realism." These intentions may never have the opportunity to manifest in an outside job—but the idea of risk is predicated on the fact that what we intend may not be effectively achieved. Nonetheless, risk presents an act of rebellion against power, against structural sin by seizing hope in a better world that has been denied. Like Payton's clients, we must refuse to let the sin of normalcy define what is possible or not.

One final note on some limits to Scott's work that Payton's practices raise: although Payton has programs and policies that are informed by the curriculum of normalcy, the power structures are more complicated: the line between the dominant class and subordinate class is far blurrier at Payton than in Scott's examples of slaves and plantation owners. While it is easy to conceive of the clients at Payton as an oppressed class, it takes far more work to see the (underpaid, overworked) staff and administration at Payton as a dominant class. Even if they are those with the most immediate interpersonal power, it is not rightfully said that staff and administration are trying to maintain their power *qua* power.

The staff's sense of the "status quo" is generally critical, even if resigned. I raise this point to follow through on a criticism that Ortner makes of Scott: attention to power in practice theory must be ethnographically thick, in the sense that it does not flatten out the power dynamics among different classes.[41] This is especially the case when the racial and gender dynamics of direct support professionals and training supervisors are taken into account: the vast majority of care work is done by women of color in economically fragile positions.[42] Normalcy shapes not only the clients' lives and the projects they can pursue but also dictates the value of the human labor that supports clients' lives and projects. Many training supervisors enforce normalcy because they need the job, because of their own disempowered position. This provides a profound insight into just how enmeshed sin and sins are in the communal life of Payton, and also how important sites of resistance to that sin become.

---

[40]Perske, "The Dignity of Risk and the MR," 26, emphasis in original.

[41]Ortner, *Anthropology and Social Theory*, 46.

[42]For a further discussion, see: Arlee Russell Hochschild, "Global Care Chains and Emotional Surplus Value," in *On the Edge: Living with Global Capitalism*, ed. W. Hutton and A. Giddens (London: Jonathan Cape, 2000); for a theological assessment see: Sullivan-Dunbar, *Human Dependency and Christian Ethics*.

"Soft Agencies": Tactics in Search of Place

Where Scott's work attends to communal signs of resistance, Michel de Certeau looks more closely at "everyday life" as a response to Foucauldian depictions of panoptical power. Indeed, de Certeau's own metaphorical imagery makes critical homages to Foucault, both recognizing the role of the panopticon and also challenging its absolute nature. Both men are similarly focused on the quotidian—de Certeau describes his work as attending to the "microphysics of power"[43]—but where Scott looks at culturally shaped transcripts, de Certeau examines the "ordinary language" of people and popular culture.[44] Indeed, the script may not even be necessary for de Certeau. The role of intentionality in de Certeau falls to the "soft" end of Ortner's spectrum, in large part because his interest is in the actions, or uses of consumers, not their subjectivity, per se.[45] De Certeau understands resistance as something that happens in the process of making a life for oneself, finding a place to call one's own in the midst of larger structures of power.

De Certeau unpacks agency through a set of two dichotomies: place and space; and strategies and tactics. The former (place and strategies) are practices visible in the foreground of society; the latter (space and tactics) are always present but do not structure social power the way place and strategies do. "Place" refers to holding a position of power, specifically a position of power over time: a proper place allows a kind of control, the ability to claim an "us" against "them" or "that." From the vantage of place, one can employ strategies: "the calculus of force-relationships which becomes possible when a subject of will and power [corporate or individual] can be isolated from the environment."[46] Strategies rely on a certain kind of strength, power, and most importantly, sense of self-possession.

Social power may be organized through places and strategies, but de Certeau also proposes that there are: "innumerable other practices that always remain 'minor,' always there but not organizing discourses and preserving the beginnings or remains of different (institutional, scientific) hypotheses for that society"[47] These "minor" practices sow the seeds of alternatives to what power dictates is possible: for Payton, that means imagining alternatives to normalcy. In this respect, de Certeau shares some

---

[43]Michel de Certeau, *Practice of Everyday Life*, trans. Steven Rendall (Berkeley: University of California Press, 1988), xiv.

[44]de Certeau, *Practice of Everyday Life*, xiii.

[45]This is evident in the first sentence of de Certeau's *Practice of Everyday Life* (xi), but is noted in secondary literature, as well. See: Ian Buchanan, *Michel de Certeau: Cultural Theorist* (London: Sage, 2000), 86–125; and John Frow, "Michel de Certeau and the Practice of Representation," *Cultural Studies* 5, no. 1 (1991): 52–60.

[46]de Certeau, *Practice of Everyday Life*, xix.

[47]de Certeau, *Practice of Everyday Life*, 48.

affinities with Scott's hidden transcript: like Scott, de Certeau rejects the idea that hegemonies and ideologies ever have total control over society. From the panopticon, it may seem as if normalcy rules, but in actuality, there are always remnants of alternative ways to organize society, ways that reject the very values normalcy upholds. This is what constitutes tactics—tactics being less intentional and more improvised than strategies, and operating in "spaces" outside the purview of place. If a *place* is a century-old skyscraper looking out over New York City, *space* is street level: with all the motion, chaos, sound, and struggle that is invisible from the top of the Empire State Building.

Clients employ tactics in the space of Payton in ways that start to make Payton resemble a place of their own. The layers of dependency relationships that shape their comings and their goings often mean that clients' day-to-day lives are shaped by factors in which they have little to no input. So Payton Workshop presents the possibility of occupying *place*: whether through the relative autonomy a client might have from family or through using the wages earned to buy objects of their own desire. Clients celebrate payday (every other Friday), happily anticipating the purchase of everything from a soda to a personal TV using the money they earned. Some clients use their earnings to buy into the subsidized recreation events that Payton hosts, such as mini-golf, an arcade trip, or a weekend spent camping, where they see friends and build community. The possibility of community employment amplifies this: the main benefit for clients is the increased spending power and the independence (and further opportunity for tactics) that brings. Clients are very aware of the power that money holds. In this sense, clients comply with normalcy (in that they want to be productive workers), but for their own projects and serious games.

At the same time, forming a place can also lead to a rejection of outside jobs. Gemma would be an ideal candidate for a community job: her supervisor relies on her for more complex jobs, and Gemma knows this. It is a point of pride, and she is eager to take up the tasks she can do well. She likes earning money, and she really likes spending that money. Yet, she refuses to seek an outside job, and she claims (counter-intuitively) that it is because of money. Like many clients, Gemma is on Supplemental Security Income (SSI), and this imposes strict earning limits. Shortly before the vocational classes began, Gemma told me her parents were asked to refund $70 of the SSI check she receives, because of the money she made at the workshop.[48] Her mom (so Gemma reported) told her to quit her job. When Gemma brought this up in her voc rehab class, Sandra explained that some financial planning

---

[48]Current SSI benefits are $783/month for a single person. Any income that Gemma earns counts against this—any job she holds lessens the amount of SSI her family receives on her behalf. See: "Supplemental Security Income," Social Security Administration, *SSA.gov*, available online: https://www.ssa.gov/ssi/text-income-ussi.htm (accessed July 29, 2020).

could take care of the issue. Gemma's parents would just need to better anticipate Gemma's potential wages (whether through Payton or her outside job) when reporting income for SSI. Implicit in Sandra's response was the assumption (shared with normalcy) that earning a wage is preferable to receiving government benefits—but normalcy to Gemma's parents prefers the low-risk guarantee of the SSI funds.

Gemma refused to quit. She told me, "I can't help how hard I work"—a statement that both denies her agency while asserting it. *No, I won't quit*—but *I can't control how I work*. It is her claim to helplessness that enables Gemma's resistance to parental demands. And they listened—Gemma was not forced to quit. Nonetheless, two weeks later in the vocational class, she announced, again: "I can't get an outside job, I'll lose my benefits." Despite asserting her desire to work against her parents' wishes, Gemma still ceded to some of the limits that her parents and material resources impose.

That being said, there are more reasons than money that cause Gemma to prefer Payton Workshop. For a start: it is regular, stable, and predictable. Transportation is relatively easy. And of course, the friendships she has are an important factor, too—friendships she negotiates with tactics that implicitly, if unreflectively reject the values of normalcy. In this respect, Gemma illustrates de Certeau's theory of "usage." Despite the fact that elites in a capitalist system have control of visible production, usage functions when workers enact their own hidden production: an example of this is *la perruque*, a French term for "the worker's own work disguised as work for his employer," which de Certeau sees as an instance where the workers take control of the one thing that is theirs: time.[49] So Gemma takes the long way to the bathroom to see her friends; when Gemma is out of work, she colors pictures that she then gives to friends or even sometimes supervisors as gifts. This converges with Scott's hidden transcript: subordinate, but not passive classes can to some degree manipulate the system imposed on them. Yet, this differs from Scott in that it lacks the same kind of intentionality that the hidden transcript may display: Gemma's tactics are not resisting power the way Marie says "you're gonna be nice to me." Still, they serve Gemma's own projects, which do not necessarily align with normalcy.

Take, for example, one afternoon when the art project at hand was creating decorative "koi fish" by covering toilet paper rolls with layers of scales made out of brightly colored tissue paper. It was tricky work since the tissue paper was thin and not taking well to the wet glue. I was working with Gemma, and we had developed a system where I cut out the scales and she placed them on the roll with craft glue. She had used as much of her favorite color—pink—as possible. The finished product had multiple upside-down scales and wrinkled paper.

---

[49]de Certeau, *Practice of Everyday Life*, 25.

"That looks cool. That looks gooooood," Gemma proclaimed, sincere despite significant flaws to a "normal" observer. And, as she does with most of the crafts, she began to plan which of her friends to which she would gift the fish. This "usage" (in de Certeau's parlance) becomes a new mode of production, a transaction in relationships beyond the control of the staff. This is not to claim that Gemma *intends* a refutation of normalcy by either her proclamation or her gift. A stick-it-to-the-man intention is not necessary for *la perruque*. The fish operates much like Gemma's treatment of workshop rules: Gemma is simply looking after her own interests, attending to her friendships through the use of her time and gifts. And yet, the very value that Gemma places on these friendships—primarily with other clients (although an occasional craft is given to her mother or her supervisor) exists as a de facto refutation of normalcy that does not value either relationships with people with IDD, or the people themselves.

Yet, there is one dissonance between de Certeau's *la perruque* and a client at Payton Industries worth examining: possession of time. Because the clients at Payton earn their wage by the pieces they produce, they don't control their time in the same way that de Certeau assumes a French worker does. That is, they are not paid for idle time. A worker with an hourly wage who sneaks in time working on independent projects (or perhaps browsing Facebook) is charging the employer to do work that does not benefit the employer's profit. Piece-rate wages do not operate the same way.

Moreover, the abundance of time is often a source of complaint. Clients become frustrated not about a lack of time, but a surplus—they are often resentful when they are told to color and do puzzles instead of earning money. This flips *la perruque* on its head—clients want to participate in the production of goods. They understand their agency not in manipulating labor, but in having the option to labor at all. The meager piece-rate wage is incredibly important to clients. This is the weakness of tactics: they are susceptible to time, to circumstance. Tactics lack the luxury of power or place, and they must respond to opportunity—this is why they exist in space. They must jump at opportunities; they must take *risks* in the hope that eventually they can build a place of their own.

Finding Place in Spaces of Normalcy

Despite the unpredictability of tactics, de Certeau contends that tactics can start to forge a place, illustrating this through the example of a North African immigrant and refugee in France. This immigrant, despite the restrictions of language and low-income housing "creates for himself a space in which he can find ways of using the constraining order of the place or of the language. Without leaving the place where he has no choice but to live and which lays down its law for him, he establishes within it a degree of plurality and creativity. By an art of being in between, he draws unexpected results from his situation."[50] An immigrant, making his own way in a land where the language itself excludes him. Clients at Payton have limited fluency in the language of normalcy, and the lives they build for themselves often present precisely the kind of fluid, tactical hybridity that de Certeau describes. Sin has dealt them a bad hand. Still, Gemma and Tim play along, looking for a place to take a tactical advantage—a new job, or maybe money from their father's wallet.

Over five years ago, when I started this project, I wrote the following about one of the clients at Payton for a version of this chapter to be distributed at a workshop:

> Marie was in the process of doing just that [making a place for herself] during my time with Payton Center. In early April, I first heard her announce that she was getting her own apartment. She hadn't even entered the art room yet, but told people as soon as she walked in the large, automatic double doors in the hall. Her red button down shirt was disheveled (and might've been missing either a button or a hole), but her grin was bright. "I'm getting my own apartment, and I'm going to the movies this weekend."
>
> I congratulated her. She had been in one of the group homes run by the Payton Center and it appeared this move would be to supported living, an increase in independence. She would have two roommates, and, she assured us, "My mom will still bring me to Rec events."
>
> In the weeks leading up to her move, during Payton Act rehearsals, Marie gave us a countdown. "I'm moving in two weeks," she interjected into moments of quiet backstage. And then: "I'm moving next Saturday." And finally: "I'm moving this weekend."
>
> The next time I saw her, the Tuesday after she had moved, she was waving cheerfully as she emptied out of the Payton van that transported several clients to rehearsal. "I'm in my new apartment now!" She announced.
>
> I smiled, responding, "Right, you moved Saturday?"
>
> My question went unaffirmed, but her answer pointed to another hazard of more independent living: "There's a list in my apartment, I'm gonna have a lotta chores to do from now on." I wasn't sure how much of her voice was excitement or nervousness, but either way, I understood.
>
> And her plans didn't stop there. During our pizza dinner the night of the first performance of The Lorax, Marie asked if I was going to be at art class this year. I told her yes—at least before Christmas. After Christmas I'm less certain. With my candidacy exams on the horizon, I explained that "I have a really big test that I need to study for."

---

[50]de Certeau, *Practice of Everyday Life*, 30.

She took this in stride, also unsure how long she'll still be going to art Class. "I'm trying to get another job."

"Really?"

"Yeah, I'm tryin' to get a job at the W——" I don't recognize the name of the place, but Marie continued, explaining: "I can shop for the residents, they give me a list and I get the stuff." In a sense, this is apropos. She speaks frequently about managing her money, about what she'll buy at trips to the games arcade and pumpkin farms. These are her tactics of agency, the ways she takes advantage of the opportunities that the Rec program provides. And they may also be a vehicle of strategy, a way to look forward in time.

A new job, new roommates, and a new apartment—Marie's life seemed on the "right" track—at least as normalcy would have it. So I was surprised when I started my fieldwork at Payton Workshop, about nine months after I wrote the earlier passage, and did not see Marie there.

Art was on a long break for the summer at that point, so I did not see Marie again until I had been observing at Payton Workshop for a few months. Even so, by that time I was wrapped up in the people who actually were at Payton Workshop, and had forgotten about the people I expected to be there. So it was a couple of months still, before Marie said something that jolted my memory:

"There's a picture of me riding a bike in the hall!" Marie announced this to the classroom as a whole. No one else commented on the significance.

I looked up from helping someone else at her table. "Oh, where were you riding your bike?"

"At Day Program." She issued her trademarked, high-pitched giggle. Day program was for clients at Payton who are not considered good candidates for vocational rehab.

At this moment I remembered that she ought to have been at the workshop—curiosity piqued, I asked: "You used to work at Payton Workshop, right?"

"Yeah, but I didn't do okay there. I had a lot of behaviors." No giggle. Marie did not have a reputation for emotional volatility, though she was known to form really strong attachments and perhaps push too far in terms of boundaries. She was once reprimanded for too frequently (as in multiple times a day) calling another client she wanted to be romantically involved with. I overheard her consent to the reprimand with a genuine "I am sorry, and I will work on my behavior"—a line that felt memorized, but nonetheless earnest.

"Oh, well do you like Day program?"

"Oh yes!" Her laughter peeled through the room.

I recalled another part of her earlier story: "Are you still living in your own apartment?"

"No, my Dad got sick and my Mom couldn't afford it anymore, so I live at home, now." No giggle. At this, more than the move to Day program, my heart broke for Marie—even if her own wasn't.

Resistance and Complicity

As I write this, I continue to remain unsure if my disappointment on Marie's behalf (which she does not appear to share) is rooted in my own susceptibility to normalcy. In spite of what felt—to me, only—like a failure, Marie is still making a life of her own, attending Day program and art class, telling staff to be nice to her, and calling friends on the phone in the evening. The same goes for Gemma or Tim, as well as Danny, Betty, and Camilla. We've seen, with the help of Scott and de Certeau, the ways that clients resist the limitations of normalcy—we've also seen ways in which they comply with it. The issue of complicity is not just a matter of working with social sins—it's a way in which clients try to sort out their own agency in a world that wants to deny it.

Still, there is one last level of sin, beyond normalcy and institutions, that begs our attention, and that is clients' personal sins. In resistance and complicity alike, clients can hurt one another and commit sins against their neighbors. Gemma's theft at the start of this chapter is only one among many examples. Exaggerations and lies are interwoven with client gossip; even truths can be bitter and aimed to hurt or devalue a friend. Betty fights with her boyfriend. This is infrequent, but the buildup is visible over a few weeks. She bosses her boyfriend around a bit, and strictly enforces the expectation that he sit next to her at lunch, which he will go through phases of resenting. Regularly, I hear Betty smack loudly on the chair next to her if he was being too slow, a demanding gesture. One afternoon, I came late to lunch after an interview, and I saw Betty on the opposite side of the cafeteria from her friends—sitting by herself, silently eating lunch. I asked someone what happened, and was told that she and her boyfriend had a fight. He said something that really upset her, and she moved. Her boyfriend laughed and joked with his friends as usual.

And yet the next day, Betty was back in her regular spot, smacking the chair next to her. A fight like this could be a result of sins on both parties' behalves: whatever her boyfriend said to her, and Betty's own bossiness and tendency to ignore his desires. And still, they moved on—whether by tacit agreement or an explicit apology and forgiveness remains unknown.

I am a part of this network of complicity, too.

After a summer of humidity and rain, autumn presented dryer days, still warm enough to eat (and for some clients, smoke) outside. Tim had been paying more attention to me lately, often asking questions about whether I would be at art class that week while misaddressing me as "Mariah." I was sitting on a bench under a tree adjacent to the clients, fielding a car insurance problem while still trying to watch the general tenor of the social interactions. With one ear, I listened to a voicemail—with the other, I heard the pitch of voices raise, and saw a group of standing clients tense, group into a tighter circle.

Tim was in the middle of the circle, yelling at another client. The supervisors reacted swiftly, trying to de-escalate. They verbally commanded Tim to stand down. Another supervisor placed herself physically in front of Tim, between him and the other client. The other client slinked away, and the group dispersed.

All that happened in a matter of a few moments. Finished with my phone call, I sat on the bench and looked down at my lap, jotting a few notes about the incident. Tensions between Tim and the other client had been rising for a few days. Tim seemed to feel provoked by him, but the cause was never clear to me.

I had only written a few words of my observations when I felt someone hover over me: Tim.

"He called me a, a, a—" Tim stumbled over the words finally getting to: "a mother."

Startled, I jumped up, but the backs of my knees were pressed against the bench and there was nowhere for me to go. Tim was only a few inches taller than me, but leaned over me, getting closer with each repeated explanation that he had been called a "mother," the second profane word of the phrase always implicit. He seemed to want some action from me, but there was nothing I could do other than sympathize.

"I'm not a supervisor, Tim. I can't help you, Tim." I repeated this a few times—again, all of this happened in just a few moments—seconds, really—before I heard one of more senior supervisors yell at Tim.

"Inside, Tim. You have to go inside. Now." They weren't telling him to back away from me, they weren't chastising his actions directly. They were trying to redirect, a strategy I had seen numerous times before.

But still, Tim was leaning over me, and I felt my heart race, remembering the pain of his innocent high-fives too clearly. He was still stumbling over the offending phrase, quivering and tense, like he could explode at any moment. His anger and frustration read clearly through his body language; the fear in my own didn't register with him.

The supervisor came over to us, standing just to my right, still not touching Tim but verbally commanding him inside. The proximity of the supervisor seemed to work, and he backed away a few steps. Taking advantage of the space, she stepped between me and Tim, walking him backward toward the door by virtue of her presence.

I lingered outside as the rest of the client group moved indoors, startled by and reflecting on my own reaction to Tim. On a certain level, it makes sense—women generally read men invading their space as a threat, for a host of reasons. Still, I couldn't figure out why I was so certain Tim would hurt me. I had never seen him hurt another client, and still I felt that harm was imminent.

Despite the fact that I had cast Tim as unfairly targeted by the clients' self-policing, I wondered if I had come to see him as a threat, regardless. And the brutal truth is that Tim could have hurt someone—he was certainly strong enough to do so. Tim has been at Payton for a good chunk of his life, but I had only known him a couple of years. It is possible that he seemed harmless only because the policing of his behaviors had been so effective.

Is what Tim did that afternoon a sin? It does not seem properly comparable to Gemma's theft—Tim was probably frustrated, and he saw me, if mistakenly so, as a resource to enact some sense of justice. Though I am not sure what he wanted, he did not actually hurt me. Perhaps the sin in question is my own complicity in normalcy, a normalcy that sees people with IDD as a problem, facilitating the immediacy with which Tim went from "harmless" to "threat." That my reaction may have been colored by race and gender only compounds the role that structural sin played.

Still, I do not want to let Tim off the proverbial hook. Nor do I want to let the clients that have targeted Tim off that same hook. Same for Betty, or Gemma, or others in their respective sins. The last stranglehold that normalcy may have is our refusal to recognize that agency for liberation also means an agency that risks sin.

Ortner suggests that the "agency of projects is from certain points of view the most fundamental dimension of the idea of agency . . . that the less powerful seek to nourish and protect by creating or protecting sites, literally and metaphorically, 'on the margins of power.'"[51] We see "agency as project" in the field at Payton, as clients create their own scripts, their own places on the margins of the power of normalcy—perhaps, one could say, on the margins of sin. As Ortner notes: "the possibility of resistance is a more shadowy and of course not always realized part of the structure [of agency and power], but it is part of the structure nonetheless."[52]

For Christian ethics, we can take this message about resistance to heart with sin: even where it seems that sin shapes all our choices, even where it seems that culpability for sins is inevitable, those limits on agency are still shaped by the possibility of resisting: by hope, and the risk of imagining a different world. The recognition of how normalcy, of how sin and sins affect us also presents an implicit recognition that there could be another way, even when it seems there is not.

Theologians must carry this lesson as we trace out the deep entanglements of structural sin and personal sins. We can name both sin and sins, we can be frustrated and even harmed by choices made by ourselves and others, and yet we can find grace (daresay, hope) in acts that might seem otherwise.

---

[51]Ortner, *Anthropology and Social Theory*, 144.
[52]Ortner, *Anthropology and Social Theory*, 149.

Weaver calls on theologians to name moral acts, and I want to name some now. Gemma's theft is sinful: it damages her relationship with her parents and herself. The treatment of Tim by other clients is also sinful, whether they are cognizant of normalcy, passing, and even race, or not. If we think beyond the clients, we may even begin naming culpability for those who enforce normalcy via budgeting lines and funding requirements. The impact of these acts, intentional or not, reasoned or not, is real. Trust is broken and relationships are harmed. Yet, to assess their actions—daresay, anyone's actions—*solely* in light of culpability is to negate the concrete impact that sin has on the world. We must confront those effects as a part of the necessary work to resist them.

Conclusion

Voices United

Throughout this book, I have set—and hopefully, humbly met—the goal of using ethnography to think theologically about Payton and the people who make up its community. Yet, in the course of presenting and discussing my work over the years, my choice of a secular field site has sometimes resulted in the question: well, how is this doing the work of specifically *Christian* ethics? Setting aside for the moment a much longer conversation about boundaries of what is specifically Christian or not, I do want to return to one of my original goals in this work: improving the work of inclusion within faith communities.

That task benefits from the growing research in practical and pastoral theology around inclusion. The mixed-methods work of people like Erik Carter and the Faith and Flourishing project have offered insightful overviews of inclusive practices among a wide range of congregations. Even as I draw on this work, I also develop a narrower focus on my own faith tradition: Roman Catholicism. In my work as both a scholar and a Catholic lay minister, I often hear recognition of the importance of inclusion (and the desire to do better), but those in the position to make change are often stymied by obstacles that are not unsimilar to Payton: namely, limits on time, labor, and material resources. Well-intentioned as Catholic ministers (lay and ordained) may be, without very specific training and education about disability, they are often blithely unaware of the ways their churches and ministries fail at the tasks of inclusion, let alone creating a sense of belonging. To that extent, this conclusion asks (1) where current inclusive practices of faith communities reflect the principles of normalization, in both positive and negative senses, and (2) how a greater dialog between faith communities and social services could serve to thicken this understanding of inclusion, agency, and grace itself. Indeed, this was something hoped for by Wolfensberger, even if he took a decidedly negative view of the contribution of social services. Despite his misgivings, a mutual dialog is nonetheless beneficial for both religious and secular communities to reject sin and injustice and pursue grace and flourishing.

Catholic Institutions and Inclusion

To begin our dialog, we need to ask what role the institutional Roman Catholic Church has played with respect to intellectual disability and inclusion. The USCCB has written on several occasions about the need for justice and inclusion of people with disabilities. The 1978 "Pastoral Statement of US Catholic Bishops on People with Disabilities" shows an early adoption of "people-first" language in reference to people with disabilities; the statement was updated in 1998 under the title "Welcome and Justice for Persons with Disabilities."[1] In 1995, the American bishops released a document detailing rubrics that promoted the reception of sacraments for people with disabilities, notably asserting this with an appeal to rights language embedded in the Catholic Code of Canon Law: "Catholics with disabilities have a right to participate in the sacraments as full functioning members of the local ecclesial community (Cf. canon 213)."[2] In contrast to popular perception regarding people with IDD, the USCCB states that "Cases of doubt [about reception of communion] should be resolved in favor of the right of the baptized person to receive the sacrament. The existence of a disability is not considered in and of itself as disqualifying a person from receiving the eucharist."[3] These powerful statements express a presumption of belonging for people with IDD—furthermore, they run contrary to generations of poor catechesis. Many parents of children with IDD confess to confusion about whether their children can receive communion, believing that a certain level of "rational understanding" concerning the real presence in the Eucharist is required for reception.[4]

Although these public documents present a strong impulse toward inclusion in sacraments and parish life, there are other practices and policies that create strong barriers to belonging. Some data from a 2016 report by the Center for Applied Research in the Apostolate will be illuminating:[5]

[1]USCCB, "Welcome and Justice for Persons with Disabilities: A Framework of Access and Inclusion," *National Catholic Partnership on Disability*, November 16, 1998, available online: https://www.ncpd.org/views-news-policy/policy/church/bishops/welcome-and-justice (accessed June 5, 2017).

[2]USCCB, "Guidelines for the Celebration of the Sacraments with Persons with Disabilities," *USCCB Website*, par. 20, June 16, 1995, available online: http://www.usccb.org/beliefs-and-teachings/how-we-teach/catechesis/upload/guidelines-for-sacraments-disabilities.pdf (accessed June 5, 2017).

[3]USCCB, "Guidelines for the Celebration of the Sacraments with Persons with Disabilities," par. 20.

[4]Kristin Peterson, "Tough Love: Having a Child with Special Needs Can Test One's Faith in God and in the Parish Community," *U.S. Catholic* 74, no. 4 (2009): 27–32.

[5]M. A. Jonathon Holland, S. J. Patrick Gilger, and S. J. Thomas P. Gaunt, "Disabilities in Parishes Across the United States: How Parishes in the United States Accommodate and Serve People with Disabilities," *CARA*, 2016, available online: https://cara.georgetown.edu/product/special-report-summer-2016/.

- Only 51 percent of parishes have accessible sanctuaries, which means any liturgical role that takes place there—depending on the setup, this could be lectors, altar servers, sacristans, or EMs—cannot be done by someone with either a wheelchair or in many cases, even someone with a wheeled walker.
- Only 43 percent of parishes keep a list of resources for referrals to local organizations for disability assistance.
- Only 17 percent and 16 percent of parishes have any type of faith-sharing or support groups specifically for families of disabled people or disabled people themselves, respectively.
- While 72 percent of parishes report having volunteers with disabilities, only 48 percent report having disabled ministers, and only 17 percent report having disabled staff members.

Even the good news is limited. While 96 percent of parishes report having parking and accessible entrances, it can be dubious as to what counts as "accessible." I will use an example I garnered from a seminarian I taught in a class module about inclusive ministry, where everyone had been assigned to complete a brief accessibility survey. He noted that in order to enter the chapel for one of the campus dorms, a student using a wheelchair would have to take an elevator to a basement, actually exit the building, and then enter the chapel from a side door with a ramp. That "accessible" paths are often drastically longer and more complicated than inaccessible paths is a common issue, especially in older architecture (yet again exempted from the ADA).

Another visible, highly debated example of the religious exemptions to the ADA was the ill-received Hosanna-Tabor case of 2012 concerning the ministerial exemption.[6] In 2020, two cases concerning Catholic schools generated more controversy: *Our Lady of Guadalupe School v. Morrissey-Berru* and *St. James School v. Biel* (eventually both cases were consolidated

---

[6]Cheryl Perich, a teacher in the Hosanna-Tabor Evangelical Lutheran Church and School, was given temporary leave for health problems related to narcolepsy. When she received her doctors' clearance, she sought to return to her job, but was told by the principal that she had been replaced. Perich threatened to sue for discrimination under the ADA; the community then officially fired her from the teaching position, under the argument that it was against ecclesial rules for her to go to an outside source (the courts) for conflict resolution within the church community. John Robinson gives an extended analysis of Hosanna-Tabor, based in the argument that the religious exemption within the ADA is an extension of the First Amendment, and prevents government from infringing on religious practices of internal governance. Robinson's argument makes sense in terms of legal theory, though much of the controversy about this particular case concerned whether Perich's firing was genuinely a matter of "internal governance" or if that was a cover for discrimination against Perich on the basis of her disability. John Robinson, "Neither Ministerial Nor an Exception: The Ministerial Exception in Light of Hosanna-Tabor," *Harvard Journal of Law & Public Policy* 37 (2014): 1151.

under the first title, *Guadalupe*). In each case, the teachers whose employment was terminated claimed discrimination based on disability (i.e., a breast cancer diagnosis) or age; the schools countered with the claim that the teachers were ministers, and therefore subject to the ministerial exemption. These cases represent one of the ongoing fears of disability advocates: the refusal of a job to someone based on their (in this case temporary) disability, coupled with an unreflective lack of mercy and empathy on behalf of the Catholic community in question.

However, it is important to note here that the claim was not to justify whether the schools could discriminate—rather, the claim was to dismiss the lawsuits outright because of the ministerial exemption. This meant there was no need to investigate whether discrimination had occurred because ministry positions are not subject to any oversight by anti-discrimination bodies like the EEOC. This subtle, but important difference gets at the heart of the problem with the religious exemption: it may be a tricky ecclesiological problem to assert whether the Roman Catholic Church, at least in the United States, should be accountable to the ADA, but it is an issue of *justice* to assert that Catholics should be pursuing practices that are in line with the ADA, that promote the integration, participation, and full-bodied inclusion of people with disabilities. Even if there are strong legal precedents for religious exemptions, it may prevent church communities from more deeply examining what ableist biases might exist in their policies. Where the ADA operates as an extrinsic motivating force, Catholic institutions are expected to promote inclusion out of intrinsic motivation—because, without disabled persons the Body of Christ is quite literally incomplete.

Despite these known tensions around inclusion concerning the institutional Catholic Church, Roman Catholicism is not limited to the actions of its magisterium. Faith-based organizations like L'Arche, although interreligious by practice, are undeniably shaped by Catholic roots and serve as a powerful example of what inclusion can look like. L'Arche communities consist of people with and without disabilities living side-by-side. Those with disabilities, the core members, are paired with the nondisabled, an assistant. They live, eat, and pray together—and since they exist across the globe, their communities are frequently sites of interfaith community and prayer.

Many who are suspicious of liberalism and rights when it comes to people with IDD raise up L'Arche as an exemplar of a particularly Christian moral response to IDD. Stanley Hauerwas has also used L'Arche as a countercultural exemplar of being church, and Jason Reimer Greig highlights L'Arche's communities as counter-narratives to medical models that see disability as primarily a deficiency and devaluation.[7] The mutual

---

[7]For just one example among many, see Stanley Hauerwas, "The Politics of Gentleness," in *Living Gently in a Violent World*, ed. Stanley Hauerwas and Jean Vanier (Downer's Grove: InterVarsity Press, 2008); Greig, *Reconsidering Intellectual Disability*.

vulnerability embraced by assistants and core members is juxtaposed against the autonomy and independence sought by the disability rights movement. Interestingly, this emphasis on vulnerability is also identified by disability advocates, who are often more critical of L'Arche for operating in a perceived "charity" paradigm.[8] The stakes in this conflict have been raised in light of the recent revelations about founder Jean Vanier: L'Arche's own independent investigation in 2019 found that allegations of his sexual misconduct and abuse were credible, and he covered up the abuse of his spiritual director, Fr. Thomas Philippe.[9] While the evidence does not indicate that they abused disabled women, these revelations nonetheless demand careful interrogation (sadly, beyond the scope of this conclusion) of how vulnerability—and specifically theologies that idealize vulnerability—can be used as instruments of violence.

Yet, when we take L'Arche outside the long shadow of its founder, we see how the organization is also intertwined with the material and philosophical goals of the disability rights movement. Like Payton, L'Arche is not currently structured as an advocacy organization, but it does rely on the infrastructure that legislation like the ADA has put into place: for example, core members of L'Arche need to be on the Medicaid HCBS waiver. L'Arche cannot support its core members without the funding that disability rights activists have lobbied for. Given the emphasis that L'Arche places on financial stability when discerning whether or not to open a new community, it seems unlikely that any new communities could develop without that source of income.[10] While it is the case that the organization has focused more on creating highly localized spaces of inclusions and belonging, rather than advocating for broader policies and social justice transformation, Madeline Burghardt argues that L'Arche "contradicts many of the edicts of a capitalist society,

[8]Madeline Burghardt, "Brokenness/Transformation: Reflections on Academic Critiques of L'Arche," *Disability Studies Quarterly* 36, no. 1 (2016). https://dsq-sds.org/article/view/3734/4214.
[9]L'Arche USA, "Summary Report of L'Arche International," *Larcheusa.org*, February 22, 2020. available online: https://www.larcheusa.org/news_article/summary-report-from-larche-international/.
[10]Reimer-Grieg's narrative about L'Arche highlights their reliance on generosity and the Spirit in the origins of the movement (Reimer Greig, *Reconsidering Intellectual Disability*, 204–11). Nonetheless, as the federation of L'Arche communities has grown, their longstanding emphasis on discernment has rightfully focused on being sure that a community will be self-sufficient enough to adequately care for the core members it takes on. See, for example, the following FAQ from the "Friends of L'Arche" community in Fort Collins, CO that lists the starting costs of a L'Arche program: "The amount of funds needed will depend on whether or not a home is purchased, specifically constructed for individuals with intellectual disabilities, or donated. Construction of a one-level home capable of housing 4 to 6 adults can be expected to cost between 0.5 to $1 million. We estimate the annual operational costs for one L'Arche home with three core members, three volunteer assistants, one full time executive/fund development director and one full time administrative/budget assistant to be around $200,000." Full FAQ available online: http://friendsoflarchefc.org/FAQ.pdf.

several of which have come to define the way in which services for people with disabilities are both 'consumed' and delivered."[11] That is to say, the micropolitics of L'Arche can never be fully divorced from the macropolitics (and victories) of the disability rights movement. Burghardt goes on to suggest that L'Arche could make valuable contributions to broader political movements (if it were to become more involved in them) precisely because its experience and knowledge can make a "stronger voice" for the IDD community within the work of advocacy and justice.[12]

Whose Job Is It Anyways? Tensions in Disability Services

With that brief (and limited) overview of Catholic resources on inclusion, we turn to social services—which have their own limitations on inclusion (as this book has attested). The divide between the church institutions and social services is arguably the result of several generations distancing between spirituality and medicine. Organizations such as the American Association on Intellectual and Developmental Disabilities (AAIDD) provide comprehensive models for diagnosis, support, and quality of life for people with IDD, and yet do not include faith and spirituality as a component to be addressed.[13] Current assessment tools within social services have difficulty getting past capabilities and deficits to what is meaningful in a person's life.[14]

Moreover, current structures for most of these services rely heavily on public funding, which necessitates (for good reason) what Bill Gaventa describes as a "professional injunction to avoid proselytizing." This renders social workers, counselors, and direct support professionals nervous about even mentioning religion—something we saw in my interview with Faith in Chapter 3.[15] The general perception of the privatization of religion is probably also a factor. Social services exist in the "public" sphere, and religion exists in the "private" sphere. As Erik Carter notes in his assessment of best practices, the reluctance of service providers to address spirituality is often because they believe it is someone else's responsibility to take care of, someone more intimately connected with the client: family, perhaps, or a state-appointed guardian.[16]

---

[11]Burghardt, "Brokenness/Transformation: Reflections on Academic Critiques of L'Arche."
[12]Burghardt, "Brokenness/Transformation: Reflections on Academic Critiques of L'Arche."
[13]William C. Gaventa, *Disability and Spirituality: Recovering Wholeness* (Waco: Baylor University Press, 2018), 34. It's worth noting that the AAIDD does have a dedicated division on spirituality and religion. Also of interesting note is that the WHO—a global organization—does include spirituality and religiosity in its model.
[14]Gaventa, *Disability and Spirituality*, 34.
[15]Gaventa, *Disability and Spirituality*, 178.
[16]Erik W. Carter, *Including People with Disabilities in Faith Communities* (Baltimore: Paul H. Brooks Publishing, 2007), 151.

Yet, given that the care work associated with disability often crosses into areas we would see as primarily private (grooming, toileting, and even sexuality), spirituality should not seem so out of place.

Church institutions also contribute to this divide. At times, religious practices have actively harmed and worked to exclude people with IDD from the table. Gaventa somewhat cheekily describes an "oral tradition" passed on among service providers of the negative stories, the "what not to do" stories of how faith communities have responded to disability.[17] Roman Catholicism is not immune from this: families have left the church when children with IDD were denied confirmation, denied communion, repeatedly told to leave mass because they were creating a "disturbance," or even (in one drastic example shared by a previous director of the National Catholic Partnership on Disability) denied baptism.[18] Today, these might seem like exceptions to the rule—if so, I'm glad—but for those who have been involved with this ministry over time, they were frequent and common experiences for families already feeling frustrated and isolated while dealing with the unfriendly bureaucratic red tape of therapies and support services.

I highlight these failures not to accuse either churches or social services of failing to act in good faith—quite the contrary. My research thus far indicates a significant uptick in the desire for inclusion. Rather, there's a difficulty in making inclusive ministry a priority among the many competing needs that a parish or a diocese will face. One of the primary obstacles is simply the issue of visibility. Nondisabled people who can use stairs do not check to see where the ramp may be; nondisabled people who can read regular text do not check to see if there are labels in braille or large print hymnals. Not, that is, until the temporarily abled-bodied lose vision as they age, or break a leg, or have a stroller with two toddlers to get inside the church.

As I've spoken with ministers and taught ministry students, I often find a great willingness to work with anyone who came forward expressing needs. The problem is that this is a reactive stance, not a proactive stance. Messages of exclusion are often subtle and unnoticed by the nondisabled. Carter reminds us that many barriers "prevent people with disabilities from ever coming to your congregation in the first place. Perhaps they were never extended an invitation, they lack reliable transportation, residential staff members have not supported their involvement, or they have never been guided in exploring their own spirituality"[19] To paraphrase a quote from a parent interviewed: church institutions need to play offense, not just defense.[20]

---

[17]Gaventa, *Disability and Spirituality*, 177.
[18]Personal Interview, July 22, 2019.
[19]Carter, *Including People with Disabilities in Faith Communities*, 9.
[20]Payton volunteer and parent, Personal Interview, October 2, 2015.

In light of this gap in inclusion, there are three key principles that I want to highlight as fruitful for parishes and ministries to consider: (1) being proactive, not just reactive; (2) being attentive to the dependency relationships that enable inclusion and participation; and (3) pursuing community partnerships that not only advocate for the importance of spirituality but also serve the whole human flourishing of people with IDD.

Playing Offense

It is one thing for a pastor to be willing to work with people and families that express needs on a case-by-case basis, but it is another thing entirely for families to know ahead of time that there are resources available. While a certain level of individualization is necessary—person-centered planning is as applicable in ministry work as it is in social services—the unfortunate truth is that the life of someone with a disability is filled with obstacles for basic material needs. When families, guardians, and paid dependency workers spend their time navigating any number of funding and resource issues, the last place they want to have to take that fight is to their church.

Carter's work provides a helpful breakdown of the kinds of barriers to address, which I have laid out in table form, as follows.[21] For the moment, I want to focus on "attitude" and the passive obstacles for the present discussion.

Barriers to Inclusion and Outreach Strategies (Summarized from Erik Carter)

Active Barriers	Passive Obstacles	Proactive Outreach
• Architecture • Attitude • Communication • Programmatic • Liturgical	• Limited Transportation • Past Experience • Unreceived Invitations • Unexplored Preferences • Partitioned Professional Roles • Unfamiliarity with a Faith Community • Uncertain Responses	• Accessible Statements on Inclusion • Advisory Committees for Self-evaluation (that Include People with IDD) • Clearly Identified Resource Team/ Point Person • Earmarked Funding • Organize Meetings or Conferences • Personal Invitations with Follow-Ups

---

[21]Carter, *Including People with Disabilities in Faith Communities*, 9–25.

First, despite the well-meaning intentions I encounter in this research, I still find myself surprised by the frequency with which I encounter stigma around intellectual disability. These are rarely blatant actions or statements, but more insidious attitudinal barriers expressed by the reluctance or nervousness of the nondisabled to directly engage people with IDD: not looking them in the eye, addressing their caregivers or staff persons instead of the person themselves, treating adults like children, side-eyeing someone who gets "too noisy" during mass, or openly expressed skepticism that someone with IDD connects in a meaningful way to the liturgy.[22] The second element of attitudinal barriers is the presumption that people with IDD are recipients of ministry, not ministers themselves. As one deacon who runs disability ministry for his diocese told me in describing his dearest hopes for the future of inclusive ministry:

> The sacraments of vocation probably need to be worked on. . . . And then there are a number of guys here who would like to be priests or deacons, and they're told, "You just don't have the academic abilities." And I'm not advocating one way or the other, but I'm thinking there are some people of such strong faith. Could we not direct them to something that they could serve the Lord, and if they want to, religiously? There was a guy . . . . He wanted to be a priest. I mean, he really can't read that well, so it wouldn't work. And then he talked about being a deacon, and he tells me, "Well, they told me I couldn't do that." . . . Maybe that will be the next thing on the horizon. . . . I think, in many ways, we have moved so that folks with disabilities are more involved in the life of the parish, whether it's greeters, choir members, ushers, and the like. I'm wondering if there could be more involvement in parish life.[23]

If one of the complaints about social services is that they focus on deficits, rather than gifts in people with IDD, perhaps we need to unseat that presumption in our own work.[24] What would it look like to name gifts and draw them forward into ministry, and design our programs not around filling a need but expressing an abundance? These questions need to be a part of any proactive, "playing offense" response to inclusive ministry.

Understanding Support Structures

The passive obstacles that Carter highlights connect to my second observation: inclusion is not possible without attention to the structures that

---

[22]Carter, *Including People with Disabilities in Faith Communities*, 11–12.
[23]Personal Interview, July 18, 2019.
[24]Gaventa, *Disability and Spirituality*.

enable it, in both public and private spheres. This means attending to the multiple forms of dependency relations that support people with IDD. Most of the best practices for inclusive ministry stress the importance—in line with normalization—of "natural supports." Generally, this term is meant to refer to relationships that people with IDD might develop organically (e.g., families, friends, coworkers, etc.). One of the great benefits of improving inclusion in faith communities is that it expands the possibilities of the "natural" support network someone with IDD might draw on. Carter notes a "gradual shift away from an over-reliance on paid supports" among service providers that creates opportunities for churches to step into.[25]

Carter is right in naming this opportunity, but as we saw in Payton's history in Chapter 1, the shift in Medicaid waiver funding from paid supports to "natural supports" may have been monetary, rather than morally driven. In fact, I find that "natural supports" can often operate as a loosely euphemized "free support." It means natural support is anything or anyone that is not paid to perform care and dependency work. And I would be remiss in not noting, as discussed in the previous chapters, that unpaid care work is typically the labor of women: mothers, sisters, aunts, and daughters. Many disability advocates themselves express preferences for paid support, precisely because the professional status of a paid worker is supposed to make self-determination and choice easier—a paid worker is less likely to paternalize or project onto their client.[26] As Payton has shown us, the issue of ethics in the client-dependency worker relationship is complex; nonetheless, I raise this point to make it clear that people who serve as "natural supports" are not actually "free labor" and also deserve consideration of justice, just like paid workers.

Furthermore, what goes underappreciated in the discussion of both natural and paid support is the role of time as a resource. Those who do dependency work are often managing a lot of competing demands on time, which is a limited, zero-sum resource. Any amount of time that a person gives to one activity is time lost to any other number of needs. An hour at bible study with a client is an hour that the direct support worker (or parent, or sibling) cannot use on keeping house, planning groceries, doing homework, or spending time with other family members. Practically speaking, this means that parishes looking to be more inclusive can begin by taking into consideration the competing needs to which dependency workers are accountable. Offering transportation or forms of respite care might actually

---

[25]Carter, *Including People with Disabilities in Faith Communities*, 22.
[26]Sara Charlesworth and Donna Baines, "Understanding the Negotiation of Paid and Unpaid Care Work in Community Services in Cross-National Perspective: The Contribution of a Rapid Ethnographic Approach," *Journal of Family Studies* 21, no. 1 (January 2015): 7–21.

be the easiest place to start, as it both generates new relationships that can overcome stigma and meets some of the greatest needs.[27]

Moreover, parishes and other ministries need to consider the kinds of "dependency work" that their own volunteers might have to do, in order to facilitate inclusion. Given the aforementioned nervousness of the nondisabled, some level of reflection and training may well be pastorally useful and necessary. If, for example, a catechetical program uses individual volunteer assistants to facilitate learning for people with IDD, how well supported and trained are the volunteers? What kinds of resources are these volunteers given in order to help them serve people with IDD? How are their frustrations and limitations attended to? These kinds of dependency relationships are imperative for the inclusion and participation of people with IDD, and deserve care and attention, too.

Belonging, Normalization, and Human Flourishing

The current language in inclusive ministry is the term "belonging" rather than inclusion—an effort to sideline the potentially paternalistic overtones of "inclusion" as something the nondisabled do for the disabled. Belonging implies, instead, a place that has been lost, not a place that needs to be made. Moreover, like social services, the push among Catholic ministry is fully integrated ministries. Much as mainstreaming has taken precedence over special education classrooms, and sheltered workshops are closing in favor of community employment, the National Catholic Partnership on Disability hopes to see people with IDD in the "most natural environment," namely, alongside the nondisabled.

The first and second chapters have already detailed the many, many problems of segregating and sidelining the disability community, so I want to affirm the moral impulse behind "belonging." However, I also want to issue one warning for reflection, among ministers and theologians alike: we must be sure that our understanding of "belonging" is not colored by normalcy, the dark side of normalization. Working to ensure access for people with IDD to all that the nondisabled can access is absolutely important. But we need to ensure that we don't assume integration is superior simply because of the presence of the nondisabled.

Put another way: the removal of all disability-only spaces may not only be impractical (some people with IDD may always need more support than a nondisabled classroom, job, or catechumenate can offer), but it also may be an *ethical* mistake. People with IDD value relationships with one another.

---

[27]Carter, *Including People with Disabilities in Faith Communities*, 138–9.

There are benefits to spaces for communities with a shared identity: HBCUs, for example, or single-sex education in both secondary and post-secondary education. To make claims that disability-only spaces are either unnecessary or somehow second-rate is to neglect the benefits that people with IDD might reap from knowing others who share their experiences, who know—far better than any nondisabled person—what it is like to navigate their lives.

When churches work toward inclusion, they need to keep in mind the whole person. Both Carter and Gaventa recommend that churches try to partner with community organizations, not just to improve the integration of spirituality into disability services, but because it is a part of the church's role in the world to promote justice. So, perhaps it's time to think beyond catechesis, and beyond liturgy: how can we promote a more just, more inclusive world? What would it look like for churches to back advocacy for disability rights, today? To support initiatives for a living wage for direct support workers, or the expansion of the Autism services waiver to all forms of IDD? Following the ADA, churches were accused of deciding to be "excused from the table" of disability justice. Now is the time to earn back our place, and join our voices together for the work of inclusion.

BIBLIOGRAPHY

"61 Assembly May Convert Institution: Children's Hospital Would Be Solely For Retarded." *South Bend Tribune*. January 1, 1961.

Abel, Emily K. "A Historical Perspective on Care." In *Care Work: Gender, Labor, and the Welfare State*, edited by Meyer Madonna Harrington, 8–14. New York: Routledge, 2000.

"Allen Opposes Integration of Logan School." *South Bend Tribune*. January 28, 1954.

Amado, Angela Novak, and Roger J. Stancliffe. "Social Inclusion and Community Participation of Individuals with Intellectual/Developmental Disabilities." *Intellectual and Developmental Disabilities* 51, no. 5 (2013): 360–75.

Antaki, Charles, W. M. L. Finlay, and Chris Walton. "Choices for People with Intellectual Disabilities: Official Discourse and Everyday Practice." *Journal of Policy and Practice in Intellectual Disabilities* 6, no. 4 (2009): 260–6.

Armenia, Amy, Mignon Duffy, and Clare L. Stacey. "On the Clock, Off the Radar: Paid Care Work in the United States." In *Caring on the Clock: The Complexities and Contradictions of Paid Care Work*, edited by Clare L. Stacey, Amy Armenia, and Mignon Duffy, 3–13. New Brunswick: Rutgers University Press, 2015.

"Ask $462,000 for Hospital." *South Bend Tribune*. June 24, 1964.

Avalos, Hector, Sarah J. Melcher, and Jeremy Schipper. *This Abled Body: Rethinking Disabilities in Biblical Studies*. Atlanta: Society of Biblical Literature, 2007.

"Begin Shift of Patients: Retarded Children Move Begins to South Bend." *South Bend Tribune*. March 3, 1958.

Bersani Jr., Hank. "Wolf Wolfensberger." *Journal of Religion, Disability & Health* 4, no. 2–3 (2001): 1–9.

Bogenschutz, Matthew D., Amy Hewitt, Derek Nord, and Renee Hepperlen. "Direct Support Workforce Supporting Individuals With IDD: Current Wages, Benefits, and Stability." *Intellectual and Developmental Disabilities* 52, no. 5 (2014): 317–29.

Boshoff, Kobie, Deanna Gibbs, Rebecca L. Phillips, Louise Wiles, and Lisa Porter. "Parents' Voices: 'Our Process of Advocating for Our Child with Autism.' A Meta-Synthesis of Parents' Perspectives." *Child: Care, Health & Development* 44, no. 1 (January 2018): 147–60.

Bray, Anne, and Sue Gates. "Community Participation for Adults with an Intellectual Disability: Review of the Literature Prepared for the National Advisory Committee on Health and Disability to Inform Its Project on Services for Adults with an Intellectual Disability." *National Advisory Committee on Health and Disability*, 2003. Available online: http://www.donaldbeasley.org.nz/assets/Uploads/publications/NHC-CommunityPart.pdf (Accessed May 18, 2017).

Brock, Brian. *Wondrously Wounded: Theology, Disability, and the Body of Christ*. Waco: Baylor University Press, 2019.

Buck, Pearl S. *The Child Who Never Grew*. New York: J. Day, 1950.

Burghardt, Madeline. "Brokenness/Transformation: Reflections on Academic Critiques of L'Arche." *Disability Studies Quarterly* 36, no. 1 (2016). https://dsq -sds.org/article/view/3734/4214.

Campbell-Reed, Eileen R., and Christian Scharen. "Ethnography on Holy Ground: How Qualitative Interviewing Is Practical Theological Work." *International Journal of Practical Theology* 17, no. 2 (2013): 232–59.

Carey, Allison C. *On the Margins of Citizenship: Intellectual Disability and Civil Rights in Twentieth-Century America*. Philadelphia: Temple University Press, 2009.

Carlson, Licia. *The Faces of Intellectual Disability: Philosophical Reflections*. Bloomington: Indiana University Press, 2010.

Carter, Erik W. *Including People with Disabilities in Faith Communities: A Guide for Service Providers, Families, & Congregations*. Baltimore: Paul H. Brookes Publishing Co., 2007.

Charlesworth, Sara and Donna Baines. "Understanding the Negotiation of Paid and Unpaid Care Work in Community Services in Cross-National Perspective: The Contribution of a Rapid Ethnographic Approach." *Journal of Family Studies* 21, no. 1 (January 2015): 7–21.

"Cost of Expansion Estimated at $782,000." *South Bend Tribune*. June 29, 1962.

"COVID-19 Cases At Group Homes, Institutions Going Untracked." *Disability Scoop*. May 11, 2020. Available online: https://www.disabilityscoop.com/2020 /05/11/covid-19-cases-at-group-homes-institutions-going-untracked/28313/ (Accessed June 1, 2021).

Creamer, Deborah Beth. *Disability and Christian Theology Embodied Limits and Constructive Possibilities*. York: Oxford University Press, 2009.

Crocker, Jillian. "'We Will Handle It Ourselves': The Micropolitics of Resistance in Low-Wage Care Work." *Sociological Perspectives* 62, no. 1 (2019): 42–58.

Cuddeback-Gedeon, Lorraine. "'Nothing About Us Without Us': Ethnography, Conscientization, and the Epistemic Challenges of Intellectual Disability." *Practical Matters Journal* 11 (2018): 1–18.

Cummins, Robert A., and Anna L. D. Lau. "Community Integration or Community Exposure? A Review and Discussion in Relation to People with an Intellectual Disability." *Journal of Applied Research in Intellectual Disabilities* 16, no. 2 (2003): 145–57.

Cushing, Pamela. "What Counts as a Community? Alternative Approaches to Inclusion and Developmental Disability." *International Journal of Developmental Disabilities* 61, no. 2 (2015): 83–92.

Davis, Lennard. *Enabling Acts: The Hidden Story of How the Americans with Disabilities Act Gave the Largest US Minority Its Rights*. Boston: Beacon Press, 2015.

Davis, Lennard. *Enforcing Normalcy: Disability, Deafness, and the Body*. New York: Verso, 1995.

de Certeau, Michel. *Practice of Everyday Life*. Trans. Steven Rendall. Berkeley: University of California Press, 1988.

Dill, Jeanette S. "Are Frontline Healthcare Jobs 'Good Jobs'? Examining Job Quality across Occupation and Healthcare Settings." In *Caring on the Clock:*

The Complexities and Contradictions of Paid Care Work, edited by Clare L. Stacey, Amy Armenia, and Mignon Duffy, 54–66. New Brunswick: Rutgers University Press, 2015.

"Directors in Meeting Vote Unanimously." *South Bend Tribune*. August 16, 1946.

Dreyer, Elizabeth. *Manifestations of Grace*. Wilmington: M. Glazier, 1990.

Duffy, Mignon. "Beyond Outsourcing: Paid Care Work in Historical Perspective." In *Caring on the Clock: The Complexities and Contradictions of Paid Care Work*, edited by Clare L. Stacey, Amy Armenia, and Mignon Duffy, 14–26. New Brunswick: Rutgers University Press, 2015.

Eiesland, Nancy. *The Disabled God: Toward a Liberatory Theology of Disability*. Nashville: Abingdon Press, 1994.

Eiesland, Nancy L. and Don E. Saliers, eds. *Human Disability and the Service of God: Reassessing Religious Practice*. Nashville: Abingdon Press, 1998.

England, Paula, Michelle Budig, and Nancy Folbre. "Wages of Virtue: The Relative Pay of Care Work." *Social Problems* 49, no. 2 (2002): 455–73.

"First of Three Articles." *South Bend Tribune*. May 28, 1972.

Fleischer, James, and Doris Zames. *The Disability Rights Movement: From Charity to Confrontation*. Philadelphia: Temple University Press, 2001.

Fricker, Miranda. *Epistemic Injustice: Power and the Ethics of Knowing*. Oxford: Oxford University Press, 2007.

Friedman, Carli. "Direct Support Professionals and Quality of Life of People With Intellectual and Developmental Disabilities." *Intellectual and Developmental Disabilities* 56, no. 4 (August 2018): 234–50.

Fulkerson, Mary McClintock. *Places of Redemption Theology for a Worldly Church*. New York: Oxford University Press, 2007.

Gaventa, William C. *Disability and Spirituality: Recovering Wholeness*. Waco: Baylor University Press, 2018.

Goodley, Dan. "Empowerment, Self-Advocacy and Resilience." *Journal of Intellectual Disabilities* 9, no. 4 (2016): 333–43.

Gray-Stanley, J. A. N. Muramatsu, T. Heller, S. Hughes, T. P. Johnson, and J. Ramirez-Valles "Work Stress and Depression Among Direct Support Professionals: The Role of Work Support and Locus of Control." *Journal of Intellectual Disability Research* 54, no. 8 (2010): 749–61.

Greig, Jason Reimer. *Reconsidering Intellectual Disability: L'Arche, Medical Ethics, and Christian Friendship*. Washington: Georgetown University Press, 2016.

Gutiérrez, Gustavo. *A Theology of Liberation: History, Politics, and Salvation*. 15th Anniversary Edition. Maryknoll: Orbis Books, 1988.

Haslam, Molly Claire. *A Constructive Theology of Intellectual Disability: Human Being as Mutuality and Response*. New York: Fordham University Press, 2012.

Hauerwas, Stanley. *Suffering Presence: Theological Reflections on Medicine, the Mentally Handicapped, and the Church*. Notre Dame: University of Notre Dame Press, 1986.

Hauerwas, Stanley and Jean Vanier. *Living Gently in a Violent World: The Prophetic Witness of Weakness*. Downers Grove: IVP Books, 2008.

Hill, Faith. "The Pandemic is a Crisis for Students With Special Needs." *The Atlantic*. April 18, 2020. Available online: https://www.theatlantic.com/education/archive/2020/04/special-education-goes-remote-covid-19-pandemic/610231/ (Accessed June 1, 2021).

Hochschild, Arlie Russell. "Global Care Chains and Emotional Surplus Value." In *Justice, Politics, and the Family*, edited by D. Engster and T. Metz, 249–61. New York: Routledge, 2014.

Holland, Jonothan, S. J. Patrick Gilger, and S. J. Thomas P. Gaunt. "Disabilities in Parishes Across the United States: How Parishes in the United States Accommodate and Serve People with Disabilities." *CARA*, 2016. Available online: https://cara.georgetown.edu/product/special-report-summer-2016/

Iozzio, Mary Jo and Miguel Romero. "Preface: Engaging Disability." *Journal of Moral Theology* 6, Special Issue 2 (2017): 1–9.

Isasi-Díaz, Ada María. *En La Lucha = In the Struggle: A Hispanic Women's Liberation Theology*. Minneapolis: Fortress Press, 1993.

Isasi-Díaz, Ada María. "Solidarity: Love of Neighbor in the 1980s." In *Feminist Theological Ethics a Reader*, edited by Lois Daly, 77–87. Louisville: Westminster John Knox Press, 1994.

Kamstra, A., A. A. J. van der Putten, and C. Vlaskamp. "The Structure of Informal Social Networks of Persons with Profound Intellectual and Multiple Disabilities." *Journal of Applied Research in Intellectual Disabilities* 28, no. 3 (2015): 249–56.

Kelly, Christine. "Care and Violence Through the Lens of Personal Support Workers." *International Journal of Care and Caring* 1, no. 1 (2017): 97–8.

Kittay, Eva Feder. "Caring for the Long Haul: Long-Term Care Needs and the (Moral) Failure to Acknowledge Them." *International Journal of Feminist Approaches to Bioethics* 6, no. 2 (2013): 66–88.

Kittay, Eva Feder. *Learning from My Daughter: The Value and Care of Disabled Minds*. Oxford: Oxford University Press, 2019.

Kittay, Eva Feder. *Love's Labor: Essays on Women, Equality, and Dependency*. New York: Routledge, 1999.

Koval, Patricia. "Untitled." *South Bend Tribune*. April 24, 1969.

Koval, Patricia. "Untitled." *South Bend Tribune*. September 10, 1969.

Lafferty, Attracta, Roy McConkey, and Laurence Taggart. "Beyond Friendship: The Nature and Meaning of Close Personal Relationships as Perceived by People with Learning Disabilities." *Disability & Society* 28, no. 8 (2013): 1074–88. doi: 10.1080/09687599.2012.758030.

Levinson, Jack. *Making Life Work: Freedom and Disability in a Community Group Home*. Minneapolis: University of Minnesota Press, 2010.

Liebeler, Dolores. "Untitled." *South Bend Tribune*. November 26, 1972.

MacIntyre, Alasdair. *Dependent Rational Animals: Why Human Beings Need the Virtues*. Chicago: Open Court, 1999.

Mahar, Alyson L., Virginie Cobigo, and Heather Stuart. "Conceptualizing Belonging." *Disability & Rehabilitation* 35, no. 12 (2013): 1026–32.

Mairs, Nancy. *Waist-High in the World: A Life Among the Nondisabled*. Boston: Beacon Press, 1997.

"Mentally Ill Children to Receive Aid." *South Bend Tribune*. November 16, 1949.

Milner, Paul, and Berni Kelly. "Community Participation and Inclusion: People with Disabilities Defining Their Place." *Disability and Society* 24, no. 1 (January 2009): 47–62.

Morin, D., M. Rivard, A. G. Crocker, C. P. Boursier, and J. Caron. "Public Attitudes towards Intellectual Disability: A Multidimensional Perspective." *Journal of Intellectual Disability Research* 57, no. 3 (March 2013): 279–92.

Nichols, John. "Hospital Windows Symbolic." *South Bend Tribune*. January 25, 1973.

Nielsen, Kim E. *A Disability History of the United States: Revisioning American History*. Boston: Beacon Press, 2012.

"No Decision on Retarded at Children's: Hospital and State Deny Muscatatuck Transfer." *South Bend Tribune*. September 13, 1957.

"Northern Indiana Children's Hospital Opens Doors Today." *South Bend Tribune*. March 15, 1950.

Ortner, Sherry B. *Anthropology and Social Theory: Culture, Power, and the Acting Subject*. Durham: Duke University Press, 2006.

Overmier, J. Bruce. "On Learned Helplessness." *Integrative Physiological And Behavioral Science: The Official Journal Of The Pavlovian Society* 37, no. 1 (March 1, 2002): 4–8.

Pelka, Fred, ed. *What We Have Done: An Oral History of the Disability Rights Movement*. Amherst: University of Massachusetts Press, 2012.

Perske, Robert. "The Dignity of Risk and the MR." *Mental Retardation* 10, no. 1 (1972): 24.

Peterson, Kristin. "Tough Love: Having a Child with Special Needs Can Test One's Faith in God and in the Parish Community." *U.S. Catholic* 74, no. 4 (2009): 27–32.

Piepzna-Samarasinha, Leah Lakshmi. *Care Work: Dreaming Disability Justice*. Vancouver: Arsenal Pulp Press, 2018.

"Plan Increase at Hospital: Retarded Children Figure Will Rise to 80." *South Bend Tribune*. March 16, 1960.

"Presentation Made to Gates by Kiwanians." *South Bend Tribune*. November 29, 1946.

Reimer-Barry, Emily. "The Listening Church: How Ethnography Can Transform Catholic Ethics." In *Ethnography as Christian Theology and Ethics*, edited by Christian Scharen and Aana Marie Vigen, 97–117. New York: Continuum, 2011.

Reinders, Hans S. *Receiving the Gift of Friendship: Profound Disability, Theological Anthropology, and Ethics*. Grand Rapids: William B. Eerdmans Publishing Co., 2008.

Reinders, Hans S. *The Future of the Disabled in Liberal Society: An Ethical Analysis*. Revisions. Notre Dame: University of Notre Dame Press, 2000.

Reinders, Hans S. "The Power of Inclusion and Friendship." *Journal of Religion, Disability & Health* 15, no. 4 (2011): 431–6.

"Retarded Child Needs New Aid." *South Bend Tribune*, November 19, 1953.

"Retarded Child Project Aided, [Company] Local to Pay Teacher for One Year." *South Bend Tribune*, August 2, 1950.

"Retarded Pupil Center Planned." *South Bend Tribune*. May 22, 1950.

Reynolds, Thomas E. *Vulnerable Communion: A Theology of Disability and Hospitality*. Grand Rapids: Brazos Press, 2008.

Rivera, Geraldo. *Willowbrook; a Report on How It Is and Why It Doesn't Have to Be That Way*. New York: Vintage Books, 1972.

Robinson, John. "Neither Ministerial Nor an Exception: The Ministerial Exception in Light of Hosanna-Tabor." *Harvard Journal of Law & Public Policy* 37 (2014): 1151.

Rosen, Christine. *Preaching Eugenics: Religious Leaders and the American Eugenics Movement*. New York: Oxford University Press, 2004.

Scharen, Christian. "Ecclesiology 'From the Body': Ethnographic Notes toward a Carnal Theology." In *Perspectives on Ecclesiology and Ethnography*, edited by Pete Ward, 50–70. Studies in Ecclesiology and Ethnography. Grand Rapids: William B. Eerdmans Publishing Co., 2012.

Scharen, Christian, ed. *Explorations in Ecclesiology and Ethnography*. Studies in Ecclesiology and Ethnography. Grand Rapids: William B. Eerdmans Publishing Co., 2012.

Scharen, Christian, and Aana Marie Vigen, eds. *Ethnography as Christian Theology and Ethics*. New York: Continuum, 2011.

Scharen, Christian and Aana Marie Vigen. "Roundtable on Ethnography as Christian Theology and Ethics: Ethnography Audacious Enough to Witness." *Practical Matters Journal* 6 (2013): 1–7.

Scheper-Hughes, Nancy. "The Primacy of the Ethical: Propositions for a Militant Anthropology." *Current Anthropology* 36, no. 3 (1995): 409–40.

"School Board Denies Neglect, Complainants' Aid asked in Retarded Child Program." *South Bend Tribune*. May 13, 1952.

"School Plan Receives Help, Retarded Children to Get Special Training." *South Bend Tribune*. June 25, 1950.

Scott, James C. *Domination and the Arts of Resistance: Hidden Transcripts*. New Haven: Yale University Press, 1990.

Scott, James C. *Weapons of the Weak*. New Haven: Yale University Press, 1985.

Shakespeare, Tom, and Nicholas Watson. "The Social Model of Disability: An Outdated Ideology?" In *Exploring Theories and Expanding Methodologies: Where We Are and Where We Need to Go*, edited by Sharon Barnartt and Barbara Altman, 9–28. Emerald Group Publishing Limited, 2002.

Shapiro, Joseph P. *No Pity: People with Disabilities Forging a New Civil Rights Movement*. New York: Times Books, 1993.

Sheridan, Paula. "How Friendship Is Understood in Adults with Intellectual Disabilities across Three Life Stages." Master's Thesis. University of Limerick, 2013. Available online: https://ulir.ul.ie/handle/10344/3243 (Accessed May 18, 2017).

"Society Rents School Site, Mentally Retarded Children to be Trained." *South Bend Tribune*. June 15, 1950.

Sokol, Michael. "From the CEO: The Case for a Direct Support Professional Wage Increase." *ADEC*. February 10, 2017. Available online: http://adecinc .com/ceo-case-direct-support-professional-wage-increase/ (Accessed May 22, 2017).

Storey, Keith. "The Case Against the Special Olympics." *Journal of Disability Policy Studies* 15, no. 1 (2004): 35–42.

Stowe, Gene. *Voice: Disability and Identity at LOGAN, 1950–2010*. Notre Dame: Corby Books, 2010.

Sullivan-Dunbar, Sandra. *Human Dependency and Christian Ethics*. Cambridge: Cambridge University Press, 2017.

Sulok, Nancy. "Untitled." *South Bend Tribune*. March 15, 1973.

Swinton, John. "From Inclusion to Belonging: A Practical Theology of Community, Disability and Humanness." *Journal of Religion, Disability & Health* 16, no. 2 (2012): 172–90. doi:10.1080/15228967.2012.676243.

Swinton, John. "Who Is the God We Worship? Theologies of Disability; Challenges and New Possibilities." *International Journal of Practical Theology* 14, no. 2 (2011): 273–307. doi:10.1515/ijpt.2011.020.

Teitelbaum, Joel, Taylor Burke, and Sara Rosenbaum. "Olmstead V. L. C. and the Americans with Disabilities Act: Implications for Public Health Policy and Practice." *Public Health Reports (1974–)* 119, no. 3 (May 1, 2004): 371–4.

"These Our Children: Studebaker People Help Start School for Retarded Boys and Girls." Slide Spotlight. *South Bend Tribune.* November 1950.

Thompson, Rosemarie Garland. "Integrating Disability, Transforming Feminist Theory." *NWSA Journal* (now *Feminist Formations*) 14, no. 3 (2002): 1–32.

Trent Jr., James W. *Inventing the Feeble Mind: A History of Mental Retardation in the United States.* Berkeley: University of California Press, 1994.

United States Conference of Catholic Bishops (USCCB). "Guidelines for the Celebration of the Sacraments with Persons with Disabilities." *USCCB Website.* June 16, 1995. Available online: http://www.usccb.org/beliefs-and-teachings /how-we-teach/catechesis/upload/guidelines-for-sacraments-disabilities.pdf (Accessed June 7, 2017).

United States Conference of Catholic Bishops (USCCB). "Pastoral Statement of U.S. Catholic Bishops on People with Disabilities." *National Catholic Partnership on Disability.* November 16, 1978. Available online: https://www .ncpd.org/views-news-policy/policy/church/bishops/pastoral (Accessed June 7, 2017).

United States Conference of Catholic Bishops (USCCB). "Welcome and Justice for Persons with Disabilities: A Framework of Access and Inclusion." *National Catholic Partnership on Disability.* November 16, 1998. Available online: https://www.ncpd.org/views-news-policy/policy/church/bishops/welcome-and -justice (Accessed June 7, 2017).

"Untitled." *South Bend Tribune.* September 23, 1969.

"Untitled." *South Bend Tribune.* August 22 1972.

Vigen, Aana Marie. *Women, Ethics, and Inequality in U.S. Healthcare: "To Count among the Living".* New York: Palgrave Macmillan, 2006.

Weaver, Darlene Fozard. *The Acting Person and Christian Moral Life.* Washington: Georgetown University Press, 2011.

Wehmeyer, Michael L. *The Story of Intellectual Disability: An Evolution of Meaning, Understanding, and Public Perception.* Baltimore: Paul H. Brookes Publishing Co, 2013.

White, Katharine, and Lynette Mackenzie. "Strategies Used by Older Women with Intellectual Disability to Create and Maintain Their Social Networks: An Exploratory Qualitative Study." *British Journal of Occupational Therapy* (2015). doi:10.1177/0308022615586419.

Whitmore, Todd David. "'If They Kill Us at Least the Others Will Have More Time to Get Away': The Ethics of Risk in Ethnographic Practice." *Practical Matters* 3 (2010): 1–28.

Wolfensberger, Wolf. "Of 'Normalization,' Lifestyles, the Special Olympics, Deinstitutionalization, Mainstreaming, Integration, and Cabbages and Kings." *Mental Retardation* 33, no. 2 (1995): 128.

Wolfensberger, Wolf. "Social Role Valorization: A Proposed New Term for the Principle of Normalization." *Intellectual and Developmental Disabilities* 49, no. 6 (December 2011): 435–40.

Wolfensberger, Wolf. "Social Role Valorization And, or Versus, Empowerment." *Intellectual and Developmental Disabilities* 49, no. 6 (December 2011): 469–76.

Wolfensberger, Wolf. "Social Role Valorization Is Too Conservative. No, It Is Too Radical." *Disability & Society* 10, no. 3 (September 1995): 365–8.

Wolfensberger, Wolf. *The Principle of Normalization in Human Services*. Toronto: National Institute on Mental Retardation, 1972.

Yong, Amos. *The Bible, Disability, and the Church: A New Vision of the People of God*. Grand Rapids: William B. Eerdmans Publishing Co., 2011.

Yong, Amos. *Theology and Down Syndrome: Reimagining Disability in Late Modernity*. Waco: Baylor University Press, 2007.

INDEX

Note: Page numbers followed by "n" refer to notes.